Lecture Notes in Computer Sci

Edited by G. Goos, J. Hartmanis and J. van

T0238092

Springer
Berlin
Heidelberg
New York
Barcelona
Hong Kong
London
Milan
Paris
Singapore
Tokyo

Krzysztof Czarnecki   Ulrich W. Eisenecker

Generative and Component-Based Software Engineering

First International Symposium, GCSE'99
Erfurt, Germany, September 28-30, 1999
Revised Papers

 Springer

Series Editors

Gerhard Goos, Karlsruhe University, Germany
Juris Hartmanis, Cornell University, NY, USA
Jan van Leeuwen, Utrecht University, The Netherlands

Volume Editors

Krzysztof Czarnecki
DaimlerChrysler Research and Technology, Software Engineering Lab
Wilhelm-Runge-Str. 11, 89081 Ulm, Germany
E-mail: czarnecki@acm.org

Ulrich W. Eisenecker
University of Applied Sciences Kaiserslautern, Zweibrücken
Amerikastraße 1, 66482 Zweibrücken, Germany
E-mail: Ulrich.Eisenecker@T-Online.de

Cataloging-in-Publication Data applied for

Die Deutsche Bibliothek - CIP-Einheitsaufnahme

Generative and component based software engineering : first
international symposium ; revised papers / GCSE '99, Erfurt, Germany,
September 28 - 30, 1999. Krzysztof Czarnecki ; Ulrich W. Eisenecker. -
Berlin ; Heidelberg ; New York ; Barcelona ; Hong Kong ; London ;
Milan ; Paris ; Singapore ; Tokyo : Springer, 2000
    (Lecture notes in computer science ; Vol. 1799)
    ISBN 3-540-41172-0

CR Subject Classification (1998): D.2, D.1, D.3, F.3

ISSN 0302-9743
ISBN 3-540-41172-0 Springer-Verlag Berlin Heidelberg New York

Springer-Verlag Berlin Heidelberg New York
a member of BertelsmannSpringer Science+Business Media GmbH
© Springer-Verlag Berlin Heidelberg 2000
Printed in Germany

Typesetting: Camera-ready by author
Printed on acid-free paper   SPIN: 10720131   06/3142   5 4 3 2 1 0

Preface

In the past two years, the Smalltalk and Java in Industry and Education Conference (STJA) featured a special track on generative programming, which was organized by the working group "Generative and Component-Based Software Engineering" of the "Gesellschaft für Informatik" FG 2.1.9 "Object-Oriented Software Engineering." This track covered a wide range of related topics from domain analysis, software system family engineering, and software product lines, to extendible compilers and active libraries. The talks and keynotes directed towards this new software engineering paradigm received much attention and interest from the STJA audience. Hence the STJA organizers suggested enlarging this track, making it more visible and open to wider, international participation. This is how the GCSE symposium was born.

The first GCSE symposium attracted 39 submissions from all over the world. This impressive number demonstrates the international interest in generative programming and related fields. After a careful review by the program committee, fifteen papers were selected for presentation. We are very grateful to the members of the program committee, all of them renowned experts, for their dedication in preparing thorough reviews of the submissions.

Special thanks go to Elke Pulvermüller and Andreas Speck, who proposed and organized a special conference event, the Young Researches Workshop (YRW). This workshop provided a unique opportunity for young scientists and Ph.D. students to present their ideas and visions of generative programming and related topics and to receive thorough critique and feedback from senior experts in the field.

We are also indebted to the keynote speakers and tutorial presenters, Don Batory, Ira Baxter, Jim Coplien, and Brad Cox, for their contribution to GCSE'99. Finally, we wish to thank all who put in their efforts and helped to make this first symposium happen, especially the authors and the STJA organizers.

We hope you will enjoy reading the GCSE'99 contributions!

October 1999

Krzysztof Czarnecki
Ulrich W. Eisenecker

Organization

GCSE'99 was co-hosted with the Smalltalk and Java in Industry and Education Conference '99 (STJA'99) and organized by the Working Group "Generative and Component-Based Software Engineering" of the German "Gesellschaft für Informatik" under the auspices of the STJA Foundation.

Executive Committee

Program Chairs:
: Krzysztof Czarnecki (DaimlerChrysler Research and Technology, Germany)
  Ulrich W. Eisenecker (University of Applied Sciences Kaiserslautern, Germany)

Organizing and Publicity Chair:
: Bogdan Franczyk (University of Essen, Germany)

North America Chair:
: Don Batory (University of Texas, USA)

Eastern Europe Chair:
: Pavol Návrat (Slovak University of Technology, Slovakia)

Program Committee

Mehmet Aksit (University of Twente, The Netherlands)
Don Batory (University of Texas, USA)
Ira Baxter (Semantic Designs, Inc., USA)
Allan Brown (Sterling Software, UK)
Manfred Broy (Technical University of Munich, Germany)
Sholom Cohen, (Software Engineering Institute, USA)
Jim Coplien (Bell Labs, USA)
Serge Demeyer (University of Berne, Switzerland)
Premkumar Devanbu (University of California at Davis, USA)
John Favaro (Intecs Sistemi, Italy)
Robert Glueck (University of Copenhagen, Denmark)
Martin Griss (Hewlett-Packard Laboratories, USA)
Cristina Lopes (Xerox PARC, USA)
Pavol Navrat (Slovak University of Technology, Slovakia)
Frances Paulisch (Siemens, Corporate Technology, Germany)
Wolfgang Pree (University of Konstanz, Germany)
Mark Simos (Synquiry Ltd., USA)
Michael Stal (Siemens, Corporate Technology, Germany)
Clemens Szyperski (Microsoft Research, USA, and Queensland University of Technology, Australia)
Daveed Vandevoorde (Hewlett-Packard, California Language Lab, USA)
Todd Veldhuizen (Indiana University, USA)
Philip Wadler (Bell Labs, USA)
Roberto Zicari (University of Frankfurt, Germany)

Table of Contents

Domain Analysis and Component-Based Development

A Survey and a Categorization Scheme of Automatic Programming Systems

Wolfgang Goebl

Generali Service AG
Kratochwjlestr. 4
1220 Vienna, Austria
wolfgang.goebl@generali.at

Abstract. Automatic Programming (AP) systems have been used in a great variety of ways since the early days of software engineering. They have been used in AI related research approaches with the aim to generate computer programs from informal, incomplete, natural language-like specifications as well as in more pragmatic approaches related to 4th level languages. Terms such as "application generator", "transformational system", "code synthesizer", "generative software development" were used for naming various approaches to AP. This paper presents a categorization scheme for AP systems. In this categorization scheme, a clear distinction is made between the AI related, hard AP- and soft AP systems. After that, a broad range of AP systems as well as their position in the categorization scheme is presented. Finally we discuss the relation between AP and software reuse.

Introduction

Ever since the beginning of software development, programmers have dreamed of a way to fully automate their often tedious, laborious work. The process of converting informal specifications into an effective implementation is human labor intensive, error prone and largely undocumented [1]. Programming was, and still is, the bottleneck in the use of computers.

The old dream of computer scientists has been to combine the disciplines of artificial intelligence and software engineering to automatically generate programs from an informal specification. Rich and Waters [2] name the ultimate dream of AP the "cocktail party vision" which has the following characteristics: (i) end user oriented – the user will know only about the application domain and not about programming, (ii) general purpose – the AP system can work in a broad range of application domains, (iii) fully automatic – other than the original entry of a specification, the system requires no user assistance. This idea of AP has its roots in the very earliest software technology, but realistic applications have been elusive.

However, in addition to the "cocktail party vision"-like approaches, code generation technologies have always been used for more pragmatic approaches. These approaches typically focus on a very narrow domain, having some kind of higher level language as input. From this more pragmatic point of view, it can be said that AP has always been an euphemism for programming with a higher level language

K. Czarnecki and U.W. Eisenecker (Eds.): GCSE'99, LNCS 1799, pp. 1-15, 2000.
© Springer-Verlag Berlin Heidelberg 2000

than was presently available to the programmer [3]. All of these so called "Automatic Programming" techniques are very different from the idealistic, "cocktail party vision"-like AP systems mentioned above. It seems as if the research field just "forgot" to evolve two different terms for two different things. In our work we differ between hard AP systems and soft AP systems.

Distinct from the hard- and soft AP view to code generation technology, the software reuse community sees code generators as a software reuse technology (e.g. [4], [5], [6]), see section 5. The reused assets are patterns woven into the fabric of a generator program. Biggerstaff [6] was the first who mentioned code generators as a kind of software reuse.

The remainder of this work is organized as follows: in section 2 we present our categorization scheme for AP systems. Section 3 discusses the basic concepts of hard AP and presents a number of representative approaches. In section 4, the idea of soft AP is described as well as approaches to that more pragmatic way of AP. For each approach, its place in the categorization scheme is presented. Section 5 discusses code generation techniques as software reuse technologies. The final section presents our conclusion.

Categorization of Automatic Programming Systems

Figure 1 shows our categorization scheme for AP systems. We use the following three categories:

- The category "*Generated Code Ratio*" describes the percentage of generated code vs. manually implemented code of a system. It ranges from 0% (no longer an AP system) to 100% (the ideal of full AP).
- The category "*Generality*" ranges from AP systems, which generate code for a specific, narrow domain, to the ideal of generators that can produce code for a wide range of domains.
- The category "*Kind of Input*" subdivides AP systems by their input. Maximum automation requires a kind of input which is adequate for the users of an AP system – humans. Practice shows that the kind of input should be highly domain specific to make it easy for the user to define the program for a certain domain. A clear separation should be made between approaches using informal and incomplete specifications as input ("hard AP", see section 3) and those who use complete specifications ("soft AP", see section 4). Researchers on AP made experiments with many kinds of inputs. The values on this axis are not necessarily in the right order (AP systems using formal specifications are, for example, not necessarily "better" than AP systems using examples as input).

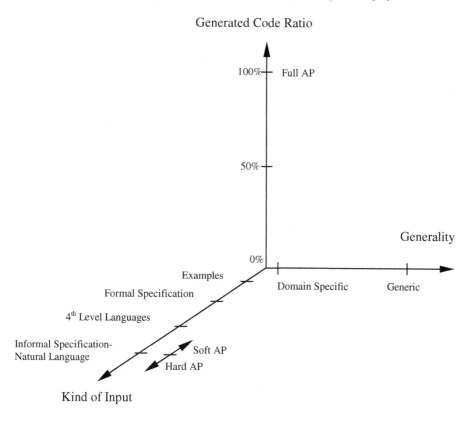

Fig. 1. A Categorization Scheme for Automatic Programming Systems

Generated Code Ratio

Rich and Waters' "cocktail party" vision of AP includes full-automation of the programming tasks. In this vision, all of the low-level code is produced from the users' input by the generator. In theory it is not surprising that full automation is an important requirement for the "cocktail party" vision, because it enables the user of an AP system not to deal with the complex details of the lower level. However, it can be observed that many practically usable AP system provide a mechanism to express things in the underlying low-level language. Vlissides [7] argues that this is because the high level metaphor that gives the code generation tool its power is rarely expressive enough to let you specify every (not-so-) little detail. The YACC parser generator, for example, uses the C language that directs program activity after a grammar rule has been reduced. Cleaveland [8] names the mechanism for expressing things in the underlying language "escape". He argues that escapes are necessary to meet a wide variety of unanticipated needs. Escapes let you take arbitrary actions at specified points in the generated program, and they dramatically increase a generator's domain width. However, they should be used very carefully because they have a number of drawbacks. A well designed input language minimizes the use of escapes and their disadvantages.

Generic vs. Domain Specific AP

The "cocktail party" vision of AP includes generality. An AP system ideally shall not be restricted to a certain domain. It is not surprising that generality is an important requirement for the ultimate vision of AP, because this prevents the need to build a new domain-specific generator for every (new) domain. Practice showed that the power of a code generation tool and its generality interact badly. Biggerstaff [6] states that code generation technologies that are very general (in that they can be applied to a broad range of application domains) have usually a much lower payoff than systems that are narrowly focused on one or two application domains. An AP system for achieving a high generated code ratio must be domain specific, both in order to interact effectively with the user and to draw upon domain-specific knowledge during the implementation process [9].

Using *generic approaches,* code for a variety of domains can be generated. Usually practicable generic approaches do not reach a very high value on the generated code ration axis. Approaches aiming at full automatic code generation and generality typically employ the most formal techniques [9]. Generic approaches with more human-friendly input, like generative CASE tools (see section 4) do not reach a large generated code ratio.

Domain specific approaches relate knowledge about the application domain to the desired software at the requirements, design or implementation phase. Using a domain specific approach results in a much higher generated code ratio than generic approaches. Application specific knowledge makes specification easier and speeds synthesis [9]. As the input language is domain-specific, it is easier for the user to specify the application. Application generators as described in section 4 are a typical example for a domain specific approach to AP.

Hard Automatic Programming

Hard AP systems represent the old dream of AP: tell your computer in natural language, what your program shall do and let it do the tedious work of programming. This approach is ultimate, because it is most appropriate for humans to communicate in their own language. Natural languages represent the way we think (informal, incomplete, redundant) as programming languages represent the way computers "think".
Barstow gives the following definition for AP systems:

Definition: Hard AP
A *(hard) AP* system allows a computationally naive user to describe problems using the natural terms and concepts of a domain in a human-friendly way, with informality, imprecision and omission of details [10].

Because of the fact that at this time no explicit distinction was made between hard- and soft AP, Barstow's definition did not include the term "hard". However, as in our terminology the definition deals with hard AP systems, we reuse his definition and add the term "hard".

The proponents of hard AP favor to use informal, human-friendly specifications. They argue that an AP system doing formalization as well as implementation achieves much higher productivity gains compared to a soft AP system. These AP systems are end user oriented - the user will know only about the application domain and not about programming. To some extent, all hard AP is an artificial intelligence problem, since its goal is to produce a computer system that performs activities that are currently unstructured and imperfectly understood [11]. Figure 2 shows the concept of a hard AP system.

Approaches to Hard Automatic Programming

A large number of research projects on hard AP can be found in literature. This section gives a brief description of some of the more important.

ΦNIX

Barstow's ΦNIX project at Schlumberger-Doll Research [13] has been investigating the use of hard AP techniques in two real-time application domains related to oil well logging.

PSI

PSI was a large AP project done by Green [14] at Stanford in the mid-70s. Its concept was to have two separate phases: a specification acquisition phase that built a specification via user interaction, and a program synthesis phase that took the specification and translated it into LISP code.

DEDALUS

DEDALUS [15] was also a transformational program synthesizer from the mid-70s, but its approach was much more logically oriented. The programs written by DEDALUS are in the domain of number theory, sets, and lists. Although it worked by refining from a high-level language to a target language implementation, much of the refinement knowledge was encoded in a small number of general rules. The specification of the rules were quite formal and unambiguous.

Programmer's Apprentice

Programmers Apprentice [16] is a large body of work done at MIT since the mid-1970s. The model of programmers apprentice is that of an assistant. The direction is supplied by the user who has the domain knowledge and will make any necessary choices in implementation. The system has knowledge about how certain tasks can be done – programming clichés that are ways to do things. During design, the system keeps track of two representations of the software being developed: the plan, which is the high-level abstraction, and the text, which is a complete or partial program in the target language and is an implementation of the plan. These two representations are connected by translators that allow translation in both directions.

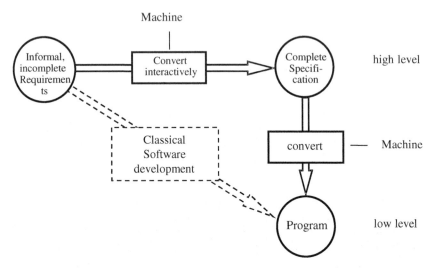

Fig. 2. Concept of Hard AP Systems: The user communicates the requirements in an informal way with omission of details. The hard AP system converts this incomplete description interactively with the user into a complete high level specification. The final conversion into executable lower level code can be done automatically without any user interaction.

Other examples for research projects on hard AP are SAFE [17], GIST [18], and PSISYN [19].

Problems of Hard Automatic Programming

The idea of hard AP has its roots in the very earliest software technology, but realistic applications have been elusive. Research approaches failed to work toward the break-even point, when it becomes easier to produce a piece of software using a hard AP system than without. Hard AP, whereby a computer system is capable of producing executable code based on informal, incomplete, and incoherent user requirements, is decades away, if ever possible [2]. Natural languages today are inherently unsuitable for the communication with computers. Today it is believed that most attempts at hard AP have either failed or enjoyed only limited success. Certainly, none of them has found its way into common software engineering practice [12]

Soft Automatic Programming

In addition to hard AP, code generation technologies have always been used for more pragmatic approaches. These approaches use complete, computer friendly input specifications. We define soft AP as follows:

Definition: Soft Automatic Programming

In a *Soft Automatic Programming* system, a user has to describe the problem in a computer-friendly, complete way, using a language appropriate for the domain. This description needs to be of some formalism and does not omit details. From this high level specification, the program is automatically converted into an executable computer program.

Soft AP techniques are very different from the idealistic hard AP systems. It seems as if our research field just forgot to evolve two different terms for two different things. Figure 3 shows the concepts of soft AP.

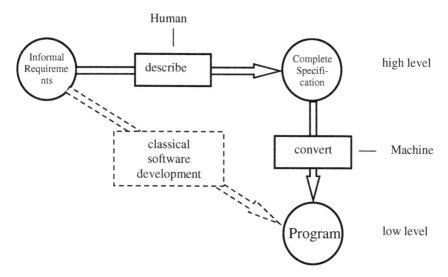

Fig. 3. Concept of soft AP: The first step is to describe the intended behavior from a source of informal requirements. After that, this complete description is converted into a form appropriate for the machine. Classical software development does both of these steps manually. A soft AP system automates the 2nd step. The main difference to hard AP is that the 1st step is done manually, because it needs human intelligence to describe a system. The conversion of this description can be done automatically. The user specifies what needs to be computed, the AP system is then used to generate executable code that describes how the computation is done.

In the late 50s systems like: Fortran, Flop, Assembly, Arithmatic etc. were named "AP systems". Most of these systems were what we today call Assembler, some were compilers. Horowitz [20] names a technology for generating low level data-access code from very high level language constructs like "*select... where...*" an "Application Generator". This paper does not mention that this "very high level language" is very similar to what has been developed at IBM a decade before – SQL.

From this background, it can be said that the term "AP" has always been a relative one. In the early days the invention of assembler was a real productivity improvement for programmers. It does not surprise that the raise of early 3rd level programming languages like Fortran made the programmers think of it as AP – a great amount of their manual, boring, error-prone low-level implementation task was automated by the compiler. Since the invention of early compilers other concepts for a better automation of programming have been introduced: database query languages, very high level languages, CASE tools etc.

Approaches to Soft Automatic Programming

Formal Specification *(general purpose, 100%, formal language)*
Formal languages like Z can be used to define the behavior of a system completely. Most approaches on AP systems using formal languages do not focus on a domain but are general purpose, and aim at full generation. The advantage of formal languages is that they can easily be transformed by transformation rules. Producing the generated code is done step-by-step. The system doing the code production process is more a transformer or synthesizer than a generator. AP systems using formal specifications are often called "Code Synthesizers" or "Transformation System".

A good example for a program synthesis system using formal specifications is the approach by Dershowitz [21]. A formal specification of the program is transformed step-by-step into executable code. The transformations are performed by synthesis rules that generate code to solve the current goal or transform the goal in one or more sub-goals. Although Dershowitz achieves the final programs using his transformation system, it requires considerable input from the user to guide the system and provide the correct goals [12].

Jia and Skevoulis [22] present an approach to synthesizing functional and robust code from object-oriented design models and Z specifications (a formal language) and operation specifications. It is based on an integrated notation of the Unified Modeling Language and a slightly extended Z notation to include object-oriented concepts and structures. The approach provides a number of choices for different design and implementation schemes from which the developer can choose the best ones for the problem at hand. Code is generated which is fully functional and can be compiled and executed without modifications. The approach does not focus on any domain. Currently there is just a research prototype, which demonstrates the feasibility of this approach.

There is a wide agreement that formal approaches have proved to be too slow and unwieldy for practical use. It is very difficult for most people to specify problems formally, and it is too computational expensive for even the fastest hardware to automatically derive programs from specifications [9]. Most formal specification languages require the same sort of care and attention to detail that traditional programming requires [10].

Compiler and Parser Generators *(domain specific, 100%, grammar)*
A very successful story of AP is the use of generators for producing compilers and parsers [23]. This kind of AP systems takes the grammar to be compiled/parsed as input and produce a complete compiler/parser. Today nearly every compiler/parser is generated by a compiler/parser generator. The most famous example for a generator for lexical analysis is LEXX [24], the most famous example for a parser generator is YACC [25]. The reason for the success of compiler/parser generators is that the domain and the input for building a concrete compiler/parser is well understood. Grammars are a very suitable specification language for defining compilers/parsers. Compiler/parser generators have grown out of the well-developed compiler theory and the ubiquitous need for compilers in computer science. Parser- and compiler

generators reuse the knowledge gained through years of research and design experience in the compiler domain, including the general theories behind lexical analysis, parsing, syntactic and semantic error analysis, and code generation. This knowledge is embedded in the design and implementation of the of the compiler/parser generator, and is reused each time a compiler/parser is generated [5].

An extension of pure compiler/parser generators are AP systems for producing whole Software Development Environments (SDEs). A SDE is a compiler for a certain programming language integrated in a development environment which for example automatically checks for the syntax of the used programming language. Jarzabek's PASCAL SDE generator [26] and "Marvel" (a Prolog SDE built at Columbia University, New York [27]) automatically produced complete software development environments from meta-environments. The meta-environment described in [26] consists of grammar-rules, some editing properties of grammar symbols, attributes of grammar symbols, relationships between grammar symbols, unparsing rules and language specific editing command for the SDE to be generated.

Examples *(domain specific, 100%, examples for input and output)*
An early idea of program synthesis is discussed by Biermann [28]: the program generation by providing examples of the inputs to the program, and the outputs generated by those inputs. From this specifications, an automatic generator would find the program, which mapped from the inputs to the outputs.

Partridge [29] suggests an approach using neural nets, which automatically generates a function that is characterized by training examples. The neural net can compute a more general function for which the training set is an example. By training on a specific example, a generalization can be achieved.

It quickly became clear that building an AP system using examples as input results in a large number of problems. For example, for any but the simplest sets of inputs and outputs, there would be a rather large number of possible programs that could perform the mappings. Furthermore only very simple programs can be defined by a manageable number of input and output parameters.

Very High Level-, Domain Specific Languages

Application Generators (AGs) (domainspecific, 100%, domain specific language)
Early application generators (AGs) were software systems geared primarily to support data-intensive application development [30]. The boom of AGs reached its top in the early eighties. AGs provide a very high level, special purpose "programming" language with a user-friendly syntax. Therefore AGs can easily be applied by the end-user, who is usually not sophisticated in computer skills [20]. Three main areas are successfully supported by AGs: 1) query-and-update languages; 2) generators of reports, screen, graphics, and dialogues; and 3) logic and arithmetic expression manipulators [31].

In his survey on application generators Horowitz [20] discusses a number of AGs that were commercially available in 1985. He mentions several AG systems (e.g.: IBM's Application Development Facility ADF, Ashton-Tate's Dbase II, National CSS's Nomad). In Nomad, "the data record can be sorted, screened by applying some very high level language constructs such as select... where...". Horowitz does not mention that this "very high level language" is very similar to what has been developed at IBM's San Jose Research Lab a decade before – SQL. All of these so called "application generators" are similar to what we would today name "database management system" with extended report capabilities.

Graphical User Interface Builders (general Purpose, few%, graphical Specification)

The rise of operating systems providing graphical user interfaces (e.g. Apple's MacOS, Microsoft's Windows, IBM's OS/2) in the late eighties made it much more comfortable for the users to work with their applications. On the other hand it also made it much more complex for the developers to build the applications. User interaction from this time on had to be done in a well designed graphical user interface. This new kind of user interface requires a new way for building the front end of an application. The low-level GUI creation APIs provided by the operating systems seemed not to be the right level of abstraction for writing applications with this new graphical interfaces. It quickly became clear that tools for graphically editing the contents and layout of such user interfaces could improve the tedious process of implementing GUIs. From this graphical specification the code for displaying is generated in a target language which calls the according GUI APIs of the operating system.

The first graphical user interface builder was *Prototyper* mentioned in [32], which did code generation from graphical user interface specifications to Pascal or C code on the Apple Macintosh platform. Prototyper lets the user design the front end without writing any code. It generates the skeletal code needed to get the application up and running. This skeletal code has to be extended using the lower level programming language to add the behavior of the dialog. Today nearly every software development environment has its own GUI builder included. They are another success story of AP.

Later GUI builders extend the graphic programming paradigm by concepts to specify the logic of the application (e.g. Digitalk's PARTS, IBM's VisualAge). These tools promise to build whole applications graphically, not just user interfaces. The vendors of these development environments suggest that by using them, whole applications are as simple to build as the pure GUIs. However, practical experience made clear that the graphic programming paradigm is very suitable for the generation of dialogs, but fails to ease the implementation of the logic of the applications. In most cases, it is less effort to implement the behavior of an application using the underlying implementation language than it is using graphical programming.

Generative Case Tools (general purpose, very few %, design documents)

CASE (computer aided software engineering) tools provide aid in the software development process. They support the analysis and design phase by offering various kinds of constructs for modeling the requirements on a software system. In addition to the modeling facilities, generative CASE tools automate parts of the implementation task. They generate some code skeletons in a target language out of the design model.

CASE tools initially were intended to be a step in the direction of AP. The (sometimes propaganda-like) advertisement of the CASE vendors in relation to the "superior AP" facilities of their tools, made some of us believe that a CASE tool can be the solution for all of the problems we face in software development. Today, after we survived the first boom of CASE, it gets clearer that CASE tools are of only limited help in the implementation of software systems. They cannot get around the fact that a generative approach gets more powerful the narrower the domain is (compare section 2).

Church and Matthews [33] who evaluated 14 object-oriented CASE tools for their generative capabilities came to the conclusion that very few tools do any more than very simple headers-only code generation. In CASE tools generating C++ for example, a complete .h file plus a .cpp file with headers and other declaration information is generated for each class, but without any executable code. To complete the implementation, the user must add the code for member function bodies. It seems as if many methodologists view the diagrams in their methods as guidelines for human developers rather than as something to be turned into precise instructions for a computer. As all of the tools evaluated have poor code generation ability, the generative capabilities of generative CASE tools are a nice tool to have rather than a technology for improving the productivity by an order of magnitude.

Aspect Oriented Programming
To date the primary idea for organizing software systems has been to break the system down into functional modules. However, many issues of concern to programmers do not cleanly follow these modularity boundaries [34]. There are many programming problems, for which neither the compositional paradigm of procedural- nor object-oriented programming techniques are sufficient to clearly capture some of the important design decisions the program must implement. This causes the implementation of those design decisions to be scattered throughout the code, resulting in tangled code that is excessively difficult to develop and maintain. In general, whenever two properties being programmed must compose differently yet be coordinated, they cross-cut each other. Because current languages provide only one composition mechanism the programmer must do the co-composition manually. This is a tedious, error-prone activity, which leads to complexity and tangling in the code.

Kiczales' idea on Aspect Oriented Programming solves this problem by allowing a programmer to express each of the different issues he wants to program in an appropriately natural form. These issues are called "aspects". In [34] the following examples for aspects in a digital library application are given: failure handling, synchronization constraints, communication strategy. As the aspects cross-cut the system's basic functionality, the usual implementation of all aspects in one piece of code necessarily results in tangled code. This tangled code is highly non-maintainable since small changes to the functionality require mentally untangling and re-tangling it. In Aspect-Oriented Programming, all such aspects are separated from each other in separate aspect definitions. Instead of manually implementing the code with all these issues "tangled" inside, the programmer expresses each of the aspects separately in a natural form. A special form of generator called an "Aspect Weaver" automatically combines these separate aspect descriptions and generates an executable form. The user works only with the well structured, separated aspect specifications. The power of the Aspect-Oriented Programming approach is that the Aspect Weaver handles the details, instead of the programmer having to do the tangling manually.

Automating Programming - A Software Reuse Technology

In the late 80s a fundamental paper was published by Ted Biggerstaff [6]. According to this paper the technologies applied to the reusability problem can be divided into two major groups that depend on the nature of the assets being reused. These two major groups are *compositional reuse* and *generative reuse*. ([35] compares the benefits/problems of these reuse approaches). Biggerstaff was the first who recognized the reuse potential of code generation techniques. From that point on, distinct from the hard- and soft AP views to code generation technology, the software reuse community has seen code generators as a software reuse technology (see [4], [5], [6]).

But how do code generators fit into the category reuse technology? What are the reused assets? Generative reuse is not as easy to categorize as compositional reuse, because the reused components are not easily identifiable as concrete, self-contained entities. The reused assets in generative reuse are patterns woven into the fabric of a generator program. The artifact being reused in a generator is the domain knowledge that is required to map a high-lêvel specification into executable code patterns. This knowledge is encoded as part of the program synthesis system in the form of interference rules, transformational rules or as domain theory [36]. Generators generalize and embody commonalties, so they are implemented once when the generator is built and then reused each time a software system is developed using the generator [5].

Basically, all approaches to soft AP can be seen as software reuse approaches. All of these soft AP systems reuse patterns inside the generators. GUI builders for example reuse the knowledge how to translate the high level graphical specification into executable code. Compiler and parser generators reuse the knowledge how to generate a compiler from the input grammar. Generative CASE-tools "know" how to build class-templates from BO-model diagrams. In our generative approach presented in [37], we reuse the mapping from the BO-model to the relational database structure (and other mappings).

Many authors of papers on generative approaches do not use the term "software reuse", maybe because they see the tools from a more transformal- than reuse point of view. The remainder of this section presents projects that have the clear intention to use generators for software reuse.

Approaches to Reuse-Oriented AP

GenVoca

Don Batory's GenVoca [38] is a general model for the generation of software. The standardized description of the basic abstractions of a domain and its interfaces are the basis for the generation of among one another compatible and replaceable components. The set of GenVoca-components implementing an abstraction or an interface are called a 'Realm'. Components are parameterized using other components belonging to other realms and generate an implementation for the abstractions of a realm. New realms can be defined from already existing realms. The composition of components takes place through the instantiation of their parameters. Design rules define restrictions for the composition of components and their ability to instantiate. The language for GenVoca is P++ - an extension of C++. GenVoca has been used to implement a number of generators (e.g. a generator for communication protocols).

Draco

The Draco-approach by J.Neighbors [39] organizes reusable software components by problem area or domain. Source-to-source program transformations, module interconnection languages, software components, and domain specific languages work together in the construction of similar systems from reusable parts. Statements of programs in these specialized domains are then optimized by source-to-source program transformations and refined into other domains. Draco uses a domain language for describing programs in each different problem area. The operations in a domain language represent analysis information about a problem domain. This analysis information is reused by the generators every time a new program to be constructed is cast in a domain language.

Conclusion

Terms like "application generator", "transformational system", "code synthesizer", "code generation tool" were used for idealistic, AI related AP approaches, as well as for soft approaches, conceptually more like 4th level languages. However, no distinction was made between hard- and soft AP. This lead to some confusion and the term „Automatic Programming" is often used for glamour, not for semantic content and has always been an euphemism for programming with a higher level language than was presently available to the programmer [3]

The fact that generators can be used as a powerful reuse technology (like in the approaches presented in section 5) is not present in common software engineering practice. Even if academia recognized that there is "another kind of reuse", it seems as if this idea hasn't found its way into the mind of most software engineers.

Looking at the state-of-the-practice of AP, it can be said that generators are more seen and implemented as a "nice tool" rather than a technology for improving productivity by an order of magnitude. Most attempts at hard AP have either failed or enjoyed only limited success. Certainly, none of them has found its way into common software engineering practice [12]. The approaches most widely used in practice are compiler/parser generators, GUI generators and generative CASE tools. All helped in improving the productivity a little, but certainly not enough to give the industry the long time required productivity boost. It can be said that the most common generators are of limited productivity benefit only. The only notable exception are compiler/parser generators, which are widely used in practice and improve the productivity by much.

References

[1]   R. Balzer, *"A 15 Year Perspective on AP"*, IEEE Transactions on Software Engineering, November 1985, pp. 1257-1267

[2]   C. Rich, R.C. Waters, *"AP: Myths and Prospect"*, IEEE Computer, August 1988, pp. 40-51

[3]   F. P. Brooks, Jr., *"No silver bullet: essence and accidents of software engineering"*, IEEE Computer Magazine, April 1987, pp. 10-19

[4]   H. Mili, F. Mili, A. Mili, *„Reusing Software: Issues and Research Directions"*, IEEE Transactions on Software Engineering, June 1995, pp. 528-562

[5]   C.W. Krueger, *„Software Reuse"*, ACM Computing Surveys, June 1992, pp. 132-183

[6]   T. Biggerstaff, C. Richter. *"Reusability Framework, Assessment and Directions"*, IEEE Software, March 1987

[7]   J. Vlissides, *"Generation gap (software design pattern)"*, C++ Report, Nov.-Dec. 1996, p. 12, 14-18

[8]   J. Cleaveland, *„Building Application Generators"*, IEEE Software, July 1988, pp. 25-33

[9]   No Author, *"Foreword"*, IEEE Software, May 1993, pp. 7-9

[10   ]D.R. Barstow, *"Domain-Specific AP"*, IEEE Transactions on Software Engineering, November 1985, pp. 1321-1336

[11]   W.T. Tsai et.al., *"A critical look at the relationship between AI and software engineering"*, Proceedings of the 1988 IEEE Workshop on Languages for Automation: Symbiotic and Intelligent Robots, p. 2-18

[12]   C. Willis and D. Paddon, *„A software engineering paradigm for program synthesis"*, Software Engineering Journal, September 1994, pp. 213-220

[13]   D.R. Barstow, R.Duffey, S. Smoliar, and S. Vestal, *"An Overview of ΦNIX"*, Amer. Ass. Artificial Intelligence, Pittsburgh, PA, August 1982

[14]   C. Green, *"The design of the PSI program synthesizing system"*, Proceedings of the 2nd International Conference on Software Engineering, October 1976, Long Beach, California, pp. 4-18, IEEE CS Press

[15]   Z. Manna, R. Waldinger, *„Dreams→Programs"*, IEEE Transaction on Software Engineering, July 1979, pp. 294-328

[16]   C. Rich, H.E. Schrobe, R.C. Waters, *"An overview of the programmers apprentice"*, Proceedings of the 6th International Joint Conference on Artificial Intelligence, August 1979, Tokyo, Japan, pp. 827-828

[17]   R. Balzer, N. Goldman, and D. While, *"Informality in Program Specification"*, IEEE Transactions on Software Engineering, March 1978, pp. 94-103

[18]   R. Balzer, N. Goldman, and D. Wile, *"Final Report on GIST"*, Technical Report of t he Institute of Information Science, University of Southern California, Los Angeles, 1981

[19]   E. Kant, D. Barstow, *"The Refinement Paradigm: The Interaction of Coding and Efficiency Knowledge in Program Synthesis"*, IEEE Transactions on Software Engineering, September 1981, pp. 458-471

[20]   E. Horowitz, A. Kemper, B. Narasimhan, *"A Survey of Application Generators"*, IEEE Software, January 1985, pp. 40-54

[21]   N. Derschowitz, *"Synthetic programming"*, Artificial Intelligence, No. 25, 1985, pp. 323-373

[22]   X. Jia, S. Skevoulis, *"Code Synthesis Based on Object-Oriented Design Models and Formal Specifications"*, Proceedings of the 22nd Computer Software & Applications Conference 1998, August 19-21, 1998, Vienna, Austria, pp. 393-398, IEEE CS Press

[23]   S. Jarzabek, *„From reuse library experiences to application generation architectures"*, ACM, Proceedings of the Symposion on Software Reuse 1995, pp. 114-122

[24]   M.E. Lesk, E. Schmidt, *"Lex: A Lexical Analyzer Generator"*, UNIX Programmer's Manual-Supplementary Documents, 7th Edition, AT&T Bell Laboratories, Indianapolis, USA

[25]   S.C. Johnson, *"Yacc: Yet Another Compiler Compiler"*, UNIX Programmer's Manual-Supplementary Documents, 7th Edition, AT&T Bell Laboratories, Indianapolis, USA

[26]   S. Jarzabek, „*Specifying and Generating Multilanguage Software Development Environments*", Software Engineering Journal, March 1990, pp. 125-137

[27]   R. Fischer, *"Zusammenfassung der 3rd SIGSOFT Conference on Software Development Environments "*, Mini Micro Magazin, April 1989, pp. 31-33

[28]   A. W. Biermann, *"Approaches to AP"*, in M. Rubinoff, M.C. Yovits, (Editors): "Advances in Computers", Academic Press, 1976 pp.1-63

[29]   D. Partridge, *"Connectionism as a software engineering paradigm"*, Advanced Information Systems, January 1993, pp. 7-14

[30]   J. Martin, *"Application Development Without Programmers"*, Prentice Hall, Englewood Cliffs, N. J., 1982

[31]   P.C. Masiero, C.A.A. Meira, „*Development and Instantiation of a Generic Application Generator*", Journal of Systems Software, 1993, Issue 23, pp. 27-37

[32]   D. Shafer, *"Automatic Pascal Code Generation with Prototyper 2.0"*, Journal of Pascal, Ada & Modula 2, March/April 1989, pp. 58-220

[33]   T.Church and Philip Matthews, „*An Evaluation of Object-Oriented CASE Tools: The Newbridge Experience*", Proceedings of the 7th International Workshop on Computer-Aided Software Engineering 1995, IEEE Computer Society Press,   pp. 4-9

[34]   G. Kiczales, „*Aspect Oriented Programming*", 8th Annual Workshop on Institutionalizing Software Reuse, WISR8, March 23-26 1997

[35]   W. Goebl, *"The Significance of Generative Software Reuse in the Domain of Data-Oriented Information Systems"*, Ph.D Thesis, Technical University of Vienna, 1999

[36]   B. Bhansali, „*A Hybrid Approach to Software Reuse*", Proceedings of the Symposion on Software Reusability 1995, ACM Software Engineering Notes, Special Issue August 1995 pp. 215-218 [37] B. Pieber, W. Goebl, *"A Generative Approach for Building Data-Oriented Information Systems"*, Proceedings of the 22nd Computer Software & Applications Conference 1998, August 19-21, 1998, Vienna, Austria, pp. 278-284, IEEE CS Press, 1998

[38]   D. Batory, B.J. Geraci, *"Validating Component Compositions in Software System Generators"*, Proceedings of the 4th International Conference on Software Reuse, April 23-26, 1996, Orlando Florida, IEEE Computer Society Press, pp. 72-81

[39]   J.M. Neighbors, „*The Draco Approach to Constructing Software From Reusable Components*", IEEE Transactions on Software Engineering, September 1984, pp. 564-574

Using Reflective Logic Programming to Describe Domain Knowledge as an Aspect[*]

Maja D'Hondt[1], Wolfgang De Meuter[2], and Roel Wuyts[2]

[1] System and Software Engineering Laboratory
[2] Programming Technology Laboratory
Brussels Free University, Pleinlaan 2, 1050 Brussels, Belgium,
mjdhondt | wdmeuter | rwuyts@vub.ac.be

Abstract. Software applications, mostly consisting of an algorithm applied to domain knowledge, are hard to maintain and to reuse as a result of their hard coded combination. We propose to follow the principles of aspect-oriented programming, separating the domain from the algorithm and describing them in a logic and conventional programming language respectively. In this paper, we report on an experiment that was conducted to validate this hypothesis, and to investigate the requirements of a programming environment for this configuration. An already existing environment that uses a logic meta-language to reason about object-oriented systems, SOUL, is used as a starting point for this experiment. The result is a working implementation in SOUL, which validates our ideas, reveals mechanisms that require more research, and points to other features that should be included.

1 Introduction

In [1] we argue that separating the *domain* from the *algorithm* in software applications, would solve a lot of maintainance and reuse problems. Applying *aspect-oriented programming* or short *AOP* [2] to model the domain as an aspect program and the algorithm as the base program, allows them to evolve independently from one another. Note that in this paper, by algorithm we mean the functionality of a software application or in general any program, whereas a domain or domain knowledge denotes concepts and constraints that model the real world and which an algorithm can be applied to [1].

Hence, following the AOP paradigm, we propose to express domain knowledge in an appropriate environment acting as an aspect language. When investigating techniques available in (amongst others) the artificial intelligence community for representing knowledge, we come across a number of languages and formalisms based on first-order predicate logic. The algorithm, on the other

---

[*] This work is partly sponsored by the *Vlaams Instituut voor de Bevordering van het Wetenschappelijk-Technologisch Onderzoek in de Industrie*.

[1] Note that, in some cases, an algorithm can also be viewed as being part of domain knowledge.

K. Czarnecki and U.W. Eisenecker (Eds.): GCSE'99, LNCS 1799, pp. 16–23, 2000.
© Springer-Verlag Berlin Heidelberg 2000

hand, is the base program and can be implemented in any conventional programming language such as C, Java and Smalltalk.

In order to conduct initial experiments investigating our hypothesis that software applications would benefit from separating the domain and the algorithm, we require a programming environment that is a symbiosis between a domain aspect language and a conventional programming language. A suitable candidate is the *Smalltalk Open Unification Language* or *SOUL* [3] [4], a declarative framework that uses Prolog to reason about the structure of Smalltalk programs. SOUL was originally developed as a validation for the use of logic meta-languages for expressing relationships in object-oriented systems. In this paper we take advantage of this construction to represent domain knowledge in the Prolog layer and algorithms in Smalltalk. Therefore, Prolog is no longer used as meta-language for reasoning about Smalltalk programs, rather it serves as an aspect language for describing aspect programs on the same level as the base programs in Smalltalk.

In the rest of this paper, we describe an experiment involving an example inspired by a real-world geographic information system (GIS). Although not originally designed for this purpose, we use SOUL and Smalltalk to turn our example into a working aspect-oriented program, thereby providing proof of concept of our ideas. In addition to this, the experiment reveals features that should be incorporated in a programming environment for AOP with domain knowledge as an aspect. Some of these features are not yet implemented in SOUL, but present a mere technical issue. Other features, however, require more investigation.

In the remainder of this text, the *slanted type style* is used to denote concepts from the domain knowledge, whereas algorithms are written in `typewriter type style`.

2   An Example

A GIS, for example a car navigation system, is applied to a vast amount of geographic data, modelled as a planar graph. The nodes, edges and areas of this graph have properties attached to them such as a hotel, a street name or an industrial area respectively. These geographic data are actually the domain knowledge of a GIS. Our example concerns *roads, cities* and *prohibited manoeuvres* (Fig. 1). The latter is modelled on two cities, signifying that it is prohibited to take the road from the first city to the last.

To this sub domain a shortest path algorithm is applied, more specifically the *branch and bound algorithm* below:

```
branchAndBoundFrom: start to: stop
    |bound|
    bound := 999999999.
    self traverseBlock: [:city :sum|
    city free ifTrue: [sum < bound ifTrue: [city = stop
```

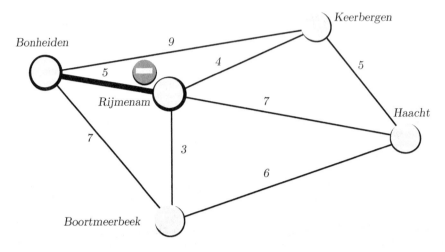

Fig. 1. A planar graph representation of the domain knowledge. The circles denote cities, whereas the lines indicate roads that connect two cities. To each road the distance between the two connected cities is attached. A prohibited manoeuvre is shown from the *city Rijmenam* to the *city Bonheiden*.

```
   ifTrue:  [bound := sum ]
   ifFalse: [self branch: city sum: sum]]]].
self traverseBlock value: start value: 0.
^bound

branch: node sum: sum
   city free: false.
   city roads do: [:road|
   (self isProhibiedFrom: city by: road) ifFalse:
      [self traverseBlock value: road next
                          value: sum + road distance].
   city free: true.
```

By way of introducing the example, we presented it programmed in a conventional way: the domain knowledge and the algorithm are both implemented in Smalltalk. Note that the algorithm implicitly selects the shortest road first, because the instance variable **roads** of a **city** is a sorted collection. Figure 2 shows a UML diagram of the domain and the algorithm.

This branch and bound program illustrates that the domain and the algorithm cannot evolve independently from each other: the domain knowledge concerning prohibited manoeuvres cross-cuts the implementation of the algorithm.

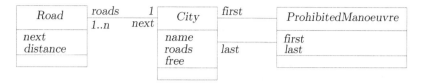

Fig. 2. An UML diagram of the branch and bound algorithm. We assume that accessors and mutators are implemented for the instance variables, which are used in the branch and bound program.

3   A First Experiment

The example, which was described in the previous section as a single Smalltalk program, is now transformed into an aspect-oriented program in SOUL. Using the Prolog layer to describe the domain knowledge, we get the following result:

Fact city (Rijmenam)
Fact city (Boortmeerbeek)
...
Fact road (city (Rijmenam), city (Boortmeerbeek), [3])
Fact road (city (Keerbergen), city (Rijmenam), [4])
...
Fact prohibitedManoeuvre (city (Rijmenam), city (Bonheiden))
Rule roads (?current, ?newResult) if
    findall (road (?current, ?next, ?distance),
    road (?current, ?next, ?distance), ?result),
    privateRoads (?current, ?result, ?newResult).
Rule privateRoads (?current, ?result, ?newResult) if
    prohibitedManoeuvre (?current, ?next),
    removeRoad (?result, road (?current, ?next, ?distance), ?newResult)
Fact privateRoads (?current, ?result, ?result)

The base program in Smalltalk looks like this:

```
branchAndBoundFrom: start to: stop
    |bound|
    bound := 999999999.
    self traverseBlock: [:node :sum|
    node free ifTrue: [sum < bound ifTrue: [node = stop
        ifTrue:  [bound := sum ]
        ifFalse: [self branch: node sum: sum]]]].
    self traverseBlock value: start value: 0.
    ^bound

branch: node sum: sum
    node free: false.
```

```
node edges do: [:edge|
  self traverseBlock value: edge next value: sum + edge distance].
node free: true.
```

Note that it is basically the same as the first version of the algorithm presented in the previous section. We have changed the variables and methods `city` to `node` and `road(s)` to `edge(s)`, to stress that domain knowledge concerning cities and roads is no longer part of the algorithm. There are still nodes and edges in this otherwise domain independent algorithm, because a branch and bound algorithm is graph-based and thus requires the use of these concepts. This imposes a constraint on the domain this algorithm can be applied to, but also indicates the *join points* between the two: *cities* map to `nodes` and *roads* map to `edges`.

Another difference with the previous conventional implementation, is that the base program is no longer responsible for the selection of the next roads to be visited: in the domain layer, the rule *roads* unifies with *?newResult* a list of next roads omitting prohibited manoeuvres. This delegation to the Prolog layer is possible, because Prolog queries can be explicitly launched from Smalltalk code. Thus, when the message `edges` is sent to the variable `node` in the base program, this is translated to a query, for example:

q *Query roads (city (Rijmenam), ?newResult)*[2]

This brings us to another point: the value at run-time of the variables `node` and `edge` in the base program. The algorithm works with placeholder objects, instances of the classes `Node` and `Edge`, which do nothing more than wrap corresponding Prolog facts, *city* and *road* respectively, thus transforming them to Smalltalk objects. Accessing these objects is delegated to the domain layer as a query (see previous example), since these objects do not actually store any values other than a Prolog fact. The mechanism of manipulating Prolog objects in Smalltalk and vice versa, necessary for fixing the join points of the aspect-oriented program, is referred to as the *linguistic symbiosis* of those two languages [5]. The idea is the following:

$$up(s) \quad = p \qquad\qquad\qquad\qquad \text{if } s = down(p)$$
$$ = smalltalkFact(s)$$

$$down(p) = s \qquad\qquad\qquad\qquad \text{if } p = up(s)$$
$$ = \texttt{Prologobject new with: } p$$

where Prolog is the up layer and Smalltalk is the down layer, and where s is a Smalltalk object and p is a Prolog fact. *Upping* a *downed* Prolog object returns the original unwrapped Prolog object. *Upping* a Smalltalk object means wrapping it in a Prolog fact *smalltalkFact*. Vice versa, *downing* an *upped* Smalltalk

---

[2] The prefix q *Query* is required by SOUL syntax.

object returns the Smalltalk object whereas *downing* a Prolog fact wraps it in an instance of the `PrologObject` class from Smalltalk. When Smalltalk sends a message to a Prolog fact, for example to retrieve edges (roads) from *city(Haacht)*, the fact is implicitly *downed* and the result is *upped* again [6]. This linguistic symbiosis is not yet implemented in SOUL and is therefore explicitly and not very elegantly programmed in this experiment, which nevertheless provides a proof of concept. Further work certainly includes embedding this mechanism in SOUL, thus making it implicit and invisible to the programmer.

However, the linguistic symbiosis to enable AOP with the domain aspect requires the *downed* Prolog facts to have a state, as the messages `free` and `free:` in the base program indicate. These messages are used to let the algorithm know if a node has already been visited in order to avoid cycles. This property attached to nodes is purely algorithmic and should not be incorporated in the domain knowledge about cities. Therefore, when a Prolog fact is *downed* for the first time, the programming environment should attach an instance variable `free` and corresponding accessor and mutator to the instance of the class `PrologObject` in Smalltalk that wraps it. This wrapper should be recycled when the same Prolog fact is *downed* again, so that the value of `free`, in other words the state of the wrapper, is not lost.

4   A Second Experiment

For the next experiment, we strip the domain knowledge of prohibited manoeuvres and add a new concept: the *priority manoeuvre* as explained in figure 3.

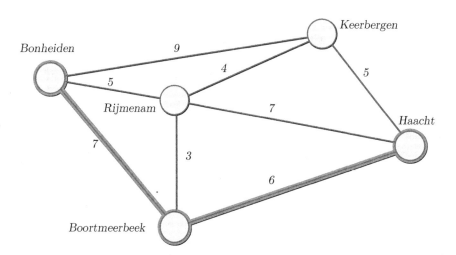

Fig. 3. The priority manoeuvre that concerns the cities *Haacht*, *Boortmeerbeek* and *Bonheiden*. When in *Boortmeerbeek* and coming from *Haacht*, the road to *Bonheiden* is preferred over any other road, even when that road is shorter.

The domain knowledge is extended and replaced with the following:

Fact priorityManoeuvre (city(Haacht), city(Boortmeerbeek), city(Bonheiden))
Rule roads (?current, ?previous, ?newResult) if
    findall (road (?current, ?next, ?distance),
    road (?current, ?next, ?distance), ?result),
    privateRoads (?current, ?previous, ?result, ?newResult)
Rule privateRoads (?current, ?previous, ?result,<road (?current, ?next, ?dis-
tance) | ?newResult>) if
    priorityManoeuvre (?previous, ?current, ?next),
    removeRoad (?result, road (?current, ?next, ?distance), ?newResult)
Fact privateRoads (?current, ?previous, ?result, ?result)

If we would implement the branch and bound algorithm applied to this domain in a conventional program, the algorithm would require the passing of an
extra parameter `previous` in order to find priority manoeuvres, as shown below:

```
branchAndBoundFrom: start to: stop
   ...
   self traverseBlock: [:previous :node :sum |
      ...
      ifFalse: [self branchFrom: previous to: node sum: sum]]]].
   self traverseBlock value: nil value: start value: 0.
   ^bound

branchFrom: previous to: node sum: sum
   ...
```

As with the `free` instance variable in the previous section, the domain knowledge cannot be burdened with this algorithmic information. But neither should
the algorithm be tangled with an extra parameter that is needed to test a domain constraint concerning priority manoeuvres. In our working implementation,
we use the domain knowledge described above and the same algorithm as was
presented in the previous section. This shows that the domain can evolve independently from the algorithm. In order to achieve this, we created an object that
runs in background in parallel with the algorithm, secretly remembering the previously visited node. Although not very elegant, our temporary solution again
hints at what kind of mechanism should be incorporated in an environment for
AOP with domain knowledge as en aspect.

5   Conclusion

This paper reports on an experiment on aspect-oriented programming with domain knowledge as an aspect, using a reflective logic language as the aspect
language. On the one hand this experiment was conducted to show that the domain and the algorithm of a program can evolve independently from one another

when using the AOP paradigm and regarding domain knowledge as an aspect. We validated this hypothesis on a small scale, since the experiment involved limited domain knowledge and a relatively simple algorithm. On the other hand, despite this small scale, the experiment immediately revealed some properties that a programming environment which supports this programming style should have. First of all, it should incorporate a language based on first-order predicate logic for representing the aspect, such as Prolog, and a more conventional programming language for the algorithm. Moreover, the programming environment should provide a language symbiosis between the aspect language and the base language, to allow transparent manipulation of objects from one language in the other. This mechanism is required in order to express the join points between objects in the aspect language (up) and objects in the base language (down). In addition to this, the algorithm should be able to attach algorithmic properties to domain knowledge objects. More precisely, the base program should have the possibility to add instance variables and methods to a *downed* domain object. Finally, this experiment showed that some kind of memory manager should be conceived that runs in the background and that passes otherwise lost information to either the algorithm or the domain layer.

References

1. D'Hondt, M., D'Hondt, T.: Is domain knowledge an aspect? ECOOP99, Aspect-Oriented Programming Workshop (1999)
2. Kiczales, G., Lamping, J., Mendhekar, A., Maeda, C., Lopes, C., Loingtier, J., Irwin, J.: Aspect-oriented programming. In Proceedings of ECOOP (1997)
3. Wuyts, R.: Declarative reasoning about the structure of object-oriented systems. In Proceedings of TOOLS USA (1998)
4. Wuyts, R.: Declaratively codifying software architectures using virtual software classifications. Submitted to TOOLS Europe (1999)
5. Steyaert, S.: Open design of object-oriented languages, a foundation for specialisable reflective language frameworks. PhD thesis, Brussels Free University (1994)
6. De Meuter, W.: The story of the simplest MOP in the world, or, the scheme of object-orientation. In Prototype-Based Programming (1998)

Aspect Weaving with Graph Rewriting

Uwe Aßmann and Andreas Ludwig

Institut für Programmstrukturen und Datenorganisation
Universität Karlsruhe, RZ, Postfach 6980, 76128 Karlsruhe, Germany
(assmann|ludwig)@ipd.info.uni-karlsruhe.de

Abstract. This paper introduces *GRS-based AOP* which explains a large subclass of AOP weavers as graph rewrite systems (GRS). The corresponding class of AOP problems has a formal background since it inherits all features of graph rewrite systems such as criteria for termination, confluence, and unique normal forms. In particular, it it shown that different kinds of rewrite rules form different weaver classes. At least two of them (EARS and XGRS weavers) have simple semantics since they always yield unique weaving results.

Aaspect-oriented programming (AOP) allows to specify parts and behaviors of components using different views, or aspects. These aspects can be specified independently from each other and are combined to the final form by a weaver tool. This composition process yields software that is better readable (since specifications are modular) and better reusable (since aspects can be recombined). However, although single instances of AOP such as Adaptive Programming [Lie96] or Compositon Filters [AWB+94] rely on formal principles the technique as such does not yet have a formal background.

This paper introduces *GRS-based AOP* which explains a large subclass of weavers as graph rewrite systems (GRS). Hence it has a formal background, inheriting all features of graph rewrite systems such as criteria for termination, confluence, and unique normal forms. In particular, it it shown that different kinds of rewrite rules form different weaver classes. Although GRS-based AOP does not cover all possible incarnations of AOP, it provides a simple formalism for aspects relying on properties that can be recognized directly from the their syntactical structure.

We start with a simple example which demonstrates that graph rewrite rules can describe simple weavings. After introducing some basic terminology we present a refined classification concering components, join points, and weavers (section 3). With GRS-based AOP, different kinds of rewrite rules form different weaver classes (section 3.1). Some of them have simple semantics since they always yield unique weaving results. For aspects that are encoded into aspect graphs, it is observed that GRS-based weaving must use context-sensitive graph rewriting (section 3.1). In particular, GRS-based AOP simplifies the construction of AOP weavers. Since tools exist which generate code for the graph rewriting specifications weavers can be generated automatically. We demonstrate this with an example with the graph rewrite tool OPTIMIX (section 4). A table comparing the different classes of GRS-based AOP concludes the paper.

K. Czarnecki and U.W. Eisenecker (Eds.): GCSE'99, LNCS 1799, pp. 24–36, 2000.

1   An Informal Example: Weaving into Method Entries

Suppose we want to weave some statements into all methods of a class that express a debugging aspect, e.g. the statements could print a message when a method is entered. To this end, a weaver should insert the corresponding statements expressing the aspect into all entries of the methods. For example,

```
public doit () {
    /* here comes the method body */
}
...
```

should be extended with a statement which prints the name of the class:

```
public doit () {
    System.out.println("entering class " + this.getClass().getName()); // debugging aspect
    /* here comes the method body */
}
...
```

The rule in Fig. 1 depicts a simple simple weaver, consisting of a simple graph rewrite system with only one rule. The weaver rule contains in its left-hand side two patterns, one that matches a class and its method (later on called the component pattern), and another one which matches a statement expressing the aspect (later on called the aspect pattern). Whenever a redex in the classes and aspect statements is found whose class name corresponds to the name mentioned in the aspect statement the statement is linked to the method as entry statement. The lower part of Fig. 1 shows two redexes in an example graph which the rule matches. The entries of the corresponding methods are extended by the statement that carries the aspect. If the statements consist of printing debugging output, and the rule system is parametrized with the appropriate class name, it transforms our example as desired.

The example hints to the insight that certain weave problems can be expressed with graph rewritings over components and aspect graphs. Before we detail this, the next section presents some basic terminology.

2   Basic Terminology

In AOP, only some basic terminology seems to be standardized [KLM+97]. The area is new and quickly developing; it is not yet known how far AOP reaches, and a preliminary fixing of the terms could hinder the development. Hence this paper relies on some basic definitions for AOP terms that seem to be generally consistent with the literature; this does not preclude that other definitions can be considered:

Components contain the primary structure of a program [Cza98]. They have a meaning of their own, i.e. do not refer to other aspects. They carry the core functional semantics of an application. *Aspects* form the secondary structure of the application and refer to components or other aspects. A *join point* is a point

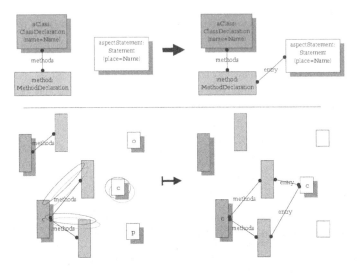

Fig. 1. Weaving a statement which realizes an aspect into a class' methods. Classes are depicted in gray, methods in gray without shade, statements in white. On top, the graph rewrite rule is depicted. Two redexes are found in this example host graph.

in a component where aspects are integrated. A *weaver* integrates aspect into components to arrive at the final program.

AOP literature distinguishes different ways how aspects are specified. This leads to different classes of aspects and aspect-oriented systems:

Script-based AOP In this operational approach, aspects are weaved in by scripts which modify the component explicitly. They are executed at weaving time in a predefined order. RG is one of those systems [MKL97]: its memoization, fusion and memory management aspect are represented by rules which are applied to the algorithmic component.

Language-based AOP In this declarative approach, aspects are described by aspect languages. [KLM+97] claims that aspect languages provide more abstraction than script-based AOP and increase the expressive power of aspect specifications. However, to interpret aspects weavers must be full-fledged compilers. AspectJ is one of these systems [Lop97].

Rewriting-based AOP It has been proposed to regard a weaver as a rewriting system which rewrites components and aspects [Aßm97] [FS98]. This approach relies on the representation of aspects in data or abstract syntax (in case the aspect was specified with an aspect language) and weaves aspects by program transformations. In consequence, it is a kind of amalgamation between script-based and language-based AOP. In rewriting-based AOP, A *component/aspect graph* is an *abstract syntax graph* of a component/aspect, i.e. an instance of the *component/aspect data model*.

A variant of this kind of AOP relies on *meta models* of components and aspects and weaves aspects by *meta-programming*.

This classification need not be complete – other weavers and weaving mechanisms are likely to be invented. In this paper, we will concentrate on a variant of rewriting-based AOP, *GRS-based AOP*; this approach describes weavers as graph rewrite systems, gives them a formal background, and – employing graph rewrite tools – an automatic implementation method. Before we detail GRS-based AOP, some basic terminology of graph rewriting has to be presented.

2.1   Graph Rewrite Systems

From the many variants of graph rewrite system in the literature, we choose *relational graph rewriting*, in which graphs uniformly represent components and aspects [Aßm96a]. Nodes represent entities of components and aspects, and are linked by multiple *relations*. As opposed to general graph rewriting [EKL90], it is not required to deal with multigraphs since relations represent predicates over the entities, and a predicate holds or does not hold [Aßm96a].

Relational graph rewriting relies on the following definitions. A *context-free pattern* is a finite connected graph. A *context-sensitive pattern* is a graph of at least two disconnected subgraphs. A *host graph* is the graph to be rewritten by a graph rewrite system. A *redex* is a subgraph of the host graph injectively homomorphic to a pattern. A *graph rewrite rule* $r = (L, R)$ consists of a left-hand side pattern L and a right-hand side graph R. r is matched against the host graph, i.e. its redex is located in the host graph. A rewriting step which replaces a redex with parts specified in the right-hand side of the rule is called *direct derivation*. A sequence of direct derivation is a *derivation*. A terminating derivation ends in a *normal form* of the host graph.

All these definitions can be formalized precisely [Aßm96a] [RV94]; due to space restrictions, we keep them abstract. It is well-known that several different semantics for graph rewrite rules exists [BFG94]. Our examples here only deal with left hand sides that match a fixed number of nodes in a 1-context embedding [SWZ95]. There are more powerful approaches which allow to match sets of nodes and arbitrary embeddings.

3   GRS-based AOP

GRS-based AOP does not cover all possible incarnations of AOP, but provides a simple formalism for the weaving of aspects which rely on properties directly recognizable from the structure of the aspect specification and the components. Based on the definitions in the previous section, certain weaving processes can be modelled with graph rewriting which gives several important AOP terms a precise and clear meaning. In the following, all defined terms should be prefixed with the prefix *GRS-based-*. This is omitted for brevity.

A *join point* is a redex of a pattern in the component graph. An *aspect fragment* is a redex of a pattern in an aspect graph. An *aspect composer* (an aspect composition operator) is a graph rewrite rule. Nodes and edges in this rule are typed with the component and aspect data model. Most often, the left-hand side contains at least one *component pattern* and one *aspect pattern*. A *component pattern* is a pattern in the left-hand side of an aspect composer matching a join point. An *aspect pattern* is a pattern in the left-hand side of an aspect composer matching an aspect fragment. A *weave operation (weaving transformation)* is a direct derivation in a system of aspect composers, attaching an aspect fragment to a join point. A *weaver* is a graph rewrite system with aspect composers, working on the component graph and a set of aspect graphs. The weaving stops when a normal form of the system is found.

Once weaving is described with graph rewriting, several classes of weavers can be defined. Weavers inherit several formal features such as termination or confluence from the kind of rule system which specifies them.

3.1   Aspect Fragment Matching Rule Systems

Weaving systems of this class matchcomponent join points as well as aspect fragments in their left-hand sides. Due to the nature of aspects, components and aspect graphs are disconnected. Rewriting relates aspect subgraphs to component subgraphs. In consequence, component patterns and aspect patterns in aspect composers must also be disconnected patterns in left-hand sides. This yields the following insight:

An aspect composer matching aspect fragments in aspect graphs must be a context-sensitive graph rewrite rule, consisting of at least two disconnected subgraphs in its left-hand side, a component pattern and an aspect pattern.

Aspect fragment matching systems have the advantage that one join point can be matched multiple times with one rule, together with different aspect fragments. Hence several aspect fragments can be related to one join point with one rule, and complex weave operations can be expressed easily.

Aspect fragment matching systems can be classified at least in the following subclasses which show different behavior in termination and congruence, thus yielding different weaving behavior.

Aspect-relating Rules (EARS Weavers)   One of the simplest classes of graph rewrite systems only constructs relations, i.e. adds edges to a set of nodes. These systems are called *edge-addition rewrite systems (EARS)* and are always *congruent* (i.e. terminating and confluent) [Aßm94]. Such specifications have a simple semantics: there will be always one unique result. If such a system is used to specify a weaver, the weaver is deterministic, and hence a function from the domains of rules, components, and aspect graphs to the weaved programs.

EARS weavers are useful when items in the component graph need to be *related* to aspects: the nodes in the component graph are not modified but related to aspect fragments. This is ideal for simple property aspects. Binary properties as persistence or distribution can be expressed by relating a component node to an appropriate aspect fragment (Fig. 2).

Clearly, our example in section 1 is an EARS weaver. Hence the weaver is terminating and deterministic, i.e. the generated program is uniquely determined.

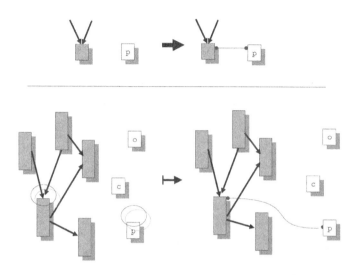

Fig. 2. Above: EARS rule, relating items of the component graph to an aspect property. Here, p means "persistence". Above left: component pattern. Above right: aspect pattern. Down: a direct derivation. Afterwards, the item in the component graph is related to the persistence property.

Aspect-additive Rules Extend Components (XGRS Weavers) Aspect-additive rules add aspect fragments to join points but do not modify the join points (Fig. 3). They match a component pattern as well as an aspect pattern but do not modify the component redex. In consequence, redexes are never destroyed. Such systems are strongly confluent since their direct derivations are commutative [Aßm96a]. If the system terminates, it yields a unique result and the weaving process is deterministic as in the case of EARS weavers.

Termination for additive graph rewrite systems has been proven in [Aßm96b]. When a system completes a subgraph of the host graph and does not add nodes to it, it terminates. Those systems are called *exhaustive GRS (XGRS)*. For weaving, this means that the aspect-additive rule system completes a subgraph in the component graph to which it does not add nodes. In consequence, a weaver consisting of an XGRS is congruent and always yields a unique weaving result. We call such systems *XGRS weavers*. Similar to EARS weavers, they have a simple and deterministic semantics.

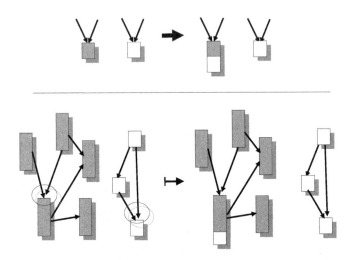

Fig. 3. Additive aspect weaving rules are context-sensitive graph rewrite rules which do not destroy join points since components are not modified.

Component-modifying Rules Weaving may require to exchange parts of components. Then an aspect composer needs to modify its component pattern, i.e. the component pattern is not rule invariant (Fig. 4).

Also with component-modifying rules, termination may be provable with the XGRS criterion, but confluence is lost. Modifying rules destroy join points in components. If two rules refer to the same parts of a join point, such a rule system produces overlaps, i.e. non-commutative direct derivations. In consequence, the system cannot be strongly confluent nor yields unique normal forms. Then, the weaving process is indeterministic since several normal forms may exist.

Indeterministic weaver specifications only make sense if all normal forms are semantically equivalent which may be proved for a particular specification[1]. Otherwise it has to be proved that a weaver specification is confluent.

3.2   Aspects in Rules Only

Aspect weavers can also rely on rules which do not contain disconnected component and aspect patterns. For instance, aspects can be encoded in rules themselves. Then the aspect fragments which are to be introduced in join points are encoded in the right-hand sides of rules $(R \setminus L)$ and a specification of aspects apart from the weaving rules is not necessary. Hence these systems are very similar to script-based AOP systems (section 2).

---

[1] Also program optimization is an indeterministic process. However, there are always variants of the program with the same semantics. If the optimization only yields such equivalent variants, it is semantically sound.

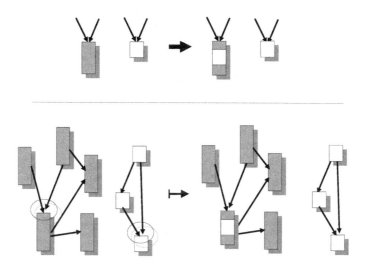

Fig. 4. A rule modifying a component with an aspect fragment. The component pattern is not rule-invariant.

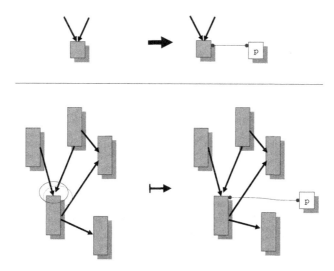

Fig. 5. Aspects specified in right hand sides of rules. Above: rule with aspect in $R \setminus L$. Down: aspect is introduced into the component graph by executing the right hand side of the rule

3.3   Intra-component Weaving Rules

One class of weavers results when rules rewrite the component graph only (*intra-component rules*), i.e. contain only component patterns. Such systems may modify join points, may add parts of join points to other join points, or may move code from one place of the component to another (Fig. 6). Hence they can also be classified as EARS-based, additive or modifying, inheriting the same formal features.

An example for such a *code-motion weaver* is RG, which optimizes the control- and data-flow aspect in a component [MKL97]. Such systems resemble standard code motion optimizations in compilers since they move code within the component [Aßm96b]. Their join points correspond to code statements in the component graph.

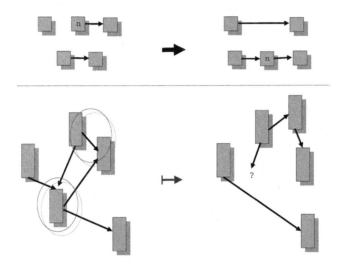

Fig. 6. Rules weaving intra-componently. Here, the rule moves a node n to another place.

This concludes our classification of GRS-based AOP weavers. It is likely that more classes will be found, which differ in their weaving semantics since they have different formal features as graph rewrite systems.

4   Weaving with GRS Tools

In GRS-based AOP, weaver specifications can be fed into a graph rewrite tool to generate a weaver implementation. One example for such a tool is OPTI-MIX which produces C and Java code from rule specifications in textual form [Aßm96b] [Aßm99]. Figure 1 would be specified as follows:

```
grs WeaveAspectStatement(ClassDeclarationList classDeclarations, Identifier Name,
                  StatementList aspectStatements) {
  range aClass <= classDeclarations;        // instantiation of aClass, component data
        aspectStatement <= aspectStatements; // instantiation of aspectStatement, aspect data
  rules
    if // look for join point (aClass,method) in all classes (component pattern)
       aClass.name == Name and method in aClass.methods
       // aspect pattern
       and aspectStatement.place == Name
    then // add the statement to the method of the class
       aspectStatement in method.entry;
} grs
```

The rule system `WeaveAspectStatement` consists of one rule. Its precondi-
tion (between `if` and `then`) consists of a list of conjunctive predicates which
correspond to the edges of the left-hand side from Fig. 1. The generated algorithm searches all redices (join point and aspect fragment pairs) starting
from a range of nodes (all classes in list `classDeclarations` and statements
in `aspectStatements`). The rule rewrites a redex, adding the `aspectStatement`
to the entry of the `method`. Hence in the modified class graph, each time a
method from class with name `Name` from list `classDeclarations` is called, the
aspect statement is executed.

For the rule system, OPTIMIX generates a Java method which contains
the weaver. Basically, this weaver applies the rules until a fixpoint is reached.
Also, OPTIMIX finds out that `WeaveAspectStatement` is an EARS and applies
certain optimizations to improve the efficiency of the generated weaver.

The generated weaver can be applied for weaving of arbitrary aspects into
method entries, such as mixing in diagnostic print statements – as in our example
–, or event signalling statements for program animation. Also, the system can
be extended with more rules so that more complex aspect weavings are possible,
e.g. complete method wrappings.

Not all aspect weavings can be reduced to GRS-based AOP. However, we
believe that we have identified an important subclass of AOP which has a precise
semantics: the weaving is based on graph rewriting, join points are redices, the
weaver consists of the graph rewrite system, and weaver implementations can be
generated automatically.

5   Related Work

It is well-known that AOP can be modeled with meta-programming [KLM+97].
Although GRS-based AOP also relies on a data model (meta model) of both
aspects and components, it has not been realized yet that aspect composers can
be modeled by graph rewrite rules.

[Zim97] develops the idea to use design patterns as transformation operators
on the class graph. In [Aßm97], we have extended this work: design patterns are
regarded as graph rewrite rules modifying class graphs. Since design patterns
refer to certain aspects of systems it is only a small step towards the work
presented in this paper.

The most closely related work is [FS98]. Here aspect composition is explained as a program transformation on abstract syntax trees, i.e. as *term rewriting system*. This is similar to our approach, however, we claim that graph rewriting is more apt for aspect composition since it has to deal with *class graphs*. Secondly, whenever aspects are represented explicitly in an aspect graph, term rewriting is not sufficient since context-sensitive rules are required. Fradet and Südholt also claim that aspect compositions that preserve semantics are closely related to program optimizations. This is supported by our approach since we use essentially the same graph-rewriting approach that has been found useful as a uniform framework for program optimizations [Aßm96b].

In this paper, we have considered automated, i.e. *chaotic* graph rewriting. In contrast, *programmed* graph rewriting a la PROGRES [SWZ95] allows to program a control-flow on rewrite rules. This helps to structure otherwise non-confluent or non-terminating rule systems, but sacrifices the declarative semantics of general graph rewriting.

6   Conclusion

This paper presented GRS-based AOP, an approach in which aspects, join points, and weavings have a well-defined and precise semantics since they are all defined in terms of graph-rewriting. Aspect composition is described by graph rewrite rules, weave operations are direct derivations, and weaved programs are normal forms of the rewrite systems. Formal features, such as termination or confluence criteria are inherited to weaving. A classification of the aspect composers leads to two classes of simple weaving systems which have a deterministic semantics (EARS weavers and XGRS weavers). Aspect composer systems can be fed into graph rewrite tools such as OPTIMIX which generate weavers automatically. Hence for GRS-based AOP, it is not necessary to write weavers by hand.

The following table summarizes our classification of GRS-based AOP and the features of its classes.

System	terminating?	deterministic?	Aspect graph
Aspect Fragment Matching			
Aspect-relating (EARS)	yes	yes	yes
Aspect-additive	if XGRS	yes	yes
Component-modifying	if XGRS	normally not	yes
Aspects in Rules	depends	depends	no
Intra-component	depends	depends	no

Clearly, GRS-based AOP does not cover all AOP incarnations. Also, specific instances may have more appropriate formalizations. In particular, it should be investigated how specific formalizations, e.g. of Adaptive Programming, relate to GRS-based AOP. In general, AOP requires more research: How are aspects described which do not only rely on syntactical properties? How can we relate, reuse, modify, (de)compose aspects? To answer these questions, GRS-based AOP provides a good starting point.

References

[Aßm94]   Uwe Aßmann. On Edge Addition Rewrite Systems and Their Relevance to Program Analysis. In J. Cuny, H. Ehrig, G. Engels, and G. Rozenberg, editors, *5th Int. Workshop on Graph Grammars and Their Application To Computer Science, Williamsburg*, volume 1073 of *Lecture Notes in Computer Science*, pages 321–335, Heidelberg, November 1994. Springer.

[Aßm96a] Uwe Aßmann. Graph Rewrite Systems For Program Optimization. Technical Report RR-2955, INRIA Rocquencourt, 1996.

[Aßm96b] Uwe Aßmann. How To Uniformly Specify Program Analysis and Transformation. In P. A. Fritzson, editor, *Compiler Construction (CC)*, volume 1060 of *Lecture Notes in Computer Science*, pages 121–135, Heidelberg, 1996. Springer.

[Aßm97]   Uwe Aßmann. AOP with design patterns as meta-programming operators. Technical Report 28, Universität Karlsruhe, October 1997.

[Aßm99]   Uwe Aßmann. OPTIMIX, A Tool for Rewriting and Optimizing Programs. In *Graph Grammar Handbook, Vol. II*. Chapman-Hall, 1999.

[AWB+94] Mehmet Aksit, Ken Wakita, Jan Bosch, Lodewijk Bergmans, and Akinori Yonezawa. Abstracting object interactions using composition filters. In O. Nierstrasz, R. Guerraoui, and M. Riveill, editors, *Proceedings of the ECOOP'93 Workshop on Object-Based Distributed Programming*, LNCS 791, pages 152–184. Springer-Verlag, 1994.

[BFG94]   Dorothea Blostein, Hoda Fahmy, and Ann Grbavec. Practical Use of Graph Rewriting. Technical Report Queens University, Kingston, Ontario, November 1994.

[Cza98]   Krzysytof Czarnecki. *Generative Programming: Principles and Techniques of Software Engineering Based on Automated Configuration and Fragment-Based Component Models*. PhD thesis, Technical University of Ilmenau, October 1998.

[EKL90]   H. Ehrig, M. Korff, and M. Löwe. Tutorial introduction to the algebraic approach of graph grammars based on double and single pushouts. In H. Ehrig, H.-J. Kreowski, and G. Rozenberg, editors, *4th International Workshop On Graph Grammars and Their Application to Computer Science*, volume 532 of *Lecture Notes in Computer Science*, pages 24–37, Heidelberg, March 1990. Springer.

[FS98]   Pascal Fradet and Mario Südholt. AOP: Towards a Generic Framework Using Program Transformation and Analysis. In *Workshop on Aspect-oriented Programming, ECOOP*, July 1998.

[KLM+97] Gregor Kiczales, John Lamping, Anurag Mendhekar, Chris Maeda, Cristina Lopez, Jean-Marc Loingtier, and John Irwin. Aspect-oriented programming. In *ECOOP 97*, volume 1241 of *Lecture Notes in Computer Science*, pages 220–242. Springer-Verlag, 1997.

[Lie96]   Karl J. Lieberherr. *Adaptive Object-Oriented Software: The Demeter Method*. PWS Publishing, 1996.

[Lop97]   Christina Videira Lopes. *D: A Language Framework for Distributed Programming*. PhD thesis, College of Computer Science, Northeastern University, November 1997.

[MKL97]   Anurag Mendhekar, Gregor Kiczales, and John Lamping. RG: A Case-Study for Aspect-Oriented Programming. Technical report, Xerox Palo Alto Research Center, 1997.

[RV94]   Jean-Claude Raoult and Frédéric Voisin. Set-theoretic graph rewriting. In Hans Jürgen Schneider and Hartmut Ehrig, editors, *Graph Transformations in Computer Science*, volume 776 of *Lecture Notes in Computer Science*, pages 312–325, 1994.

[SWZ95]   Andreas Schürr, Andreas J. Winter, and Albert Zürndorf. Graph Grammar Engineering with PROGRES. In *European Software Engineering Conference ESEC 5*, volume 989 of *Lecture Notes in Computer Science*, pages 219–234, Heidelberg, September 1995. Springer.

[Zim97]   Walter Zimmer. *Frameworks und Entwurfsmuster*. PhD thesis, Universität Karlsruhe, February 1997.

Aspects in Distributed Environments

E. Pulvermüller, H. Klaeren, and A. Speck

Wilhelm-Schickard-Institut für Informatik
University of Tübingen
D-72076 Tübingen

Abstract. We illustrate how to combine CORBA as a distributed system with aspect-oriented programming (AOP) and the resulting positive impacts. In particular, we focus on the question how AOP can be applied to a CORBA application aiming at a better separation of concerns.
The paper shows with implementation examples a practical way to package the distribution issues of a CORBA application into separated aspects (with AspectJ). This supports the distributed application design and leads to increased flexiblity.

1 Introduction

A system with distribution is characterized by a substantial amount of complexity. When designing distributed applications additional issues compared to centralized systems have to be considered. Some of these issues are fragmentation, replication, naming, concurrency, failure, configuration and communication [25].

There are different approaches to manage this inherent complexity in distributed systems:

One way is to aim at *transparency* to build models which are very close to those of centralized systems. Distribution related issues are hidden to the user and the application programmer [3]. However, there are many cases where full transparency is not desirable or reachable. In [9] it is even pointed out that distribution transparency is impossible to achieve in practice.

In a fully transparent communication environment the application developer has at best limited possibilities to influence the way of communicating or to improve network performance, respectively. The flexibility to fully exploit communication knowledge is restricted.

Other approaches aim at supporting the development of distributed applications by offering a *process* or *method*, respectively. In [25] a stepwise development process is shown. The different concerns (fragmentation, replication, naming, concurrency, failure, configuration, communication) are handled transparently according to the idea of separation of concerns.

Besides transparency and the application of an appropriate software development method, the usage of *patterns* [7], [2], [19], particularly those for distributed systems as in [16] is an established means to ease and improve application design [22]. Patterns provide architectural or design solutions for known problems.

K. Czarnecki and U.W. Eisenecker (Eds.): GCSE'99, LNCS 1799, pp. 37–48, 2000.

Distributed application development can furthermore be simplified using a *framework*. Examples for such frameworks are CORBA implementations [18], [24] and ACE [23]. A framework is a semi-finished set of cooperating classes which are the main components to create systems [6], [19], [20]. A developer customizes the framework to a particular application.

Leaving fully transparent systems out of account due to their lack of flexibility, there still remains in all approaches the necessity to inject additional code into objects. Distribution issues like communication, naming, etc. are implemented this way. This is one primary source of complexity in distributed applications which can be addressed with aspect-oriented programming (AOP) [13], [14]. AOP is a concept to achieve separation of concerns. Reusable objects are designed and coded separately to cross-cutting code. An aspect weaver is responsible for merging both design elements. AOP is one research area in the field of generative programming [5], [4].

In the remainder of this paper we show how a CORBA environment can be profitably combined with aspect-oriented programming. We take JavaIDL (together with the IDL compiler `idltojava`) [26] as an almost CORBA 2.0 [18] compliant distributed object technology provided with the Java Development Kit (JDK) 1.2. For the AOP part we use AspectJ 0.3beta1 [28]. This is an aspect-oriented extension to Java developed at Xerox PARC. AspectJ 0.3beta1 supports additional syntax to define aspects, separated from the Java class code. Currently, the weaving output is pure Java which can be automatically compiled with JDK.

2   Combining CORBA and AOP

When combining two technologies the question raises how one technology can take advantage of the other. With AOP and CORBA systems there are multiple answers to this question:

1. Applying aspects to cross-cutting issues of the problem domain
   Aspect-oriented programming can be applied to application objects running in a CORBA environment in the same way as in centralized applications. Cross-cutting code resulting out of the problem domain is collected in aspects (cf. figure 1)[1]. After the weaving process (e.g. with AspectJ) the resulting pure Java application can run distributed in a CORBA environment that supports the Java language mapping (e.g. JavaIDL from Sun Microsystems or VisiBroker from Inprise).
2. Implementing CORBA related code in distributed applications as aspects
   Regarding a CORBA distributed application, both client and server are supplemented with more or less code referring to ORB and Common Object

---

[1]   Weaving should be regarded just as one phase of the compilation process [12]. Throughout this paper we present the weaving as a separate primary phase in order to stress it.

Services (defined in COSS [17]) or even Common Facility (CF) functionality. Program parts concerning distribution issues could be separated from the original objects by means of aspects (cf. figure 1).

3. Distributing aspects using CORBA

Many objects can reuse the same aspect. In a distributed environment this means that these objects could be distributed. Therefore, the reused aspects have to be made available in the whole distributed environment. This increases complexity since the suitable aspect has to be found in a network of computing units. The emerging complexity caused by the need to manage those distributed aspects could be handled by a kind of aspect repository similar to an Interface Repository. This could help managing those distributed aspects. Especially graphical tools could ease locating the aspects in the network.

In figure 2 an *Application* at location C can find the appropriate aspects via the aspect repository (e.g. *Aspect1* and *Aspect2*). With dynamic aspects as proposed in [15], [11] the process of searching and choosing aspects can be done even at run-time.

4. Using aspects to implement or extend a CORBA (like) system

In [10] a CORBA-compliant middleware architecture for distributed systems is described. The idea of this adaptable and configurable middleware, called AspectIX, is to extend CORBA to a more open and flexible model. In AspectIX a client may configure (even dynamically) functional and nonfunctional properties of the objects semantics by means of aspects.

Section 3 concentrates mainly on the question in which ways CORBA related code can be put into aspects (item 2). Since distribution related code has to be injected into object code this is a major source of complexity. Therefore, applying AOP to distributed CORBA applications this way addresses one of the most urgent problems.

3   Aspects for CORBA Communication Code

In this section we want to work out in which ways aspects could be applied to applications using a CORBA-compliant ORB implementation for communication purposes. The question is whether AOP can help to improve problem understanding, coding and reuse. The CORBA program parts have to be investigated in order to find the possible positive impacts which aspects have on the resulting CORBA code.

In the following a simple client/server application exchanging a string is investigated[2]. With the simple example the impacts of AOP can be shown.

The implementation uses JavaIDL as an almost CORBA-compliant implementation from Sun Microsystems and AspectJ 0.3beta1 from Xerox as an AOP mechanism.

---

[2] Both error handling and debugging functionality are classical examples for the usage of aspects [28]. They are not regarded in this paper.

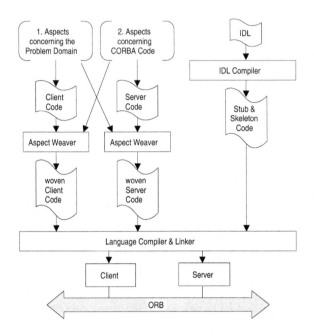

Fig. 1. Cross-cutting Code relating to (*1.*) Problem Domain and (*2.*) CORBA as Aspects

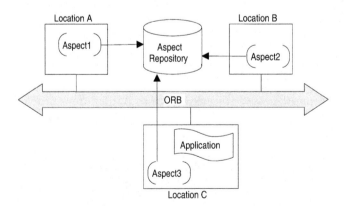

Fig. 2. Distributed Aspects

3.1   The Client Side

The client can be coded almost as if it were a pure local client.

```
import App.*;

public class Client
{
  static Interface_Name ref;

  public static void main(String args[])
  {
    try{

      // Call server object and print result
      String aString = ref.get();
      System.out.println(aString);

    } catch(Exception e) {
        System.out.println("ERROR : " + e);
        e.printStackTrace(System.out);
      }
  }
}
```

The variable `ref` holds a reference to the `Servant`. The servant implements an interface called `Interface_Name` which defines the `get()` operation. In the distributed version the interface is generated out of the `.idl` file. `App` is a package containing the stubs generated with the IDL compiler `idltojava` or other application specific packages in a local version.

Additional code for a local version is encapsulated in the following aspect:

```
/**
 * The ClientLocal aspect injects code before method main
 * of class Client to run the Client locally.
 */
aspect ClientLocal {
  advise void Client.main(String args[]){
    static before {
      try{
        ref = new Servant();
      } catch(Exception e) {
          System.out.println("ERROR : " + e);
          e.printStackTrace(System.out);
        }
    }
  }
}
```

For the interaction with a server in the CORBA environment the communication and the name server issues are localized in a client communication aspect. It is assumed that the corresponding server works with the COS naming service [17] of JavaIDL.

```
/**
 * The ClientComm aspect injects CORBA code before
 * method main of class Client.
 */
import org.omg.CosNaming.*;
import org.omg.CORBA.*;

aspect ClientComm {
```

```
advise void Client.main(String args[]){
  static before {
    try{
      // Create and initialize the ORB
      ORB orb = ORB.init(args, null);

      // Get the root naming context
      org.omg.CORBA.Object objRef
        = orb.resolve_initial_references("NameService");
      NamingContext ncRef = NamingContextHelper.narrow(objRef);

      // Resolve the object reference
      NameComponent nc = new NameComponent("Name", " ");
      NameComponent path[] = {nc};
      ref = Server_InterfaceHelper.narrow(ncRef.resolve(path));
    } catch(Exception e) {
        System.out.println("ERROR : " + e);
        e.printStackTrace(System.out);
    }
  }
 }
}
```

Now, the corresponding server may run locally or in the CORBA distributed environment. For a locally running server (class `Servant`) the client has to be woven with the `ClientLocal` aspect whereas a distributed server leads to the need to weave with the `ClientComm` aspect.

3.2   The Server Side

Further advantages of AOP can be exploited if it is applied to the server code. Whereas distribution issues were separated on the client side, the main advantage considered on the server side is flexiblity. With AOP, the application developer can combine the appropriate aspects into the server compilation process, which results in a server with a special functionality.

In our example we demonstrate how a server can provide either a name server or a file based (stringified object reference [18] stored in a file) functionality depending on the aspects chosen in the compilation process. Obviously, a client using this functionality has to implement the corresponding code (at best encapsulated in an aspect, as well).

The application can be divided into kernel code and some flexible, interchangeable code fragments packed into aspects as depicted in figure 3.

The `Server` is responsible for creating a `Servant` instance which serves the request from the client.

```
import App.*;
import org.omg.CORBA.*; // CORBA specific classes.

class Servant extends _Interface_NameImplBase
{
  public String get()
  {
    return "\n A String \n";
  }
}

public class Server
```

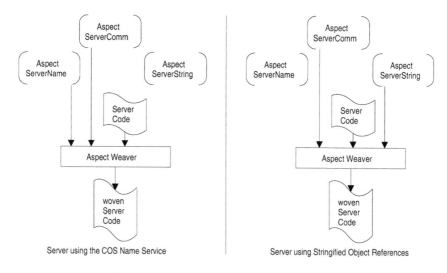

Fig. 3. Flexible Programming with Aspects

```
{
  static Servant ref;

  public static void main(String args[])
  {
    try{
      // Create the servant
      ref = new Servant();
    } catch(Exception e) {
        System.err.println("ERROR: " + e);
        e.printStackTrace(System.out);
      }
  }
}
```

As shown in figure 3 there is an aspect implementing the CORBA related code using the name server functionality:

```
/**
 * The ServerName aspect injects name server
 * functionality after method main of class Server.
 */
import org.omg.CosNaming.*; // naming service.
import org.omg.CosNaming.NamingContextPackage.*;
import org.omg.CORBA.*;

aspect ServerName {
  advise void Server.main(String args[]) {
    static after {
      try{
        // Create and initialize the ORB
        ORB orb = ORB.init(args, null);
        orb.connect(ref);

        // Get the root naming context
        org.omg.CORBA.Object objRef
                = orb.resolve_initial_references("NameService");
        NamingContext ncRef = NamingContextHelper.narrow(objRef);
```

```
      // Bind the object reference in naming
      NameComponent nc = new NameComponent("Name", " ");
      NameComponent path[] = {nc};
      ncRef.rebind(path, ref);
    } catch(Exception e) {
        System.out.println("ERROR : " + e);
        e.printStackTrace(System.out);
      }
    }
  }
}
```

The `ServerString` aspect implements the CORBA related code, as well. Instead of using the name server it saves a stringified reference into a file out of which the client can extract the reference.

```
/**
 * The ServerString aspect injects stringified reference
 * code after method main of class Server.
 */

import java.io.*;
import org.omg.CORBA.*;

aspect ServerString{
  advise void Server.main(String args[]) {
    static after {
      try{
        // Create and initialize the ORB
        ORB orb = ORB.init(args, null);
        orb.connect(ref);

        // stringify the ref and dump it in a file
        String str = orb.object_to_string(ref);
        String filename = System.getProperty("user.home")
           +System.getProperty("file.separator")+"IOR";
        FileOutputStream fos
           = new FileOutputStream(filename);
        PrintStream ps = new PrintStream(fos);
        ps.print(str);
        ps.close();
      } catch (Exception e) {
          System.err.println("ERROR: " + e);
          e.printStackTrace(System.out);
        }
    }
  }
}
```

The `ServerComm` aspect can be reused. It contains the code responsible for waiting for a client request. This implementation is used both in a server working with the name server and in the server using the stringified reference approach.

```
/**
 * The ServerComm aspect injects the wait for request
 * code after method main of class Server.
 * (must be inserted after ServerString or ServerName).
 */
import org.omg.CORBA.*;

aspect ServerComm {
  advise void Server.main(String args[]){
    static after {
      try{
```

```
    // Wait for invocations from clients
    java.lang.Object sync = new java.lang.Object();
    synchronized(sync){
      sync.wait();
    }
  } catch(Exception e) {
      System.out.println("ERROR : " + e);
      e.printStackTrace(System.out);
    }
  }
 }
}
```

These examples show that aspects are a promising and powerful means to achieve flexible programming by choosing and combining the necessary aspects.

Furthermore, an aspect can implement a non CORBA-compliant functionality. When exchanging this aspect with a CORBA-compliant one an application easily can be ported to a CORBA system. Besides this exchange of aspects no further changes may be necessary if the CORBA related code is completely concentrated into separated aspects.

There are other approaches aiming at a good separation of concerns. One way would be to use abstraction, i.e. to encapsulate CORBA related code in functions. This requires to insert an appropriate function call into the client or server code. Unlike the aspect solution the developer is obliged to change this call within the code when functionality has to be changed. With aspects, the developer has a clearly separated and therefore flexible programming construct. Moreover, a solution with aspects is orthogonal to the abstraction provided by the functions.

4   Experiences with AspectJ in a CORBA Environment

JavaIDL seems to be a very promising and almost CORBA-compliant ORB since it is integrated into JDK 1.2. According to Sun JavaIDL supports the basic CORBA-compliant ORB interfaces as well as a COS Naming Service [26]. However, currently not all CORBA features are implemented in JavaIDL[3] and it is available on a very limited number of platforms (Solaris and Windows). It may be expected that the significance of JavaIDL will increase due to the fact that Sun Microsystems has announced that it will support the porting of JDK 1.2 to other platforms (e.g. Linux).

Though all the distributed applications using JavaIDL have been tested on Windows NT 4.0, weaving with AspectJ 0.3beta1 is also possible on Linux if appropriate JavaIDL packages exist.

Despite promising advantages there remain some minor problems:
Multiple existing aspects can be woven with application objects. This requires the possibility to specify the order of the aspects that are woven into the application code. The weaving priority in AspectJ 0.3beta1 is determined by the aspect name. A language construct to express this order explicitly would ease the aspect management.

---

[3] The Interface Repository, for example, is not yet implemented.

In the case of an error during compilation, the error report of the compiler refers to the woven file. The error information currently has to be manually mapped back into the source code.

Our examples have shown how CORBA functionality can be extracted into aspects. This concept of separating CORBA communication issues from the application objects by using AOP leads to clear structured code. The programmer can concentrate on the implementation of problem domain issues.

Furthermore, functionality concerning distribution can easily be reused if placed into aspects (this was shown in section 3.2 with aspect `ServerComm`).

5   Conclusion

Our goal was to examine how AOP can be combined with CORBA. The work focused on the question whether and how aspect-oriented programming can improve distributed application development in a CORBA environment. It has led to the result that packaging the distribution issues of a CORBA application into separated aspects can support the application developer.

Aspect-oriented programming with AspectJ applied to a CORBA system proved to be a helpful means to achieve both a kind of transparency by separation of concerns and flexibility for the application programmer. CORBA related code can be extracted and encapsulated in aspects. When implementing the objects concerning the problem domain the programmer is not confused with distribution issues. Despite encapsulating distribution issues flexibility is preserved. The application programmer can fully decide about CORBA related issues when implementing the aspects. Furthermore, available aspects containing CORBA related code may be exchanged easily.

Further work should be done to find a general way how all CORBA ORB and COS related code could be placed into aspects. This could ease and improve CORBA application development. Furthermore, the application of AOP to CORBA system development (which is only touched in this paper) should be investigated in detail. Especially the problem of semantically interacting CORBA services may be addressed by AOP to support the CORBA system designer.

In this paper we concentrated on AOP via the application of AspectJ. A variety of other AOP mechanisms exist (e.g. Composition Filters [27]). Each of them may lead to improvements if used for CORBA applications or systems.

Moreover, a network wide (re)use of aspects should be supported. This may be realized by additional tools similar to an Interface Repository for interfaces in CORBA. Graphical tools could be helpful.

Dynamic aspects as proposed in [15], [11] could improve flexibility. Therefore, aspects implementing specific CORBA functionality could be exchanged not only at compile-time.

The examples in this paper show that a mechanism assuring the correct combination of aspects is necessary. In section 3.2 we introduced the aspects `ServerString` and `ServerName` for the remote communication between client and server. We have to assure that only one of both aspects is chosen. Moreover, weaving the `ServerName` aspect requires that `ServerComm` is woven as well and that the client is woven with an aspect containing the name server issues instead of the stringified issues. Composition validation algorithms as proposed in [1] for the composition of components may be useful to address this problem. The concept of assertions [8] may contribute to a solution, as well.

Another open question is how to distribute objects. Effective distribution strategies are needed to achieve goals like maximizing performance and minimizing costs. There exist only a few guidelines for effective object distribution [21]. When distributing aspects, a similar problem occurs. Further research in this field is necessary.

Guidelines for good aspect design would be extremely helpful. Such guidelines may be embedded into a software development method which considers the usage of aspects.

Acknowledgments. We would like to thank Prof. Eisenecker and Krzysztof Czarnecki for inspiring discussions as well as Gregor Kiczales and the AspectJ team for their support and advices.

References

1. Batory, D., Geraci, B. J.: Composition Validation and Subjectivity in GenVoca Generators. In: IEEE Transactions on Software Engineering. Special issue on Software Reuse (1997) 67 – 82
2. Buschmann, F., Meunier, R., Rohnert, H., Sommerlad, P., Stal, M.: Pattern-Oriented Software Architecture. John Wiley, Chichester, New York, Brisbane, Toronto, Singapore (1996)
3. Coulouris, G. F., Dollimore, J.: Distributed Systems: Concepts and Design. Addison-Wesley (1988)
4. Czarnecki, K., Eisenecker, U. W.: Synthesizing Objects. In: Proceedings of ECOOP'99, 13th European Conference on Object-Oriented Programming. Lecture Notes in Computer Science LNCS 1628. Springer-Verlag, June (1999) 18 – 42
5. Eisenecker, U. W.: Generative Programming GP with C++. In: Mössenböck, H.-P. (ed.): Proceedings of Modular Programming Languages JMLC97. Lecture Notes in Computer Science LNCS 1204. Springer-Verlag, Heidelberg, March (1997) 351–365
6. Fayad, M. E., Schmidt, D. C.: Object-Oriented Application Frameworks. In: Communications of the ACM. vol. 40, no. 10, October (1997) 32 – 38
7. Gamma, E., Helm, R., Johnson, R., Vlissides, J.: Design Patterns: Abstractions and Reuse of Object-Oriented Software. Addison-Wesley, Reading, MA (1994)
8. Gough, J., Klaeren, H.: Executable Assertions and Separate Compilation. In: Mössenböck, H.-P. (ed.): Proceedings Joint Modular Languages Conference. Lecture Notes in Computer Science LNCS 1204. Springer-Verlag, Berlin Heidelberg New York (1997) 41–52
9. Guerraoui, R., Fayad, M.: OO Distributed Programming Is Not Distributed OO Programming. In: Communications of the ACM. vol. 42, no. 4, April (1999) 101 – 104

10. Hauck, F., Becker, U., Geier, M., Meier, E., Rastofer, U., Steckermeier, M.: AspectIX: A Middleware for Aspect-Oriented Programming. In: Object-Oriented Technology, ECOOP98 Workshop Reader. LNCS 1543. Finland. Springer-Verlag (1998) 426 – 427

11. Kenens, P., Michiels, S., Matthijs, F., Robben, B., Truyen, E., Vanhaute, B., Joosen, W., Verbaeten, P.: An AOP Case with Static and Dynamic Aspects. In: Proceedings of the Aspect-Oriented Programming Workshop at ECOOP98. Brussels (1998)

12. Kiczales, G.: Private Communication. June, 1999

13. Kiczales, G., Lamping, J., Mendhekar, A., Maeda, C., Lopes, C.V., Loingtier, J.-M., Irwin, J.: Aspect-Oriented Programming In: Proceedings of ECOOP'97, European Conference on Object-Oriented Programming. Lecture Notes in Computer Science LNCS 1241. Springer-Verlag, June (1997)

14. Lopes, C. V., Kiczales, G.: Recent Developments in AspectJ. In: Proceedings of the Aspect-Oriented Programming Workshop at ECOOP98. Brussels (1998)

15. Lunau, C. P.: Is Composition of Metaobjects = Aspect Oriented Programming. In: Proceedings of the Aspect-Oriented Programming Workshop at ECOOP98. Brussels (1998)

16. Mowbray, T. J., Malveau, R.C.: Corba Design Patterns. John Wiley and Sons, Inc., New York, Chichester, Weinheim, Toronto, Singapore, Brisbane (1997)

17. Object Management Group: CORBAservices: Common Object Services Specification. December (1998)

18. Object Management Group: The Common Object Request Broker: Architecture and Specification. February (1998)

19. Pree, W.: Design Patterns for Object-Oriented Software Development. Addison-Wesley, Reading MA (1994)

20. Pree,W.: Komponenten basierte Softwareentwicklung mit Frameworks. dpunkt, Heidelberg (1997)

21. Purao, S., Jain, H., Nazareth, D.: Effective Distribution of Object-Oriented Applications. In: Communications of the ACM. vol. 41, no. 8, August (1998) 100 – 108

22. Schmidt, D.C.: Experience Using Design Patterns to Develop Reusable Object-Oriented Communication Software. In: Communication of the ACM. Special Issue on Object-Oriented Experiences. vol. 38, no. 10, Brisbane, Australia (1995)

23. Schmidt, D. C.: ADAPTIVE Communication Environment: An Object-Oriented Network Programming Toolkit for Developing Communication Software. http://www.cs.wustl.edu/~schmidt/ACE.html. New Orleans (1999)

24. Siegel,J.: OMG Overview: CORBA and the OMA in Enterprise Computing. In: Communications of the ACM. vol. 41, no. 10, October (1998) 37 – 43

25. Silva, A. R., Sousa, P., Marques, J. A.: Development of Distributed Applications with Separation of Concerns: In: IEEE Proceedings of the 1995 Asia-Pacific Software Engineering Conference APSEC95. Brisbane, Australia (1995)

26. Sun Microsystems: JavaIDL Documentation. http://java.sun.com/products/1.2/docs/guide/idl/, (1999)

27. University of Twente: Homepage of the TRESE Project. The Netherlands. http://wwwtrese.cs.utwente.nl/, http://wwwtrese.cs.utwente.nl/sina/cfom/index.html, (1999)

28. XEROX Palo Alto Research Center: Homepage of AspectJ. http://www.parc.xerox.com/aop/aspectj, (1999)

Lightweight and Generative Components I: Source-Level Components

Sam Kamin, Miranda Callahan, and Lars Clausen

{kamin,mcallaha,lrclause}cs.uiuc.edu
Computer Science Department
University of Illinois at Urbana-Champaign
Urbana, IL 61801

Abstract. Current definitions of "software component" are based on abstract data types — collections of functions together with local data. This paper addresses two ways in which this definition is inadequate: it fails to allow for lightweight components — those for which a function call is too inefficient or semantically inappropriate — and it fails to allow for generative components — those in which the component embodies a *method* of constructing code rather than actual code. We argue that both can be solved by proper use of existing language technologies, by using a higher-order *meta-language* to compositionally manipulate values of type *Code*, syntactic fragments of some *object language*. By defining a client as a function from a component to *Code*, components can be defined at a very general level without much notational overhead.

In this paper, we illustrate this idea entirely at the source-code level, taking *Code* to be string. Operating at this level is particularly simple, and is useful when the source code is not proprietary. In a companion paper, we define *Code* as a set of values containing machine-language code (as well as some additional structure), allowing components to be delivered in binary form.

1 Introduction

The programming world has long sought methods of dividing programs into reusable units, fundamentally altering the way in which programs are created and dramatically increasing productivity. Current notions of components as abstract data types (such as classes and, on a larger scale, COM objects and the like) have been very successful. However, we believe that to take the next step in increased productivity, two types of components will need to be accommodated that do not find a place in current component technologies. One of these is "lightweight" components — those that cannot, either due to cost or for semantic reasons, be implemented as function calls. Another are the "generative" components, those which are used to build other programs. We are particularly interested in the latter, as we believe the only way to effect major change in how software is constructed is to find a way to implement *methods* of computation — algorithms, idioms, patterns — rather than just programs.

The thesis of this paper is that a method for implementing such components is within our grasp, using existing programming technologies. Our proposal is both general and conceptually simple. Define a *Code* type, whose members represent the "values" of syntactic fragments of an imperative *object language*. Suppose these values can be built compositionally — that is, that the values of compound fragments can be derived from the values of their sub-fragments. Then, embed the *Code* type within a higher-order *meta-language*. The language will provide a variety of types that can be built over the *Code* type, such as lists of *Code* values, functions from *Code* to *Code*, etc. A client is then just a function from a component to *Code*, and the component can be any value that is useful to the client. Given a quotation/anti-quotation mechanism for defining constants of type *Code*, this proposal provides a powerful, general, and notationally clean mechanism for writing clients and components.

This paper introduces very little new technology. Rather, it demonstrates how existing technologies can be adapted to overcome the shortcomings of current software components. We do not pretend to present a complete solution, but rather to sketch a plausible approach, one which is marked by its simplicity and generality. A complete and practical solution would need to contend with issues of security and portability; would ideally be notationally even cleaner than what we have done; and would, of course, have a robust and efficient implementation. Some technical problems standing in the way of realizing these goals are discussed in the conclusions.

We operate here entirely at the source-code level. For us, *Code* is just "syntactic fragment" or, more simply, "string." Components are sets of values that aid in the construction of source programs. (Think of them as higher-order macros.) Source-level components can be useful in "open source" environments, and also provide the simplest setting in which to illustrate our thesis. A companion paper [6] extends this to binary-level components.

The next section elaborates on the basic idea of the paper and gives our first example. Sections 4 and 5 present two more examples. Section 6 discusses related work. The conclusions include a discussion on future research suggested by these ideas, as well as a brief synopsis of the work described in the companion paper.

2   *Code* and Components

Our central thesis is that a powerful component system can be obtained by the expedient of defining an appropriate *Code* type in a functional language (called the *meta-language*). This type represents the "value" of programs and program fragments in some *object language*. The "value" may be the code produced by that fragment, or the function it calculates (in the denotational semantics sense), or anything else, so long as values can be built compositionally — that is, the value of a compound fragment must be a function of the values of the fragments it contains.

Given the definition of *Code*, the meta-language provides a variety of useful type constructions, such as lists and functions, and is itself a powerful and concise language in which to program. A component is a value in the language, and a client is a function from the type of the component to *Code*. The implementation of a quotation/anti-quotation mechanism to facilitate the creation of *Code* values also add notational convenience. In this paper, we give *Code* the simplest possible definition: *Code* = *string*. A more abstract approach would be to define code as abstract syntax trees, but it would make little difference for the examples in this paper; see the end of section 6 for a further discussion of using AST's.

All syntactic fragments correspond to values of type *Code*. There is no distinction made between different kinds of values: expressions, statements, etc. However, for clarity of exposition, we will use subscripts to indicate the intended kind of value. Bear in mind that *there is only one type of Code*; the subscripts are merely comments.

In our examples, the meta-language is a functional language similar to Standard ML [5], called Jr, and the object language is Java [4]. One syntactic difference between Jr and Standard ML is the anti-quotation mechanism of Jr, inspired by the one in MetaML [9]. Items occurring in double angle brackets << ⋯ >> are syntax fragments in the object language. Thus, they can be thought of as constants of type *Code*, except that they may contain variable, "anti-quoted" parts, introduced by a backquote ('); these are Jr expressions that must evaluate to *Code*.

A simple example is this "code template:"[1]

```
fn whatToPrint =>
   << public static void main (String[] args) {
        System.out.println('whatToPrint);
     }>>
end
```

---

[1] The notation "fn *arg* => *expr* end definitions a one-argument function in Jr. Note that the function is anonymous. It can be given a name, like any other value, by writing val *funname* = fn .... A more conventional-looking alternative syntax is fun *funname* *arg* = *expr*.

This template is a function from an expression of type String to a function definition; i.e., the template has type $Code_{expr.\ of\ type\ String} \rightarrow Code_{function\ def.}$. To get the function definitions, we can apply it to a simple expression like <<"Hello, world!">>, or something more elaborate, like <<args.length>0?args[0]:"">>.

To summarize: what appears inside the double-angle brackets is in Java syntax and represents a value of type *Code*; within these brackets, the backquote introduces an anti-quoted Jr expression returning a value of type *Code*, which is spliced into the larger *Code* value.

3   A First Example: Sorting

Suppose we wish to provide a sorting function as a component. Our idea of a general-purpose component is that the programmer should be able to use the component with a minimum of bureaucracy, whether there are two data items to sort or a million; regardless of the types of the components; and with any comparison function.

To get started, here is the simplest version of this component, a procedure to sort an array of integers, using a simple but inefficient algorithm:

```
// Component:
val sortcomp =
  <<class sortClass {
      void sort (int[] A) {
        for (int i=1; i<A.length; i++) {
          int temp = A[i];
          int j = i-1;
          while ((j >= 0) && (temp < A[j]))
              { A[j+1] = A[j]; j--; }
          A[j+1] = temp;
        }
      }
  }>>
```

The client will use this component by loading it and then calling it in the usual way.[2]

---

[2] The let construct introduces a temporary name for a value. Using _ as the name simply means the expression is being evaluated for its side effects and the value will not be used. Function application is denoted by juxtaposition.

```
// Client:
let val _ = load sortcomp
in
  <<class SortClient {
      void useSortComponent() {
        int[] keys; ... sortClass.sort(keys); ...
      }
    }>>
end;
```

The load function turns a value of type $Code_{class}$ into an actual, executable, class definition.

To avoid the necessity of matching the type of the client's array with the type expected by the component, we abstract the type from the component:

```
// Component:
fun sortcomp typenm =
  <<class sortClass {
      void sort ('typenm[] A) {
        for (int i=1; i<A.length; i++) {
          'typenm temp = A[i];
          ... as above ...
        }
      }
    }>>;
```

The client must supply the type as an argument when loading the component, but otherwise does not change:

```
// Client:
let val _ = load (sortcomp <<int>>)
in  ... as above ...
```

To abstract out the comparison function, we could pass it as a second argument to the sort function. However, that is both inefficient and bureaucratic, particularly since Java does not allow functions as arguments; instead, we abstract the comparison function from the component as a function of type $Code_{exp} \rightarrow Code_{exp} \rightarrow Code_{comparison}$:

```
// Component:
fun sortcomp typenm compareFun =
  <<class sortClass {
     void sort ('typenm[] A) {
        ...
        while ((j >= 0) && ('(compareFun <<temp>> <<A[j]>>)))
        ...
} } >>;
```

Note that, since the arguments to compareFun are of type *Code*, in the body of the sort procedure they must be quoted. The client passes in an argument of the correct type:

```
// Client:
let val _ = load (sortcomp <<int>> (fn i j => <<'i<'j>> end))
in ... as above ...
```

The comparison function itself is a Jr function, so it is not quoted; however, it returns *Code*, so its body is quoted.

"Lightweight" components are those that, like macros, do not entail the creation of a new function or class, but simply add new code in-line. A lightweight sorting component would put a statement in the place of the call. In preparation for such an example, we now define the sort component in such a way that it provides two *Code* values: the sort procedure (optional) and a statement to be placed at the point of the call. More specifically, the second value is a function from the array being sorted to a statement. So we now think of the component as having type

$$Code_{type} \rightarrow (Code \rightarrow Code \rightarrow Code)_{comparison}$$
$$\rightarrow Code_{fundef} \times (Code_{argument} \rightarrow Code_{call})$$

This can accommodate either an in-line sort or a call to the provided sort routine, as above. Here is how we would provide exactly the functionality of our previous version of the component:[3]

```
// Component:
fun sortcomp typenm comparefun =
  [ <<class sortClass { ... as above ... } >>,
    fn arg => << sortClass.sort('arg); >> end ];
```

---

[3] The [·, ·] notation creates a pair of values. The function fn [x, y] => ... expects its argument to be such a pair, and binds x and y to its two elements.

Now the client must use the provided sort-calling code:

```
// Client:
fun sortclient [sortproc,sortcall] =
   let val _ = load sortproc
   in
     <<class SortClient {
         void useSortComponent() {
            ... int[] keys; ... '(sortcall <<keys>>) ...
       } }>>
   end;


sortclient (sortcomp <<int>> (fn e1 e2 => <<'e1 < 'e2>> end));
```

In this case, the effect is exactly as in the previous version: the call to
sortClass.sort is inserted directly into the client code (and the less-
than comparison is inserted directly into the sort procedure).

Using the type given in (1), it is possible to insert in-line code beyond just
a function call. We exploit this capability in the following component,
adding an additional integer argument indicating the length of the array.
If the length is 2 or 3, the sort is done in-line; if less than 100, the sort
is done by insertion sort; otherwise, the component uses quicksort.

```
// Component:
fun sortcomp typenm comparefun size =
  if (size < 4) // place in-line
  then
  let fun swap e1 e2 =
      <<if (!'(comparefun e1 e2)) {
          'typenm temp = 'e1; 'e1 = 'e2; 'e2 = temp;
       }>>
  in [<<>>,  // no auxiliary class in this case
     fn arrayToSort =>
       if (size < 2) then <<>>
       else if (size == 2)
       then swap <<'arrayToSort[0]>> <<'arrayToSort[1]>>
       else // size == 3
         <<{ '(swap <<'arrayToSort[0]>> <<'arrayToSort[1]>>)
             '(swap <<'arrayToSort[1]>> <<'arrayToSort[2]>>)
             '(swap <<'arrayToSort[0]>> <<'arrayToSort[1]>>)
          }>>
      end ]
  end
```

```
else // don't in-line
  let val callfun =
     fn arg => << sortClass.sort('arg); >> end
  in [<<class sortClass {
           void sort ('typenm[] A) {
              '(if (size < 100)  // use insertion sort
                  then <<... as above ...>>
                  else // size >= 100 - use quicksort
                       <<... definition of quicksort ...>>)
        } }>>,
      callfun]
  end;
```

The client calls the component just as before, but with the additional argument. Note that this argument is not a *Code* argument, but an actual integer.

Using `sortclient` defined above, the result of the call

```
sortclient (sortcomp <<int>> (fn e1 e2 => <<'e1<'e2>> end) 2);
```

would be to load nothing (there being no auxiliary class in this case) and to transform the client to

```
class SortClient {
  void useSortComponent() {
    ... int[] keys; ...
    if (!(keys[0] < keys[1])) {
      int temp = keys[0];
          keys[0] = keys[1];
          keys[1] = temp;
} ... } }
```

4   Example: Caching

If a programming technique can be formalized, it can be made into a component. One example is the technique of caching, which can have a dramatic impact on the running time of an algorithm.

Given a function **f**, we cannot simply define a new function, **cached_f**, to be the caching version of **f**. The reason is that **f** may have recursive calls that must be changed to calls to **cached_f**. To allow for these calls to be changed, the client must supply a function of type $Code_{recursive\ call} \rightarrow Code_{function\ body}$. In somewhat simplified form, the creator of the cached function does this:

$$\mathcal{F} = \texttt{fn f =>} \ \texttt{<<...'f(x)...>>} \ \texttt{end} \mapsto$$

```
cached_f (x) {
  if (x not in cache)
    cache entry for x =
      F <<cached_f>>(x)
  return cache entry for x
```

The caching component is presented below. This version handles caching only for functions of a single integer, though versions for arbitrary arguments of arbitrary types can be developed fairly easily.

```
fun cacheComponent thecode cachesize unusedval =
  <<class cacheMaker {
    static int [] ncache = new int['(cachesize)];

    static int original (int x) { '(thecode <<cacher>>) }

    public static int cacher (int x) {
      if ((x < '(cachesize)) && (ncache[x] != '(unusedval)))
        return ncache[x];
      else {
        int newres = original (x);
        if (x < '(cachesize)) ncache[x] = newres;
        return newres;
      }
    }
```

```
    static int setupcache (int x) {
      int i=0;
      while (i < '(cachesize)) ncache[i++] = '(unusedval); }
      return cacher (x);
    }
}>>;
```

A caching version of the Fibonacci function is shown below. The code
fragment (a) shows how the use of the caching component, and fragment
(b) is the resulting code.

```
(a) let fun fibonacci recursefn =
      <<if (x < 2) return x;
        else return ('recursefn(x-1) + 'recursefn(x-2)); >>
    in cacheComponent fibonacci <<20>> <<-1>>
    end;
```

```
(b) class cacheMaker {
      static int [] ncache = new int[20];

      static int original (int x) {
        if (x < 2) return x;
        else return (cacher(x-1) + cacher(x-2));
      }

      public static int cacher (int x) {
        if ((x < 20) && (ncache[x] != -1)) return ncache[x];
        else {
          int newres = original (x);
          if (x < 20) ncache[x] = newres;
          return newres;
      } }

      static int setupcache (int x) {
        int i=0;
        while (i<20) { ncache[i] = -1; i++; }
        return cacher (x);
      }
} }
```

5   Example: Vector Operations

Figure 1 shows a component that provides vector-level operations: multiplication by a scalar, vector addition, (component-wise) vector multiplication, and vector assignment. It is very simple to provide a class containing such operations, particularly in Java, where arrays are heap-allocated. Part (a) of Fig. 1 shows such a component in outline.

The problem is that this component is quite inefficient. For one thing, it allocates a new array for each intermediate result, though this problem could be alleviated, at some cost in convenience, by providing each operation with an additional argument, the target array. The more difficult problem is that it calculates each intermediate vector separately, using a separate loop. It does no "loop fusion."

The component shown in part (b) of Fig. 1 treats each vector as a function from an index expression to a value expression. It does not perform any actual computation until a computed vector is assigned to another vector, at which point it constructs a single loop to move the calculated values to the target array. A simple client program is shown in part (c) (note that this can be a client of either version of the vector component), and parts (d) and (e) in Fig. 2 show the result of applying the client to the components in parts (a) and (b), respectively.

6   Related Work

Much of the research in programming languages can be said to concern the problem of componentizing software. Therefore, a great deal of work bears more or less directly on ours. What generally is accounted under the title of "components" nowadays are the kind of large-scale components exemplified by COM objects [8]. These are important advances in standardizing interfaces, implementing version control, and permitting component search, among other things. However, these components are not adaptable in the sense of our sort component, and by their nature, tend to be heavy-weight. Thus, though they allow for a new level of integration of software at a large granularity, they do not seem likely to change the day-to-day dynamics of programming.

We mention three other recent research efforts that are most closely related to this work: aspect-oriented programming, and Engler's 'C and Magik systems.

Aspect-oriented programming (AOP) [7] represents an attempt to change the programming process by separating *algorithms* from certain details of

```
(a) val adt_vectorcomp =
      [SOME <<class VectorOps {
                static double[] scale (double s, double[] A) {
                  double[] B = new double[A.length];
                  for (int i=0; i<A.length; i++) B[i] = s * A[i];
                  return B;
              } ... }>>,
        fn "copy"  => fn B i => B end
         | "scale"  => fn x A i => <<VectorOps.scale('x, '(A i))>> end
         | "add"    => fn A B i => <<VectorOps.add('(A i), '(B i))>> end
         | "mult"   => fn A B i => <<VectorOps.mult('(A i), '(B i))>> end
         | "assign" => fn A B => <<'A = '(B 0);>> end
        end
      ];
```

```
(b) val fusing_vectorcomp =
      [NONE,
        fn "copy"  => fn B i => <<'B['i]>> end
         | "scale"  => fn x A i => <<('x * '(A i))>> end
         | "add"    => fn A B i => <<('(A i) + '(B i))>> end
         | "mult"   => fn A B i => <<('(A i) * '(B i))>> end
         | "assign" => fn A B =>
             let val i = gensym "i"
             in <<for (int 'i=0; 'i<'A.length; 'i++)
                    'A['i] = '(B i);>>
             end end
        end
      ];
```

```
(c) fun vectorClient [vectorauxops,vectorfuns] =
      let val _ = loadif vectorauxops
          val copy = vectorfuns "copy"
          val scale = vectorfuns "scale"
          val add = vectorfuns "add"
          val mult = vectorfuns "mult"
          val assign = vectorfuns "assign"
      in <<class VectorClient {
              void useVectorOps (double[] A, double[] B, double[] C) {
                double[] result;
                '(assign <<result>>
                    (scale <<2.0>> (mult (add (copy <<A>>) (copy <<B>>))
                                         (copy <<C>>))))
                return result;
              }
          }>>
      end;
```

Fig. 1. Vector calculations: (a) Traditional; (b) Loop-fusing; (c) A client

```
(d) void useVectorOps (double[] A, double[] B, double[] C) {
      double[] result = VectorOps.scale(2.0,
                          VectorOps.mult(VectorOps.add(A, B), C));
      return result;
    }

(e) void useVectorOps (double[] A, double[] B, double[] C) {
      double[] result;
      for (int i1=0; i1<result.length; i1++)
        result[i1] = (2.0 * ((A[i1] + B[i1]) * C[i1]));
      return result;
    }
```

Fig. 2. Vector calculations (cont.): (d) The client using component (a), (e) The client using component (b)

their implementation — like data layout, exception behavior, synchronization — that notoriously complicate programs. These ancillary aspects of programs can be regarded as components in a broad sense, and indeed they are formally specified in their own aspect languages. Our approach is not as convenient notationally because the use of the other components cannot be implicit: the programmer has to know about, and plan for, the use of our components. On the positive side, our approach is fundamentally simpler in that it requires little new technology, and it is more general in that the mechanisms we use can handle any aspect.

The work of Engler, in two papers [2, 1], is particularly close to ours. The earlier of these [2] describes a C extension, called 'C with a *Code* type and run-time macros. 'C differs from our work both in overall goals — 'C is intended mainly to achieve improved efficiency rather than to promote a component-based style of programming — and in technical details. There is no functional meta-language level in 'C — meta-computations are expressed in C itself. This implies that there are no higher-order functions or other convenient data types for manipulating code values, which we have found to be indispensable.

The more recent paper [1] describes Magik, an extension to the lcc [3] C compiler that gives users access to the internal abstract syntax tree form of programs. Both AOP and Magik, by virtue of their dependence on abstract syntax tree manipulations, are inherently compile-time approaches. Our use of a *Code* type with compositional semantics, together with ordinary abstractions found in any functional language, removes the dependence on access to the abstract syntax tree. This allows the same ideas to be implemented at the level of executable binaries (as shown in [6]), at the expense of some flexibility.

7 Conclusions

We have presented an approach to software components that is simple and general, and is based on well-known ideas in programming languages. Our suggestion is that higher-order macros written in a functional meta-language, to generate code in an imperative object language, can account for lightweight (i.e. in-lined) and generative components. More broadly, the idea is that the definition of a *Code* type — representing the "values" of phrases in the object language — with a quotation mechanism to allow simple construction of those values, is all the mechanism that is needed for a powerful component facility — the meta-language provides the rest. The definition of the *Code* type can vary, so long as values can be computed compositionally. In this paper, we define *Code* to be *String*, meaning that the "value" of a phrase is its textual representation. This leads to "source-level components."

Components and clients are written in a meta-language chosen for its power and conciseness, to produce code in an object language chosen by some other criterion (efficiency, portability, compatibility, etc.). The use of a functional meta-language is of critical importance, as this leads to a much more general macro facility while keeping the notational overhead reasonable. The overall approach — using higher-order, cross-language macros to create a simple, powerful, and easy-to-implement component system — has not, to our knowledge, been previously suggested.

One area for future research is to study ways to simplify the writing of components and clients. We hasten to point out that, in this view of components, higher-order functions over *Code* — like the component that returns a function the can be used by the client to invoke methods defined by the component — are essential. So a certain irreducible level of complexity is inherent in the approach. Still, some aspects of component- and client-writing could be simplified by the judicious use of types. For example, much of the quoting and anti-quoting could be made implicit if the types of various operations were known: if f is known to have type *Code* $\rightarrow$ *Code*, then if the antiquoted fragment `(f <<x>>) appears in a program, both the anti-quote symbol and the quotations on x can be eliminated.

Source-level components are a good way to illustrate the use of a higher-order meta-language with a *Code* type. However, in practice, binary-level components are more practical. They can be distributed in those (frequent) cases when the source code is proprietary, they are generally more efficient to use, and they allow a more dynamic use of new components. We have emphasized in the paper that the key requirement is a definition of the *Code* type that allows code values to be calculated compositionally. There is no inherent reason why machine language could not be included in such a value. In [6], we define *Code* as (roughly speaking)

$$Code = Environment \to MachineLang \times Environment$$

Here, *Environment* gives the locations of variables. This definition allows for partially-compiled components and permits the components to be distributed as executables. The examples in that paper are identical in spirit, and very similar in detail, to those given here.

References

[1] Dawson Engler. Incorporating applications semantics and control into compilation. In *Proceedings of the Conference on Domain-Specific Languages*, Santa Barbara, California, USA, 15–17October 1997.

[2] Dawson R. Engler, Wilson C. Hsieh, and M. Frans Kaashoek. 'C: A language for high-level, efficient, and machine-independent dynaic code generation. In *Conference Record of POPL '96: The 23rd ACM SIGPLAN-SIGACT Symposium on Principles of Programming Languages*, pages 131–144, St. Petersburg Beach, Florida, 21–24 January 1996.

[3] Chris W. Fraser and David R. Hanson. A retargetable compiler for ANSI C. *SIGPLAN Notices*, 26(10):29–43, October 1991.

[4] James Gosling, Bill Joy, and Guy L. Steele Jr. *The Java Language Specification*. The Java Series. Addison-Wesley, Reading, MA, USA, 1996.

[5] Robert Harper, Robin Milner, and Mads Tofte. The definition of Standard ML: Version 3. Technical Report ECS-LFCS-89-81, Laboratory for the Foundations of Computer Science, University of Edinburgh, May 1989.

[6] Sam Kamin, Miranda Callahan, and Lars Clausen. Lightweight and generative components ii: Binary-level components. September 1999.

[7] Kim Mens, Cristina Lopes, Bedir Tekinerdogan, and Gregor. Kiczales. Aspect-oriented programming. *Lecture Notes in Computer Science*, 1357:483–??, 1998.

[8] Dale Rogerson. *Inside COM: Microsoft's Component Object Model*. Microsoft Press, 1997.

[9] Walid Taha and Tim Sheard. Multi-stage programming with explicit annotations. In *Proceedings of the ACM SIGPLAN Symposium on Partial Evaluation and Semantics-Based Program Manipulation (PEPM-97)*, volume 32, 12 of *ACM SIGPLAN Notices*, pages 203-217, New York, June 12-13 1997. ACM Press.

Scoping Constructs for Software Generators

Yannis Smaragdakis and Don Batory
Department of Computer Sciences
The University of Texas at Austin
Austin, Texas 78712
{smaragd,dsb}@cs.utexas.edu

Abstract. A well-known problem in program generation is *scoping*. When identifiers (i.e., symbolic names) are used to refer to variables, types, or functions, program generators must ensure that generated identifiers are *bound* to their intended *declarations*. This is the standard scoping issue in programming languages, only automatically generated programs can quickly become too complex and maintaining bindings manually is hard. In this paper we present *generation scoping*: a language mechanism to facilitate the handling of scoping concerns. Generation scoping offers control over identifier scoping beyond the scoping mechanism of the target programming language (i.e., the language in which the generator output is expressed). Generation scoping was originally implemented as an extension of the code template operators in the Intentional Programming platform, under development by Microsoft Research. Subsequently, generation scoping has also been integrated in the JTS language extensibility tools. The capabilities of generation scoping were invaluable in the implementation of two actual software generators: DiSTiL (implemented using the Intentional Programming system), and P3 (implemented using JTS).

Keywords: software generators, program transformations, generation scoping, hygienic macro expansion

1 Introduction

Program generation is the process of generating code in a high-level programming language. A well-known problem with program generation has to do with the resolution of names used to refer to various entities (e.g., variables, types, and functions) in the generated program. This is the standard scoping issue of programming languages but scoping problems are exacerbated when programs are generated automatically. For instance, often the same macro or template is used to create multiple code fragments, which all exist in the same scope of the generated program. In that case, care should be taken so that the generated fragments do not contain declarations that conflict (e.g., variables with the same name in the same lexical scope).

Avoiding scoping problems in program generation can be done manually: Lisp programmers are familiar with the gensym function for creating new symbols. Using gensym to create unique names for generated variable declarations is one of the commonly recommended practices for Lisp programmers. Unfortunately, this practice is tedious; it complicates program generation and makes the generator code harder to read and maintain. Mechanisms have been invented to relieve the programmer of the obligation to keep track of declared variables and generate new symbols for their names. These mechanisms fall under the general heading of *hygienic macro-expansion* (e.g., [7], [8], [10]) and address the scoping problem for macros: self-contained trans-

K. Czarnecki and U.W. Eisenecker (Eds.): GCSE'99, LNCS 1799, pp. 65–78, 2000.
© Springer-Verlag Berlin Heidelberg 2000

formations that are both specified and applied in the *same* program. A desirable property in this setting is *referential transparency*: identifiers introduced by a transformation refer to declarations lexically visible at the site where the transformation is defined—not where it is applied. In this paper we adapt the ideas of hygienic macro-expansion to a more general program generation setting, where referential transparency is not meaningful. Our mechanism can be used for *software generators*, which are essentially stand-alone compilers. The definition of transformations in software generators has no lexical connection to the program generated by these transformations (for instance, the generator program and the generated program may be in different programming languages). Our mechanism is called *generation scoping* and gives the generator programmer explicit and convenient control over the scoping of the generated code. (In fact, the generation scoping idea was invented independently of hygienic macro-expansion techniques, but in the process we essentially re-invented the principles that are common to both generation scoping and hygienic macro expansion.)

Generation scoping has been implemented on two language extensibility platforms: Microsoft Research's Intentional Programming system [13] and the Jakarta Tool Suite (JTS) [1]. Two component-based software generators, DiSTiL [14] and P3 [1], were built using generation scoping. In both cases, generation scoping proved invaluable, as it simplified the generator code and accentuated the distinction between executed and generated code.

2 Background: Scoping for Generated Programs

For a quick illustration of some of the scoping issues in program generation, we will use an (imaginary[1]) extension of the C language with *code template operators*. We introduce two such operators: quote (abbreviated as ') and unquote (abbreviated as $). quote designates the beginning of a code template and unquote escapes from it to evaluate a code generating expression.[2] Consider generating code to iterate over a text file and perform some actions on its data. A possible implementation in our example language is shown below, with the quoted code appearing in bold:

```
CODE CreateForAllInFile (CODE filename, CODE actions)
{ return '{ FILE *fp;
            if ((fp = fopen($filename, "r")) == NULL)
              FatalError(FILE_OPEN_ERROR);
            while ( feof(fp) == FALSE) {
              int byte = fgetc(fp);
              $actions;
            }
          }
}
```
                                                                                      (1)

---

[1] Actually, this extension of C with meta-programming constructs corresponds closely to the state of the Intentional Programming system in 1995, when generation scoping was implemented.

[2] These operators are analogous to the LISP "backquote" and "comma" macro pair or the Scheme quasiquote and unquote primitives [6].

The first scoping issue in the above code has to do with the scope used to bind the references in the generated code fragment. That is, the generated code fragment only has meaning in a lexical environment where FILE, FatalError, fopen, etc., are defined. We will disregard this issue for now and concentrate on the scope of generated *declarations*.

In the above example, two declarations are generated (these are underlined in the code). The scope of these declarations should be quite different. The first is the declaration of file pointer fp. This variable should be invisible to user code—the code fragment represented by actions should not be able to refer to fp. This is the rule of *hygienic* program generation and it ensures that no accidental capture of references can occur: the code fragment represented by actions may contain a reference to some fp, but this will never be confused with the fp generated by the code above. Obviously, this is a good property to guarantee. The fp variable is just an implementation detail and its name should be protected from accidental clashes with other names that may be in use.

The generated declaration of variable byte, on the other hand, demonstrates the need for *breaking the hygiene*. Variable byte represents the current character being read from the text file. The code represented by actions should be able to access byte—in fact, byte is the only interface for exploiting the functionality of traversing the text file.

To illustrate the above points, consider an example use of the CreateForAllIn-File function. A program can have a file pointer, fp, that points to a text file. We may want to generate code that determines whether a file is a prefix of the file pointed to by fp:

```
CreateForAllInFile(`("prefix.txt"),
                   `{if (byte != fgetc(fp)) return -1;} );
```

The fp identifier above is *not* the same as the fp introduced accidentally by the CreateForAllInFile function in (1). Nevertheless, a naive generation process will result into fp (above) accidentally referring to the internal variable of CreateForAl-lInFile. This is a scoping problem that we want to avoid, so that the client of Cre-ateForAllInFile can be oblivious to the choice of name used for the internal file pointer variable. On the other hand, the reference to byte *should* refer to the variable whose declaration is generated in (1). Clearly, it is hard to satisfy both requirements with code fragment (1), as the two declarations are never differentiated. We now discuss two existing approaches to scoping and why they are not sufficient for our purposes.

First Approach: Generating Unique Symbols Manually. The simplest way to satisfy this dual requirement is manually. We can generate a unique symbol for all declarations that should be hidden from other code. This is, for instance, a common practice for Lisp programmers, who can use the gensym function to create unused, unique names in generated code. With our example language and the code fragment in (1), we get:

```
CODE CreateForAllInFile (CODE filename, CODE actions)
{ CODE mfp = gensym();
  return `{
              FILE *$mfp;
              if (($mfp = fopen($filename, "r")) == NULL)
                FatalError(FILE_OPEN_ERROR);
              while ( feof($mfp) == FALSE) {
                int byte = fgetc($mfp);
                $actions;
              }
          }
}                                                                    (2)
```

For typical software generators, where many code fragments are created and composed, this solution is clearly unsatisfactory. The code becomes immediately harder to read and maintain, with many alternations between generated (quoted) and evaluated (unquoted) code. The intention that the mfp (for meta-file-pointer) variable holds a single variable name (and not an entire expression) is not enforced at the language level. Furthermore, understanding the code generated by code fragment (2) requires understanding the control flow of (2) (e.g., to ensure that the value of mfp never changes).

The most important disadvantage of the "manual" creation of unique identifiers, however, is that the generator programmer has to *anticipate* which identifiers may cause name clashes and need to be hidden. The most likely problem with code fragment (2) is that the generated code will be used in a lexical environment where an identifier like FILE, FatalError, etc., does not have the meaning intended by the author of (2). The only way to avoid this problem is to use unique symbol names for *all* definitions. Then the new names will have to be passed around in the generator code so that only their legitimate clients have access to them. For instance, one can imagine that the actual name for procedure FatalError will need to be a new, unique symbol (to avoid accidental capture), which is then passed as a parameter to Create-ForAllInFile, resulting in a more complicated code fragment:

```
CODE CreateForAllInFile (CODE mFatalError, CODE filename, CODE
actions)
{ CODE mfp = gensym();
  return `{
              FILE *$mfp;
              if (($mfp = fopen($filename, "r")) == NULL)
                $mFatalError(FILE_OPEN_ERROR);
              while ( feof($mfp) == FALSE) {
                int byte = fgetc($mfp);
                $actions;
              }
          }
}                                                                    (3)
```

If we take this approach to an extreme (e.g., doing the same for FILE_OPEN_ERROR, FALSE, and all other generated variables), the code will become completely unreadable and the programmer will have an obligation to keep close track of all generated declarations as well as their clients.

Second Approach: Hygienic Macros. Another way to satisfy the scoping require-ments for the two generated variables, is through a hygienic mechanism, such as those proposed in the work on hygienic macro expansion (e.g., [5], [7], [8], [10], [11]). Hygienic mechanisms work by making generated declarations *by default invisible* out-side the pattern or template (e.g., macro) that introduced them. In the example of (1), this would mean that both the declaration of `fp` and that of `byte` will be invisible to code in `actions`. Since this is not desirable in the case of `byte`, the hygiene must be explicitly broken. In the hygienic macros work, this case is considered to be a rare exception.[3] Carl's hygienic mechanism [5] even attempts to automatically detect com-mon patterns that require breaking the hygiene. Additionally, lexically-scoped hygienic macros [7][8] use the lexical environment of the generation site as the lexical environment of the generated code (a property called *referential transparency*).

The problem with using this approach in software generators is that it is not possi-ble to reliably deduce the scope of a variable from the lexical location of the code that generates its declaration. In particular there are two important differences between macros and software generators:

1. Macros are (more or less) self-contained units. There is a clear distinction between the macro code and the code that is passed as a parameter to the macro. This is not the case with software generators. The code generating a declaration is not, in general, in close lexical proximity of the code generating a reference to that declaration.

2. The lexical environment of a program-generating code fragment cannot be identi-fied with the lexical environment of the generated code in software generators. (In hygienic macro terminology: referential transparency is not meaningful.) For instance, we could even have the generator be in a different language than the generated code (e.g., unquoted code could be in Java, quoted code in C). In contrast, lexically scoped macros use the lexical environment of the macro definition to determine the binding of all references generated by the macro.

The first point is a result of observation. The transformations in most software gen-erators interleave generating code with arbitrary computation more often than macros. In this way, it is hard to identify a self-contained program fragment *in the generator* that will be identified with a scope in the generated program.

To see the second point, consider again code fragment (1), reproduced below for easy reference.

```
CODE CreateForAllInFile (CODE filename, CODE actions)
{ return `{
                FILE *fp;
                if ((fp = fopen($filename, "r")) == NULL)
                  FatalError(FILE_OPEN_ERROR);
                while ( feof(fp) == FALSE) {
```

---

[3] For instance, we read in [7]: "We here ignore the occasional need to escape from hygiene."

```
        int byte = fgetc(fp);
        $actions;
      }
    }
}
```

CreateForAllInFile has several dependencies to other generated code (e.g., the
FILE type identifier, the FatalError function, the FALSE constant, etc.). In the case
of lexically-scoped macros such dependencies are resolved at the site of the macro definition. This would be equivalent to trying to find bindings for FILE, FatalError,
etc., in the program site where CreateForAllInFile is defined. This approach is not
valid for software generators. *For instance, the* FatalError *routine may not be
declared as a routine in the generator or a standard library, but instead exist only in
the generated program.* Hence, the declaration of FatalError must be non-hygienic
so that the code fragment generated by CreateForAllInFile can access it.

3 Generation Scoping

3.1 Generation Environments

Because of the differences between macros and software generators, we cannot
hope to achieve the same degree of automation for software generators as with
hygienic lexically-scoped macros. Nevertheless, we can still do better than manually
generating new symbols, as in example (3) of Section 2. This is the purpose of generation scoping. Generation scoping is a mechanism that represents lexical environments
in the generated program as first-class entities. In this way, the generator has control of
the scoping of the generated program, beyond that offered by the target programming
language.

To support lexical environments as first-class entities, generation scoping adds a
new keyword, environment, to the language in which the program generator is written. Its syntax is:

environment (<generation-environment>) <statement>;

where statement contains one or more quoted expressions. The generation-
environment is an expression that yields a value of type ENV. ENV is a type used to
represent environments and only has a constructor and equality function defined (i.e.,
we can only create new values of type ENV and compare them with existing ones). The
constructor for environments, new_env, can take an arbitrary number of arguments
whose values are other environments. These environments become the *parents* of the
newly created environment (the *child*). All variable declarations in a parent become
visible to the child environment. Like traditional scoping mechanisms, variable bindings of the child eclipse bindings with the same name in the parent.

An example use of environment in code implementing our example text file traversal follows below:

```
CODE CreateForAllInFile (ENV p, CODE mtbyte, CODE filename,
                         CODE actions)
{
  environment(new_env(p))
    return '{
              FILE *fp;
              if ((fp = fopen($filename, "r")) == NULL)
                FatalError(FILE_OPEN_ERROR);
              while ( feof(fp) == FALSE) {
                int $mtbyte = fgetc(fp);
                $actions;
              }
            }
}                                                                  (4)
```

To generate code using the quote operator, an environment needs to be specified. In this way, the code represented by actions can never access variable fp (as fp is generated in a new environment—which becomes a child of an environment passed into the function). At the same time, if the variable represented by mtbyte is generated in the same environment as actions, they are visible to each other. This is the case with most straightforward uses of this function. For instance:

```
environment(e)
  result =
    CreateForAllInFile(global_env, 'byte, '("file.txt"),
                       'putchar(byte) );                           (5)
```

Comparing code fragments (4) and (3), we can see why using environments is more convenient than manually handling variables by creating new symbols. In particular, there are several important advantages:

1. The generator programmer does not need to explicitly state which variables get "closed" in the right lexical environment. *All* declarations generated under an environment statement will be automatically added to the corresponding environment. Additionally, the generator programmer does not need to explicitly retrieve the binding for a certain identifier. *All* references (e.g., to fp, but also to FILE, FatalError, fopen, etc., above) are interpreted relative to that environment. *This means that, if a code fragment is generated in the intended environment, it can later be used without problems in a local context, even if the local context contains different bindings for the same identifiers.* For example, in code fragment (5), above, if global_env has the intended declaration for, e.g., FILE, it will not subsequently matter if the generated code fragment is output in the middle of a function where FILE means something different. The reference will always be to the FILE type variable defined in the environment represented by global_env.

2. The alternation between executed and generated code is avoided. There is no need to unquote code just to supply a unique symbol name.

3. Declarations are treated as a group, instead of individually. In the above example there is only one variable declared, so this is not really an advantage. In quoted code with several generated declarations, however, handling environments is easier than handling all new symbols individually. Of course, the same grouping effect could be achieved by using a mapping data structure in the generator code. The advantage of generation scoping is that the data structure is now integrated in the language and insertions and lookups are implicit (i.e., the programmer never has to specify them—see the first point above).

3.2 Implementation Issues

It is perhaps worth stressing again that the main advantage of generation scoping is that the generator programmer is relieved of the responsibility of adding declarations to environments and looking up identifier bindings in those environments. That is, the implementation of `quote` will determine whether a generated identifier is actually a declaration (of a variable, function, type, etc.) or a reference to an existing entity. Each environment has a symbol table and a collection of pointers to the parent environments. In case an identifier represents a declared entity, it is added to the current environment's symbol table together with a corresponding generated unique name for the declared entity. When a generated identifier is a reference, it will be looked up in the appropriate environment's table and, if it is not there, in the parent environments recursively.[4] The result of the identifier lookup is the unique generated name for the matching declaration. In this way, no accidental reference to the wrong variable, type, function, etc., can occur, as long as the environments are set up properly.

As is well-documented in the work on hygienic macros [7][10], determining the syntactic role of an identifier (i.e., whether it is a declaration or a reference) is hard when the entire program has not yet been generated. For instance, consider the program-generating function:

```
CODE CreateDclOrRef (CODE type) {
  return `{ $type newvar = 10 };
}
```

In most programming environments,[5] it is impossible to tell before the code is generated whether the generated code declares `newvar` or refers to an existing variable of the same name. If the parameter type holds the type specifier `` `int ``, then `newvar` is being declared. If, on the other hand, it holds the operator `` `* ``, it is not. This problem has been studied extensively in the hygienic macro community and the common approach is to employ a "painting" algorithm that marks each identifier with the environment where it was created. It is easy to adapt this approach to generation scoping:

---

[4] In case a matching declaration is found in multiple parent environments, the unique name returned is determined by a depth-first search of the parent tree, based on the order parents were specified in the new_env constructor. This is, however, an arbitrary default and not fundamental to the system's operation.

[5] This is not true for the Intentional Programming system, where the most mature version of generation scoping was implemented. The system fundamentally distinguishes (at the editor level, even) between declarations and references, so that a single code fragment cannot be used to create both.

After all the code has been generated, the marked declarations can be matched to marked references (assuming they came from the same environment). Remaining references can then be just unmarked, so that they become free references and can refer to externally declared symbols. A more thorough discussion on implementing a "painting" algorithm for program generation can be found in [11].

4 Generation Scoping in DiSTiL

Generation scoping was implemented as part of IP (Intentional Programming) [13], a general-purpose transformation system under development by Microsoft Research. It was subsequently used to build the DiSTiL software generator [14] as a domain-specific extension to IP. DiSTiL is a generator that follows the GenVoca [3] design paradigm. GenVoca generators are a class of sophisticated software generators that synthesize high-performance, customized programs by composing pre-written components called *layers*. Each layer encapsulates the implementation of a primitive feature in a target domain. The DiSTiL generator is essentially a compiler for the domain of container data structures. Complex container data structures are synthesized by composing primitive layers, where each layer implements either a primitive data structure (e.g., ordered linked lists, binary trees, etc.) or feature (sequential or random storage, logical element deletion, element encryption, etc.). Code for each data structure operation is generated by having each layer manufacture a code fragment (that is specific to the operation whose code is being generated) and by assembling these fragments into a coherent algorithm.

Generation scoping was indispensable in the implementation of DiSTiL. Even relatively short DiSTiL specifications (around 10-20 lines) could generate thousands of lines of optimized code. Due to the complexity of the generated code, as well as the flexibility of parameterization (a layer could be composed with a wide variety of other layers), maintaining correct scoping for generated code would have been a nightmare without generation scoping. In fact, initially we had attempted to implement DiSTiL with manual resolution of generated references (by generating unique symbols, as in code fragment (3)). *The sheer difficulty of this task was what motivated generation scoping in the first place.*

Generation scoping is used in DiSTiL not only to ensure the correctness of references to global declarations (e.g., library functions) but also to overcome the scoping limitations of the target language (C). With generation scoping, DiSTiL effectively manages different namespaces for every layer in a composition. In this way, there are no clashes between identically named variables introduced by different layers (or different instances of the same layer). At the same time, the code is simplified by having namespaces connected appropriately so that generated code can access all the required declarations without explicit qualification.

DiSTiL data structures consist of three distinct entities: a container, elements, and iterators (called *cursors*). Generated variables are grouped together into a common environment according to the entity to which they are related. For instance, all declarations related to the cursor part of a doubly linked list will belong in a single generation environment. These variables need *not* belong to a single lexical context. For example, variables in an environment may be global, or local, or fields of a record type. Thus, variables of an environment could belong to slices of many different lexical contexts in the generated program. In this way, the environment acts as a generator-managed namespace mechanism for the target language.

Consider the following organization used in DiSTiL (and, in fact, also in P3). In general, there is a many-to-one relationship between cursors and containers (i.e., there can be many cursors—each with a different retrieval predicate—per container). So using a single generation environment to encapsulate both cursor *and* container data members is not possible. Instead, separate environments are defined for every cursor and container. The ContGeneric environment encapsulates element data members (because element types are in one-to-one correspondence with container types) and generic container-related variables (including the container identifier). The Curs-Generic environment encapsulates generic cursor-related variables (including the cursor identifier). By making ContGeneric a parent of CursGeneric, code for operations on containers (which do not need cursors) can be generated using the ContGeneric environment, while code for operations on cursors (which also reference container fields) is generated using the CursGeneric environment. Figure 1(a) depicts this relationship.

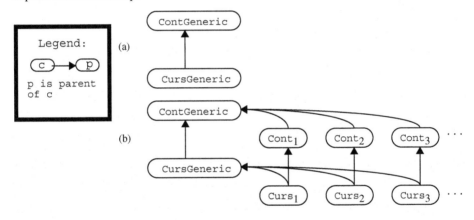

Figure 1: Hierarchical Organizations of Environments in DiSTiL

As mentioned earlier, a hallmark of GenVoca layers is that they encapsulate refinements of multiple classes. Each DiSTiL layer refines cursor, container, and element types by adding layer-specific data members. The data members added to the container and element types by layer L_i are encapsulated by environment $Cont_i$ which is a child of ContGeneric. Similarly, data members added by L_i to the cursor type are encapsulated by environment $Curs_i$ which is a child of both CursGeneric and $Cont_i$ (because cursors of layer L_i reference layer-specific container-data members as well as layer-specific cursor data members). Figure 1(b) shows this hierarchical organization of environments.

To illustrate these ideas, consider an ordered doubly-linked list layer. This layer would refine elements by adding next and prev fields, and would refine containers by adding first and last fields. This refinement can be accomplished by a Refine-

Types() method: elem_type, cont_type, and curs_type are code fragments that respectively define the set of variables (data members) in element, container, and cursor classes. When RefineTypes() is called with these code fragments as parameters, the next, prev, first, and last fields are added to the element and container types. As these fields are always used together, they are declared within a single environment Cont (which is equal to some Cont$_i$ of Figure 1):

```
void RefineTypes( CODE *elem_type, CODE *cont_type, ENV Cont) {
  environment(Cont) {
    *elem_type = `{ $(*elem_type); element *next, *prev; };
    *cont_type = `{ $(*cont_type); element *first, *last; };
  }
}
```

It is common in a composition of GenVoca layers that a single layer appears multiple times. An example in DiSTiL would be linking elements of a container onto two (or more) distinct ordered lists, where each list has a unique sort key. Every list layer adds its own fields to the element and container types. Maintaining the distinction among these fields (so that the code for the j-th list will only reference its own fields next$_j$, prev$_j$, etc.) is simple using generation environments as organized in Figure 1. Each copy of the list layer will have its own generation environments Cont$_j$ and Curs$_j$, and all code generated by that copy would always use these environment variables.

For an example, consider the Remove method for ordered doubly-linked lists, appearing below. Let Remove_Code be the code that is to be generated for removing an element from a container. The Remove method for ordered doubly-linked lists adds its code (to unlink the element) when it is called (the code that actually deletes the element is added by another layer). Thus, given Remove_Code and the environment Curs (equal to some Curs$_i$ of Figure 1), Remove() adds the unlinking code where the next, prev, etc. identifiers are bound to their correct variable definitions.

```
void Remove( CODE *Remove_Code, ENV Curs ) {
  environment(Curs) {
    *Remove_Code =`{ Element *next_el = cursor->next;
                     Element *prev_el = cursor->prev;
                     $(*Remove_Code);
                     if (next_el != null)
                       next_el->prev = prev_el;
                     if (prev_el != null)
                       prev_el->next = next_el;
                     if (container->first == cursor.obj)
                       container->first = next_el;
                     if (container->last == cursor.obj)
                       container->last = prev_el;  };
  }
}
```

Note that the bindings of identifiers cursor, container, and next in this template exist in three different generation environments: container is in ContGeneric, cursor in CursGeneric, and next in Cont$_i$. Nevertheless, all of them can be accessed from environment Curs (following its parent links), so this is the only environment that needs to be specified. Note also that there are two generated temporary declarations in this code fragment, which are completely protected from accidental reference.

This example is convenient for demonstrating the benefits of generation scoping. We attempt to show these benefits by speculating on the alternatives. Clearly the above code fragment has many external generated references, so default hygiene is not really an option. The generator writer has to explicitly create new symbols (as in code fragment (3)) for the declarations of container, cursor, etc. (not shown). Instead of managing all the new symbols individually, the generator writer could set up a data structure *in the generator (unquoted) code* to maintain the mappings of identifiers to variables. Then the writer could use explicit unquotes to introduce the right bindings. Given that declarations need to be inserted in the data structure explicitly and references need to be looked up explicitly, the code would be much more complicated. One can add some syntactic sugar to make the code more appealing. For instance, we can use $$(ds, id) to mean "unquote and lookup identifier id in bindings data structure ds". Similarly, we can use $%(ds, id) to mean "unquote and add variable id in bindings data structure ds". Even then, the code would be practically unreadable:

```
void Remove( CODE *Remove_Code, BindingDS ds ) {
  *Remove_Code =
    `{ $$(ds, Element) *$%(ds, next_el) =
         $$(ds, cursor)->$$(ds, next);
       $$(ds, Element) *$%(ds, prev_el) =
         $$(ds, cursor)->$$(ds, prev);
       $(*Remove_Code);
       if ($$(ds, next_el) != null)
         $$(ds, next_el)->$$(ds, prev) = $$(ds, prev_el);
       if ($$(ds, prev_el) != null)
         $$(ds, prev_el)->$$(ds, next) = $$(ds, next_el);
       if ($$(ds, container)->$$(ds, first) ==
           $$(ds, cursor).$$(ds, obj))
         $$(ds, container)->$$(ds, first) = $$(ds, next_el);
       if ($$(ds, container)->$$(ds, last) ==
           $$(ds, cursor).$$(ds, obj))
         $$(ds, container)->$$(ds, last) = $$(ds, prev_el); };
}
```

As outlined earlier, generation scoping improves over this code in three ways: First, no explicit data structure insertions/lookups need to be performed (e.g., there are no $$ and $% operators). Second, no explicit escapes are introduced—there is no alternation between quoted and unquoted code. Third, the grouping of variables is implicit—there is no need to repeatedly refer to a data structure like ds.

5 Related Work

Given our prior discussion of hygienic macros, here we will only touch upon a few other pieces of related work.

The environments used in generation scoping are similar to syntactic environments in the *syntactic closures* work [4][9]. In syntactic closures, environments are first-class entities and code fragments can be explicitly "closed" in a lexical environment. Nevertheless, there are significant differences between the two approaches: Syntactic closures environments can only capture the set of variables that are lexically visible at a specific point in a program.[6] In contrast, our environments can be arbitrary collections of bindings (i.e., smaller sets of lexically visible variables) and can be organized hierarchically. More importantly, however, declarations are added to generation scoping environments implicitly by generating (quoting) code that declares new variables. Thus, our approach is much more automated than syntactic closures and is ideally suited to software generators (where the lexical environment is being built while code is generated). Also, generation scoping can be used to implement the hygienic, lexically-scoped macros of [7], unlike syntactic closures, which cannot be used to implement hygienic macro expansion, as explained in [7].

Generation scoping is concerned only with maintaining correct scoping for generated code fragments. Other pieces of work deal with various other correctness properties of composed code fragments. Selectively, we mention some work on the problem of ensuring type correctness for generated programs, both for two-stage code [12] (i.e., generator and generated code) and multi-stage code [15] (i.e., code generating code that generates other code, etc.).

6 Conclusions

Program generation is a valuable technique for software development that will become progressively more important in the future. In this paper we have shown how to address the scoping issues that arise in software generators. We have presented generation scoping: a general-purpose, domain-independent mechanism to address all scoping needs of generated programs. Generation scoping can make writing and maintaining software generators easier. Its capabilities were proven in the implementation of the DiSTiL [14] and P3 [1] generators.

The future of software engineering lies in the automated development of well-understood software. Program generators will play an increasingly important role in future software development. We consider generation scoping to be a valuable language mechanism for generator writers and hope that it will be adopted in even more extensible languages and transformation systems in the future.

Acknowledgments

Support for this work was provided by Microsoft Research, and the Defense Advanced Research Projects Agency (Cooperative Agreement F30602-96-2-0226). We would like to thank an anonymous referee for his/her useful suggestions.

---

[6] In the original syntactic closures work [4] this point was almost always the site of the macro call. Later, syntactic environments were used to represent macro definition sites, as well (see, for instance, [9]).

References

[1]   D. Batory, G. Chen, E. Robertson, and T. Wang, "Web-Advertised Generators and Design Wizards", *International Conference on Software Reuse (ICSR)*, 1998.

[2]   D. Batory, B. Lofaso, and Y. Smaragdakis, "JTS: Tools for Implementing Domain-Specific Languages", *International Conference on Software Reuse (ICSR)*, 1998.

[3]   D. Batory and S. O'Malley, "The Design and Implementation of Hierarchical Software Systems with Reusable Components", *ACM Transactions on Software Engineering and Methodology*, October 1992.

[4]   A. Bawden and J. Rees, "Syntactic Closures". In *Proceedings of the SIGPLAN '88 ACM Conference on Lisp and Functional Programming*, 86-95.

[5]   S. P. Carl, "Syntactic Exposures—A Lexically-Scoped Macro Facility for Extensible Languages". M.A. Thesis, University of Texas, 1996. Available through the Internet at `ftp://ftp.cs.utexas.edu/pub/garbage/carl-msthesis.ps`.

[6]   W. Clinger, J. Rees (editors), "The Revised^4 Report on the Algorithmic Language Scheme". *Lisp Pointers IV(3)*, July-September 1991, 1-55.

[7]   W. Clinger and J. Rees, "Macros that Work". in *Conference Record of the Eighteenth Annual ACM Symposium on Principles of Programming Languages*, January 1991, 155-162.

[8]   R.K. Dybvig, R. Hieb, and C. Bruggeman, "Syntactic Abstraction in Scheme", in *Lisp and Symbolic Computation*, 5(4), December 1993, 83-110.

[9]   C. Hanson, "A Syntactic Closures Macro Facility", *Lisp Pointers IV(4)*, October-December 1991, 9-16.

[10]   E. Kohlbecker, D.P. Friedman, M. Felleisen, and B. Duba, "Hygienic Macro Expansion", in *Proceedings of the SIGPLAN '86 ACM Conference on Lisp and Functional Programming*, 151-161.

[11]   J. Rees, "The Scheme of Things: Implementing Lexically Scoped Macros", *Lisp Pointers VI(1)*, January-March 1993.

[12]   T. Sheard and N. Nelson, "Type Safe Abstractions Using Program Generators", Oregon Graduate Institute Tech. Report 95-013.

[13]   C. Simonyi, "The Death of Computer Languages, the Birth of Intentional Programming", *NATO Science Committee Conference,* 1995.

[14]   Y. Smaragdakis and D. Batory, "DiSTiL: a Transformation Library for Data Structures", *USENIX Conference on Domain-Specific Languages (DSL)*, 1997.

[15]   W. Taha and T. Sheard, Multi-stage programming with explicit annotations, *ACM Symp. Partial Evaluation and Semantics-Based Program Manipulation (PEPM '97)*, 1997.

Efficient Object-Oriented Software
with Design Patterns*

Mario Friedrich[2], Holger Papajewski[1], Wolfgang Schröder-Preikschat[1],
Olaf Spinczyk[1], and Ute Spinczyk[1]

[1] University of Magdeburg, Universitätsplatz 2, 39106 Magdeburg, Germany,
{papajews,wosch,olaf,ute}@ivs.cs.uni-magdeburg.de
[2] GMD FIRST, Rudower Chaussee 5, 12489 Berlin, Germany,
friedric@first.gmd.de

Abstract. Reusable software based on design patterns typically utilizes "expensive" language features like object composition and polymorphism. This limits their applicability to areas where efficiency in the sense of code size and runtime is of minor interest. To overcome this problem our paper presents a generative approach to "streamline" pattern-based object-oriented software. Depending on the actual requirements of the environment the source code is optimized with a transformation tool. The presented technique provides "scalable" software structures and thus reconciles reusability with efficiency of pattern-based software.

1 Introduction

Design Patterns [6] are "descriptions of communicating objects and classes that are customized to solve a general design problem in a particular context". They are widely accepted as a very useful approach to ease the design of object-oriented software. Though no specific programming language nor coding style is forced by design patterns, a pattern description typically contains a class diagram, e.g. based on OMT or UML, and sample code. The code directly reflects the class diagram in order to achieve the same reusability. It excessively utilizes "expensive" language features like object composition via pointers and polymorphism. This raises the question of the efficiency of design pattern-based software and object-oriented software in general.

In some application domains even a comparably fast object-oriented language like C++ is not fully accepted because of its expensive features like dynamic binding. An example for such domains is the embedded systems area were now the "Embedded C++"[1] standard should increase the acceptance. The same holds for the core of numerical application and (non-research) operating systems.

From our experience in the operating systems area we can state that it is hard to design and implement reusable - and at the same time efficient, overhead

---

* This work has been supported by the Deutsche Forschungsgemeinschaft (DFG), grant no. SCHR 603/1-1.
[1] Embedded C++ is a subset of C++ omitting the above mentioned expensive features.

free - object-oriented software, but it is even harder with design patterns. A pattern helps to design the class diagram of a software module. But, what is the relationship to the program code that has to be implemented? Normally the relationship is a direct mapping. Modern visual design tools generate the source code or the code is entered in the traditional way by adapting the pattern's sample code manually. This leads to flexible reusable code: Implementations and interfaces are separated by using abstract base classes and object composition is often applied to build flexible structures of objects that can be changed even at runtime. On the other hand this reusability and flexibility poses a significant overhead: abstract base classes, e.g., lead to dynamically bound (virtual) function calls. In [5] a median execution time of 5.6% and a maximum of 29% of dynamic dispatch code for a set of sample applications which quite sparingly execute virtual function calls is documented. Object composition implies pointers in every object of a specific class, thus wasting memory in the case that a dynamic modification of object connections is not needed. Last but not least the software module is often more complicated to use than a non-reusable variant which is especially trimmed to the needs of a specific application.

Our approach to overcome this problem follows the program family concept [8]. Different versions of a software module are generated to fulfill the requirements of its various application environments. Domain specific information is used to simplify the module structure as far as possible. This is done by a source-to-source transformation tool which works like an aspect weaver (see AOP [7]) with configuration information as aspect program and the module as component code. The generated code can be fed into any standard compiler which can then generate the optimized executable.

In the remaining sections of this paper we discuss the efficiency and optimization of pattern-based software in the context of application domains with hard resource constraints in more detail. This is followed by a presentation of our results and a discussion of related work.

2   Problem Discussion

Pattern-based software should be reusable and extensible without touching existing source code. A good example of how these design goals can be achieved shows the *Strategy Pattern*. The structure of this pattern is presented in figure 1 as a UML class diagram.

Fig. 1. The strategy pattern

The idea behind this pattern is to separate the interface and the implementation of some strategy. By doing this other strategies implementing the same interface can be easily integrated into the system without touching existing source code. It is even possible to change the strategy that is associated with each client object at runtime. The strategy pattern can be found as some kind of sub-pattern in many other design patterns. This makes it a very typical example to illustrate the overhead that may be posed on a software system if the implementation directly reflects the presented class diagram.

Now consider a concrete pattern instantiation: The client objects are memory managers in an operating system that know the start address and size of a memory block. They allow other objects to allocate and free pieces of memory from the pool they manage. The actual allocation can be done with different strategies like "best fit" or "first fit". The implementation of this little memory management subsystem should be reused in different operating system projects and may be extended by other strategies like "worst fit" in the future. Therefore the most flexible (pattern-based) implementation with a pointer to an abstract strategy base class is selected (figure 2).

Fig. 2. The instantiated pattern – a memory management subsystem

But this extensible and reusable implementation causes an overhead in operating system projects where the flexibility is not needed. As a first problem scenario consider a system with `MemoryManager` objects that never need the "first fit" strategy. Why should they access their associated strategy object via the abstract base class? Assuming C++ as our implementation language they could simply contain a pointer to a `BestFit` object as shown in figure 3. A special purpose design like this would omit the virtual function call needed to dynamically switch between the different strategy method implementations at runtime.

Fig. 3. Scenario 1 – single strategy class

To have an impression of the overhead that results from the abstract base class we have implemented a simple test application that creates two `BestFit` objects and a `MemoryManager` object. In this test scenario the method bodies were left empty. Only an output statement was included to track the correct behaviour. After associating the first `BestFit` object to the `MemoryManager` one of the methods of the strategy is called. Then the second `BestFit` object is associated to the `MemoryManager` and the method is called once again. The test application has been compiled in two versions: The first using the original strategy pattern (figure 2 without the `FirstFit` class) and the second using the simplified structure from figure 3. Table 1 shows the resulting static memory consumption[2]. To exclude the constant size of the startup code and the C library output function which are magnitudes bigger than our simple test modules we present only the object file sizes here.

Table 1. Scenario 1 – memory consumption

Version 1: Original Pattern					Version 2: Simplified Structure				
text	data	bss	sum	filename	text	data	bss	sum	filename
113	12	0	125	BestFit.o	36	0	0	36	BestFit.o
34	0	0	34	Manager.o	25	0	0	25	Manager.o
146	4	20	170	main.o	164	4	12	180	main.o
293	16	20	329	all	225	4	12	241	all

The sum over all sections in all linked object files in version 1 is 329 in comparison to 241 bytes in version 2. In other words, the pattern-based implementation requires about 36.5% more memory space than the specialized implementation.

Now consider a second scenario where the `MemoryManager` does not need to switch between different strategy objects at runtime because only a single global `BestFit` strategy object exists. In this case a specialized implementation can omit the abstract `Strategy` class, too. The global "best fit" strategy can be implemented by a class `BestFit` with all methods and data members declared as static. Now all strategy methods can be called without an object pointer and the `MemoryManager` objects can get rid of them. This is a significant reduction if one considers ten or hundreds of `MemoryManager` objects. But even with only a single object the memory consumption of the simplified implementation is significantly lower than the consumption of the pattern-based version. The exact numbers are presented in table 2. Here the overhead of the pattern-based implementation in this scenario is 160%.

Design patterns make the trade-offs of the different design options explicit, thus a designer can select whether to accept the overhead of the pattern-based implementation or to implement a specialized version of the subsystem. But in both cases the designer will lose. In the first case the price is mainly efficiency and in the second it is the reusability of the subsystem together with the risk to introduce errors.

---

[2] The code was generated with egcs 2.90.27 on Linux/Intel. To omit unnecessary runtime type information code the compiler options `-fno-rtti` and `-fno-exceptions` were used.

Table 2. Scenario 2 – memory consumption

Version 1: Original Pattern					Version 2: Simplified Structure				
text	data	bss	sum	filename	text	data	bss	sum	filename
113	12	0	125	BestFit.o	38	4	0	42	BestFit.o
34	0	0	34	Manager.o	29	0	0	29	Manager.o
121	4	16	141	main.o	42	0	2	44	main.o
267	16	16	299	all	109	4	2	115	all

3   Optimization

The overhead documented in section 2 cannot be tolerated in many application areas and should be avoided. Instead the complexity of the system structure should scale with the actual requirements of the subsystem's environment. It should not be ruled by possible future system extensions which may never happen. At the same time the implementation should be reusable.

To achieve this goal we combine the pattern-based software design with knowledge about the actual system requirements in a configuration phase. This input is used by an optimizer that selects a specialized system structure which is free of the pattern overhead (optimization phase). For the software developer this process is transparent. The source code directly reflects the pattern-based design, thus is as reusable and extensible as the design itself. The necessary specialization is done by a source code transformation tool in the generation phase. The complete process is illustrated in figure 4.

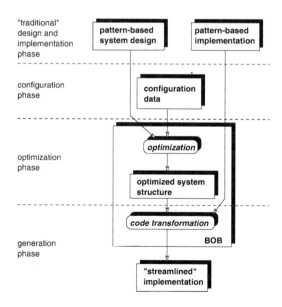

Fig. 4. The complete optimization process

The result of this approach is a tool that allows to generate a family of fine-tuned subsystem implementations from a single reusable pattern-based source code. The configuration step selects the best suited family member.

Section 4 discusses the software architecture of the "black optimizer box" (BOB) and the code transformation with further details. The remaining parts of the current section focus on the more important optimization phase and the rules and conditions guiding the optimization process.

3.1 Pattern Descriptions

An important prerequisite for the optimization of the pattern-based implementation is the documentation of the applied pattern. The documentation is needed to avoid a complex source analysis and the software developer should document instantiated patterns anyway. The pattern description consists of the pattern name, a name of the created pattern instance and list of classes building the pattern with their associated roles as shown in figure 5.

```
define CommunicationSystem decorator
{
    component: Driver;
    concrete_component: Ethernet;
    decorator: Protocol;
    concrete_decorator: IP;
    concrete_decorator: Crypt;
}
```

Fig. 5. A pattern description

Pattern instances usually can be extended without touching existing source code. With the **extend**-command (see figure 6) this is possible with the pattern description as well .

```
extend CommunicationSystem
{
    concrete_component: CAN;
}
```

Fig. 6. A pattern description extension

Having this description (pattern definition and extensions) the optimizer "knows" the names of the classes forming a pattern and implicitly how the connections between these classes are implemented, i.e. the class diagram (figure 8, top). In figure 4 this corresponds to the "pattern-based system design" box.

The example subsystem described in figure 5 is a simplified communication system. It contains some communication protocols, an ethernet and a CAN bus driver. Other hardware drivers can be added easily because of the abstract `Driver` base class.

With the decorator pattern it is possible to connect objects in a chain where method calls are forwarded to the next object. The data passed along this chain as a function parameter may be modified. This is the way how protocols in the example are implemented. The chain has to be terminated by a hardware driver. With the flexibility of this structure you can create an IP communication driver with encryption running via ethernet or any other combination that makes sense. New protocols can also be added without touching existing code.

3.2   Requirement Definitions

The pattern instance (`CommunicationSystem` in the example) is reusable in different environments. To find an optimized system structure for the pattern-based subsystem it is necessary to specify the requirements of its environment. The requirement definition that is used for this purpose corresponds to the "configuration data" in figure 4. It is provided in the configuration phase, thus can be exchanged for different application environments.

The requirement definition mainly consists of the list of class names that are used from the pattern-based subsystem and a description in what way objects are instantiated. An example is given in figure 7.

```
require CommunicationSystem
{
    IP [Protocol (Ethernet)];
}
```

Fig. 7. A pattern requirement definition

This requirement says that only the IP, `Protocol` and `Ethernet` classes are needed (directly) by the environment of the pattern-based subsystem. The `Protocol` class should contain a pointer to an `Ethernet` object, instead of a pointer to any kind of `Driver`.

Before the system structure can be modified the requirement definition is checked against the class hierarchy given by the pattern description: All classes mentioned have to be known and a relation to another class (like "`Protocol (Ethernet)`") is restricted to the subtree below the class referenced in the original class hierarchy. Inheritance relationships cannot be changed but one can change an object composition built with a pointer to an aggregation (like "`Protocol [Ethernet]`"). It is also possible to create specialized class versions with the alias feature, e.g. "`EP is Protocol [Ethernet]; CP is Protocol [CAN];`". This is needed to optimize subsystems based on patterns that contain cycles in the class relation graph.

3.3   Optimization Rules

With the description of the implemented system structure and the requirements in the actual application scenario a "streamlined" system structure can be automatically derived. The following simple rules are applied:

1. All classes, that are not mentioned in the requirement definition and that are not needed by a mentioned class, can be removed.
2. The class relation changes given in the requirement definition are applied.
3. Classes, that can't lead to a virtual function call anymore are "devirtualized", i.e. all pure virtual functions are removed and virtual functions are declared non-virtual.
4. Empty classes are removed.

The first rule is used to find out which classes are not needed in the current application scenario. The operation not only removes the code and static data of the classes that are not needed but also references to other classes. This point increases the chance for further optimizations in rule 3.

With the second rule the class relation changes are applied exactly as required, because the way how objects of the optimized subsystem are instantiated and connected by the environment and the resulting optimized code have to match. Otherwise the system would be incorrect and couldn't be compiled.

The third rule is responsible for the elimination of virtual functions and, thus, for the runtime improvements. Here a complicated code analysis is performed, because calls to virtual functions have to be found and checked if they still (after rule 1 and 2) need to be virtual.

By applying the last rule former interface classes that contain only pure virtual functions can be removed.

3.4   Optimization Example

Figure 8 shows an example of requirement definitions and the resulting system structures.

The upper part contains the structure of the sample communication system that is already known from figure 5, 6, and 7. The structure is very flexible because low-level drivers and protocols can be added without touching exisiting source code and the using environment is able to create any possible chain of protocols that is terminated by a low-level driver. The disadvantage is that every function call in this chain is a virtual function call leading to a waste of runtime and memory space for virtual function tables and dispatch code.

With the presented approach it is now possible to generate a family of implementations. If, for example, some system configuration only requires just a CAN bus driver the structure on the left can be generated. If you want to send crypted data via IP on an ethernet you can get the structure on the right. The black diamond-shaped boxes mean aggregation, so a single object can be instantiated that contains all the necessary state information and no virtual function calls take place anymore.

Pattern-based System Structure

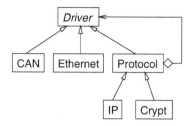

Scenario 1: Just a CAN Driver   **Scenario 2: Crypted Data via IP on Ethernet**

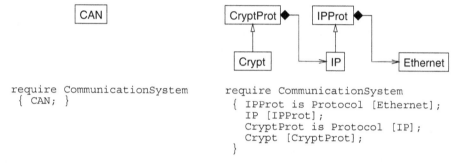

```
require CommunicationSystem        require CommunicationSystem
  { CAN; }                           { IPProt is Protocol [Ethernet];
                                       IP [IPProt];
                                       CryptProt is Protocol [IP];
                                       Crypt [CryptProt];
                                     }
```

Fig. 8. Optimized system structures

3.5 Multiple Requirement Definitions

Currently only a single requirement definition that describes the demands of the environment of the pattern instance is allowed. With this restriction the environment is forced to have a common view on the classes in the pattern. A future extension of our transformation system shall handle this problem.

As an example consider a subsystem that requires just a single CAN driver like scenario 1 of figure 8 and a second subsystem requiring an IP communication via ethernet with data encryption. Both requirements do not conflict and can be merged easily.

Even if one subsystem specifies "IP [Protocol [Ethernet]]" and instantiates its driver objects with "IP ip;" and another subsystem specifies "IP [Protocol (Ethernet)]" a common requirement can be found automatically: The second subsystem instantiates IP objects with individual ethernet driver objects like "Ethernet eth; IP ip (&eth);". An algorithm has to find the "cheapest" system structure that fulfills both requirements. In the example it is the requirement definition of the second subsystem. To have optimization transparency, the source code of the first subsystem has to be adapted by creating an Ethernet object any time the source code exhibits a creation of an IP object.

4   Implementation

Figure 4 shows two actions inside of BOB: The "optimization" and the "code transformation". These two steps directly reflect the two-level system architecture that implements the optimization process.

The upper level is responsible for the optimization. It reads and analyses the pattern descriptions and requirement definitions given in the PATCON language, that was introduced by the examples in figure 5, 6 and 7. With the optimization rules described in subsection 3.3 a list of transformation commands is generated. The whole process is done without reading or modifying the source code. This is a problem because the system configurator has to provide a lot of information that could also be automatically found in the source code. A coming redesign will take this problem into account.

The transformation commands are the input for the lower level that does the code transformation. The lower level is implemented by an aspect weaver that handles the customization of object interactions in general. The transformations allow quite complex code manipulations like "change a class reference via pointer to an aggregation" or "devirtualize a function if possible". Many of these functions require an analysis of method bodies.

The transformation functions are some kind of meta programs that drive lower-level transformations based on rewrite rules for the resolved abstract syntax trees of the component code. This work is done by "PUMA for C++", a parser and manipulator library for C++ code, which is going to be extended to an aspect weaver environment with a plug-in interface for multiple aspect weavers in the near future. With PUMA we can analyse and manipulate the code of the whole application. This is very important for the pattern optimization. It is also the reason why it is not possible to integrate the optimizations into a standard compiler. Normal compilers work with single translation units.

5   Results

A prototype implementing the algorithms and transformations described in the previous sections is running. To demonstrate the results, we have implemented a communication system like that from figure 8. The difference to that system is that we only have a single "hardware" driver which implements a simple mailbox for local inter-thread communication. Our two protocols are a checksum calculation and encryption. With this "renaming" scenario 1 is just a single mailbox and scenario 2 is checksum protocol on encrypted messages. The resulting code sizes and runtimes are presented in table 3. For the measurements again the egcs-2.90.27 on a Linux/Intel system was used. The sizes are given in units of bytes and the runtimes in Pentium II clock cycles.

The code sizes contain the complete test application consisting of two threads that communicate with each other via a shared mailbox. It also consists of classes that implement abstractions of communication addresses and data packets, the mailbox code and a lot of inlined operating system functions for thread synchronization and scheduling. All of these parts are equal in the pattern-based

Table 3. Code sizes and runtimes

	Scenario 1		Scenario 2	
	Pattern	Optimized	Pattern	Optimized
code	1532	1477	3676	3550
data	36	20	148	100
bss	20	16	208	188
sum	1588	1513	4032	3838
∅ receive time (sync.)	675	424	1694	1548
∅ receive time (async.)	314	307	675	518

and the optimized version. So results like those of table 1 and 2 could not be expected. Nevertheless there is a difference of 75 bytes in scenario 1 and 194 bytes in scenario 2. This is a reduction of about 4.8% in both cases.

The runtime data shows the number of clock cycles needed for synchronous and asynchronous receive operations. In scenario 1 in both versions no virtual function call takes place and no unnecessary constructor code is executed in the pattern-based version. So we can explain the big difference (675-424) only with a better cache hit rate because of the slightly reduced memory consumption or a better luck with the scheduling. In scenario 2 there is a speedup of 8.6% in the synchronous case where context switch times are included and 23.3% in the asynchronous case.

6   Related Work

The generation of pattern implementations is proposed in [3]. This work of IBM has much in common with our work since different implementations can be generated depending on so called "trade-offs". These trade-offs correspond to the optimization conditions in section 3. The difference is that this work mainly focuses on the increased productivity with automatic code generation tools and not the efficiency and optimization aspects.

The specialization of source code in our approach is a kind of static configuration. This can also be done with template metaprogramming as proposed in [4]. While that paper presents a general purpose implementation technique for static configuration we concentrate on design patterns. The specialized source code could also be generated with template metaprogramming, but the optimization would have to be a manual process. Our approach simplifies the software development because no template programming is necessary and only the used patterns need to be documented. The configuration information can be supplied in a problem-adequate language.

Virtual function call optimization by source-to-source transformation of C++ code was successfully applied in [1]. The optimizer described in this paper implements a class hierarchy analysis and a profile-based type feedback optimization. Similar ideas are presented in [2]. Both papers concentrate on runtime. A simplification of the whole program structure or the elimination of member variables that lead to reduced memory consumption was not documented. This would require extra knowledge about the implementation like the pattern descriptions.

7   Conclusions

We have not completed our work on this topic yet. A lot of implementation and especially documentation work still has to be done, and our experiences with the system in future projects will probably have an influence on the optimization rules and conditions, too.

Nevertheless the tools and techniques presented in this paper show how reusability and extensibility of a pattern-based software design can be reconciled with the efficiency of the resulting implementation by automatically scaling software structures. The software designer simply needs to define requirements and make the applied patterns explicit inside a pattern description file. The rest of the optimization is completely transparent. Thus we are optimistic that our approach may raise the level of acceptance of pattern-based object-oriented software in application areas with hard resource constraints. For our development of PURE [9] - a family of object-oriented operating systems that targets the area of deeply embedded systems - patterns can now be applied without risking unacceptable overhead.

References

[1] G. Aigner and U. Hölzle. Eliminating Virtual Function Calls in C++ Programs. Technical Report TRCS95-22, Computer Science Department, University of California, Santa Barbara, December 1995.

[2] D. Bernstein, Y. Fedorov, S. Porat, J. Rodrigue, and E. Yahav. Compiler Optimization of C++ Virtual Function Calls. In *2nd Conference on Object-Oriented Technologies and Systems*, Toronto, Canada, June 1996.

[3] F. J. Budinsky, M. A. Finnie, J. M. Vlissides, and P. S. Yu. Automatic code generation from design patterns. *IBM Systems Journal*, 35(2), 1996.

[4] K. Czarnecki and U. Eisenecker. Synthesizing Objects. In R. Guerraoui, editor, *Proceedings of the 13th European Conference on Object-Oriented Programming (ECOOP'99)*, number 1628 in Lecture Notes in Computer Science, pages 18–42, Lisbon, Portugal, 1999. Springer Verlag.

[5] K. Driesen and U. Hölzle. The Direct Cost of Virtual Function Calls in C++. In *OOPSLA'96 Proceedings*, October 1996.

[6] E. Gamma, R. Helm, R. Johnson, and J. Vlissides. *Design Patterns: Elements of Reusable Object-Oriented Software*. Addison-Wesley, 1995. ISBN 0-201-63361-2.

[7] G. Kiczales, J. Lamping, A. Mendhekar, C. Maeda, C. Lopes, J.-M. Loingtier, and J. Irwin. Aspect-Oriented Programming. Technical Report SPL97-008 P9710042, Xerox PARC, February 1997.

[8] D. L. Parnas. On the Design and Development of Program Families. *IEEE Transactions on Software Engineering*, SE-5(2):1–9, 1976.

[9] F. Schön, W. Schröder-Preikschat, O. Spinczyk, and U. Spinczyk. Design Rationale of the PURE Object-Oriented Embedded Operating System. In *Proceedings of the International IFIP WG 9.3/WG 10.5 Workshop on Distributed and Parallel Embedded Systems (DIPES '98)*, Paderborn, 1998. ISBN 0-7923-8614-0.

Vanilla: an open language framework

Simon Dobson, Paddy Nixon, Vincent Wade, Sotirios Terzis, and John Fuller

Department of Computer Science, Trinity College, Dublin 2, Ireland
E-mail: simon.dobson@cs.tcd.ie

Abstract. A trend in current research is towards component-based systems, where applications are built by combining re-usable fragments or components. In this paper we argue the case for building programming languages from components. We describe VANILLA, a component-based architecture for language tools. The core of Vanilla is a set of components, each implementing the type checking and behaviour of a single language feature, which are integrated within a well-structured framework to provide a programming language interpreter. Features may be extensively re-used across a variety of languages, allowing rapid prototyping and simplifying the exploration of new constructs. We describe the design and implementation of the system, and draw some general conclusions from the experience of building with components.
Subject areas: language design and implementation; frameworks.

Introduction

The move towards component-based design throughout software engineering is an encouraging trend, one which both simplifies software development through re-use and encourages the development of dynamically extensible applications and systems. It presents several major challenges to programming language research in determining the type and combinator structures which will best support such dynamic composition. However, we may also observe that programming languages themselves offer an excellent example of systems which are composed from largely orthogonal components. The individual parts of a language – arithmetic, loops, objects *etc* – are frequently compositional in nature, in the sense that the definition of one feature is only minimally (if at all) dependent on the detailed definitions of others. Given a suitable framework, we may view the construction of languages as an exercise in composition. This may be seen both as the logical consequence of minimalist language design and as a way of bringing the discipline of language design to composing components, without constraining the available combinators to be exactly those of any current language. This is vital for exploration of a field which is as yet very poorly understood.

Over the past year we have been developing VANILLA, a Java-based component architecture for language tools. The core of Vanilla is a set of components, each implementing the type checking and behaviour of a single language feature, which are integrated within a well-structured framework to provide a programming language interpreter. Since many language features appear in very similar

K. Czarnecki and U.W. Eisenecker (Eds.): GCSE'99, LNCS 1799, pp. 91–104, 2000.

guises across languages[7][9], the component-based approach maximises the re-use of language components and allows the designer to focus on what makes his language different from others. Since components can easily be added, subtract-ed and modified individually, the language designer has great scope for exploring the impact of new language features with minimal coding effort.

In this paper we describe Vanilla's architecture and discuss how combining components simplifies experiments with novel languages and features. Although our presentation concentrates on an application in language research, we believe that many of the observations apply equally to any large component-based sys-tem. We first describe the overall component architecture, concentrating on the design of the container framework. We then discuss the components of languages and show how they may be defined in isolation and then combined. We describe our current crop of components, and compare our system with other approaches to experimental language construction. We conclude with some directions for the future.

Architecture

The abstract internal architecture for compilers and interpreters is well-accepted, and is common across a range of tools from basic command-line driven tools to full visual metaphor environments. It consists of three phases:

- a *parser* converts a program's *concrete syntax* (the code the programmer writes) into a more tractable internal representation or *abstract syntax tree* (AST);
- the AST for the program is *type checked*, a static semantic analysis which ensures that the program text is correct with respect to the rules of the language;
- finally, the AST is converted into the appropriate behaviour, either directly (for an interpreter) or by generating code to be executed later (a compiler).

Although this architecture is generally accepted it is subject to a number of variations. Most seriously, there are often some tempting optimisations which, while making a particular tool more efficient, obscure the architecture and in-troduce couplings between the different phases. As such "creeping" couplings are introduced it becomes more likely that a change in one part of the system will have an undesirable side-effect on another, and the tool becomes more difficult to modify.

We took several important decisions for the overall structure of Vanilla:

Keep it clean. The design of the system was to be "clean", in the sense that no design compromises would be made on the grounds of efficiency. The intention was to produce a clearly-structured, easily-understood and well-documented tool, accepting inefficiencies in the interests of clarity.

Keep it simple. The core of the system – the type checking and interpretation phases – would be designed to be as simple and flexible as possible.

Keep it well-founded. The standard language features would be designed so
as to be well-founded. Type theorists and programmers sometimes think
about constructs slightly differently: Vanilla always favours semantic clarity
over pragmatism.

A component framework for languages

Unintended coupling of phases within a system can be avoided by setting that
system within a framework which is sufficiently flexible to avoid the need for
such compromises. There are several possible approaches which might be taken,
the most attractive of which is the *component architecture*. A component is
typically represented by a collection of classes and objects which are re-used *en
masse* to maintain their defined structure. The power of the approach comes
from integrating components within a framework defining their relationships
and interactions. It is the framework rather than the individual components
which provide the flexibility of the component architecture. This gives three
main advantages:

Clear internal architecture. The framework provides a clear decomposition
of responsibility between the different parts of the system. Since the subsystems can only interact through the framework, there is considerably less
scope for unintended coupling between modules.
Easy substitution. The framework can make it easy to add or replace functionality. Conversely (and equally importantly) it can control exactly how
replacement occurs to protect the system against uncontrolled changes.
Incremental experimentation. New components can provide new features
which make use of existing features. This reduces the complexity of experiments.

Our contention is that we may define a set of components, each defining an independent programming language feature, and combine them to construct complete language interpreters. If we consider type checking as an example, the
framework defines the key properties, operations and algorithms of type checking (free variables, substitution, sub-typing *etc*) while the components provide
the realisations of (parts of) these operations. Essentially the framework defines
what is the same for all type checkers while the components define *what is different* between individual languages. Component re-use occurs when languages
exhibit substantial commonality in their typing. The same comments apply to
interpretation and (to a lesser extent) parsing.

One possible stumbling block is that phases of the framework may over-
commit to certain algorithms. This is often necessary in order to provide a
sufficiently concrete framework in which to implement components. It has the
disadvantage that the type checker (for example) must select a particular typing
algorithm (natural deduction) within which the components work. Selecting a
new algorithm (such as one based on unification) would not be an incremental
change and would require re-implementing the entire phase. The impact of such

a change may not affect other phases – for example interpretation is probably not affected by a move to unification-based typing. This may not be the case, however: one might for example provide a dummy type checker and place the burden of type checking directly on the interpreter at run-time. The important point is that the framework allows such interactions to be localised and flexibly controlled.

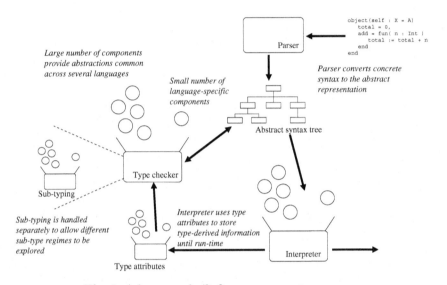

Fig. 1. A language built from components

Vanilla's architecture (figure 1) is basically a direct realisation of the three-phase architecture described above – with the important difference that the tool phases are intended to be component-based frameworks whose actual functionality is provided by components rather than being hard-wired.

The architecture centres around the abstract syntax tree of the program being processed. The AST is built by the parser phase from the source text of the program and then traversed by the type checking and interpretation phases. Traditional language parsers are monolithic, defining the complete concrete syntax of the language using a parser generator such as JavaCC. We support these, and also a system of parser combinators which allows grammar fragments to be defined separately and then combined[6]. This is useful for experimentation, although a little fragile for deployment.

A single AST will generally contain a large number of different node types, representing the various elements of languages (identifiers, loops, procedures, type declarations, *etc*), which are used to drive the rest of the system. Type attributes allow the interpreter components to record properties identified during typing for use at run-time. We separate sub-typing from typing to allow experimentation with alternate sub-typing regimes (such as name-sensitive *versus* purely structural sub-typing).

Our implementation of this architecture consists of around 100 classes, with another 70 for the parser component generator.

Component composition

A typical component architecture would use components to implement discrete functions within the system. Our requirement in Vanilla is slightly different: we want components to co-operate in implementing a single phase. A phase is built from a number of components, each providing part of the overall functionality. The definition of a component's local functionality may depend on the global functionality of the sub-system – to use type checking as an example, a component for functions might define types for function literals (its local functionality) in terms of the type of the arguments and the function body (having any type determinable by the full type checker). This allows components to offer features uniformly across all types provided by other components. A component-based phase must therefore combine a set of components to co-operate in providing the full phase, and make the capabilities of the full phase available to the components.

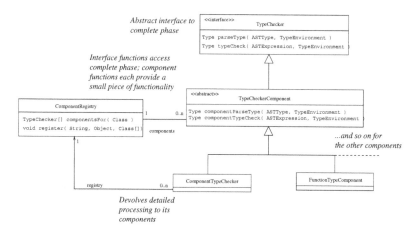

Fig. 2. Component composition pattern

The solution we devised is to drive selection of components within phases using the types of the AST nodes. Each phase implements a simple abstract interface. The implementation of a phase consists of a set of components within a harness (figure 2). When installed each component "expresses an interest"in one or more AST node types. As a phase walks the abstract syntax tree, it identifies the components interested in each encountered node type and calls them in sequence (illustrated schematically in figure 3 and through a code fragment in figure 4). (Although there may be many components in the sub-system only a relatively small number will be interested in each particular node type, so this approach rapidly prunes the space of possible components.) Using the type checker as an example, a component then has three possible actions:

1. it may determine that the expression represented by the node is type-correct and return the assigned type;
2. it may determine that the expression is type-incorrect, and throw an exception; or
3. it may decline to commit itself and allow another component to handle the node.

It is the third possibility which allows AST nodes to be overloaded: removing this option leads to a system without extensible abstract syntax. This may be desirable for some purposes, for example program analysis, but also precludes some very natural generalisations such as functions taking types as parameters and a general access operator. The structure of the component pattern means, however, that Vanilla can easily detect whether a particular language is using AST overloading and raise an error if desired.

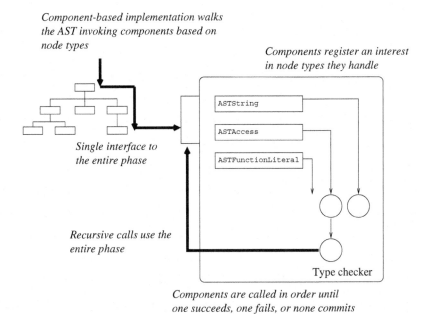

Fig. 3. Behaviour of component composition

```
public void register( ComponentRegistry reg )
{
   // register our interest in ASTIf nodes with the typing phase
   try { Class[] nodes = {
           Class.forName("ie.vanilla.pods.conditionals.ASTIf") };
        reg.register(getClass().getName(), this, nodes);
      } catch(ClassNotFoundException cnf)
        { System.out.println("PANIC! Can't load classes\n" + cnf);
          System.exit(1); }
}


public Type componentTypeCheck( ASTExpression x, TypeEnvironment tc )
   throws TypeException, UnrecognisedSyntaxException
{
   // we're interested in ASTIf nodes
   if(x instanceof ASTIf) {
      ASTIf cond = (ASTIf) x;

      // make recurive calls to the entire phase to allow
      // other pods to type-check the branches
      Type condition = typeCheck(cond.getCondition(), tc),
           trueBranch = typeCheck(cond.getTrueBranch(), tc);
      ASTExpression fb = cond.getFalseBranch();
      Type falseBranch = (fb == null) ?
         BottomType.Bottom : typeCheck(fb, tc);

      // condition has to be a boolean
      SubTypeReleation rel = getSubtypeRelation();
      if(!rel.isSubtypeOf(condition, BooleanType.Boolean, tc))
         throw (new TypeMismatchException(cond,
                                          BooleanType.Boolean,
                                          condition));

      // type is the LUB of the branches
      return rel.leastUpperBound(trueBranch, falseBranch, tc);
   }

   // we'll never be passed anything else, but this keeps
   // the compiler happy...
   else { return null; }
}
```

Fig. 4. Type checking component for conditionals

Language components

Having established a language framework, it remains to populate it with functional components. A typical programming language consists of a number of orthogonal elements – arithmetic, functional abstraction, variable binding, records and so forth. Each feature may be understood in isolation: one may describe functions without having to specify exactly what terms may appear in their bodies, for example, or describe sequential composition independently of the terms being composed. Describing a feature involves specifying its abstract structure, realisation, type rules, behaviour *etc.* Vanilla takes this principle and applies it directly to implementing interpreters. Each feature is implemented by a set of classes (which we call a *pod*) providing the structures and operations needed by that feature. A typical pod includes classes providing:

- abstract syntax tree (AST) nodes representing the abstract structures of the feature;
- representations of any types it introduces;
- any sub-type relationships between the types;
- the mapping of AST nodes to types, possibly including types introduced by other pods;
- the typing-time derivations of any attributes which should be propagated to run-time;
- representations of any run-time values introduced; and
- the mapping of a type-checked AST to a run-time result, which might again depend on other pods.

Defining a new pod involves defining Java classes for each of the structures introduced. Typically these classes derive directly from a system-defined abstract class defining the operations to be provided. For example a new type is represented within Vanilla by deriving a sub-class of the `Type` class and providing the operations to perform free variable extraction, α-conversion *etc.* Similarly an interpreter component provides an initialisation function to express the component's interest in different AST node types and another function interpreting those nodes when encountered by the interpreter, usually involving recursive calls to the interpreter to compute the values of sub-expressions. Pods may place requirements on the availability of other features in a language – for example the pod providing conditionals requires some other pod to define boolean-valued expressions – but are usually independent on exactly how these features are provided. This makes pods very loosely coupled, which in turn means that a single pod may offer its services uniformly across a range of other language structures.

We have implemented a range of pods covering a substantial fraction of the language design space, including common imperative, functional and object-oriented language features, and some more unusual typing constructs (figure 1). Excluding the rather less well-decomposed core pod a typical language feature requires around 9 classes (850 heavily-commented lines of code); the most complex pod, providing a polymorphic object model from Abadi and Cardelli[2],

Pod	Feature	Classes	LOC
Core	Common ground types and arithmetic	61	4000
Records	Ordered products with named elements	9	900
Sequences	Extensible sequences	11	1000
Loops	`for` and `while` loops	5	400
Conditionals	`if` conditionals	4	300
Variables	Assignment and retrieval	8	900
Functions	Function abstraction and application	15	1500
Named types	Type naming	7	700
Kinds	Type variables	5	400
Universals	Bounded universal types	6	600
Existentials	Partially abstract types	8	700
Autos	Dynamic typing with "self-describing" values[5]	10	900
Mu	μ-recursive types	9	700
Objects	Objects with covariant self types[2]	23	2500
Classes	Constructing objects from classes	8	1000
Simple I/O	Very simple string-based input and output	6	500
	Averages with (without) core pod	12 (9)	1100 (850)

Table 1. Some standard Vanilla pods

needs 23 classes (2500 lines of code). This illustrates that defining a new feature does not represent a substantial programming effort.

Although we have provided a standard pod set, the component architecture does not mandate any particular decomposition of the design space. Our approach has been to follow type-theoretic boundaries, which suits our own purposes but may cause problems for others. For example, the common object-oriented languages allow the definition of objects whose methods return objects of the same type as the receiver. Using our system of pods such objects are modeled using a combination of first-order object types and explicit μ-recursive types. This clearly separates the responsibilities each pod has within the language and exploits the orthogonality which the components offer: it is also rather convoluted for a non-type theorist! More pragmatic users might prefer to implement recursive object types directly, especially if there are no other recursive type structures in the language which might benefit from pod re-use.

Environments, contexts and sub-expressions

An AST encapsulates all the static information about an occurrence of a language construct in a program. In traversing the AST a phase will make use of this static information plus a certain amount of dynamic information gathered from the analysis of the tree so far. A construct might, for example, include references to "free" variables which it does not itself define: the type checker must ensure that these variables are appropriately declared elsewhere (for example in lexical containing scopes), which the interpreter must be able to access the values of these variables when they are evaluated. This dynamically-gathered information is maintained by type and interpretation environments.

The type-checking phase uses a type environment which is basically a nested look-up table mapping names to values holding the current state of type checking. Each value is keyed by a name and a sort – for example variable, named type, type variable, and hypothesised sub-type relationship. Some languages keep the different sorts in different classes, so that a single identifier may refer to a variable and a type depending on context; others keep the classes distinct. The type environment allows clients to retrieve entries by name and sort, optionally recursing up the environment hierarchy.

The interpreter phase uses a run-time environment, which is generally somewhat simpler and holds the bindings of names to values as the program executes.

Subtleties in both typing and interpretation appear in some constructs. The most interesting is the difference in type between the use of a variable in an expression and as the target for an assignment: the former has the type of its values, the latter the type of variables of that value. Languages such as ML[11] give variables a different static type and force the programmer to explicitly dereference the variable to access its value; languages such as C refer to this difference as being a *legal l-value* and "covertly" change the type as appropriate. The ML case is cleaner for the type checker and can be provided by assigning a type such as `Var Int` to variables and providing a suitable dereferencing operator, but is arguably less convenient for the programmer. The C case is a little more complex because the type assigned to an occurance of a variable (and the value returned when it is evaluated) depend on the context in which it appears.

Vanilla handles these "mode-sensitive" typings by representing contexts in the type environment, which can affect the way a construct is processed. Consider type-checking a piece of code which increments a variable:

```
elem = elem + 1;
```

The type checker will begin checking this expression in the default expression context. It needs to ensure that the left-hand side evaluates to an assignable integer variable, and that the right-hand side evaluates to an integer. It type-checks the left-hand side in an assignment context, indicating that it is looking for an assignment target. The recursive call will determine whether `elem` identifies a variable and, if so, will return the vartype of that variable (`Var Int`). The assignment will then recursively evaluate the the right-hand side in an expression context (since it is looking for a value, not an assignment target), and determine that `elem` has type `Int` when it appears in an expression. Finally the type checker will satisfy itself that the value on the right is a sub-type of the underlying type of the variable on the left.

Extensible syntax introduces the possibility of "late decisions" in the evaluation of an AST. Suppose a component implements the "dot" operator for addressing into a structure. This operator is overloaded in a number of contexts such as record access and fully-qualified naming for elements in modules, and its AST representation as the `ASTAccess` node is similarly ambiguous. A component encountering such a node cannot decide *a priori* whether it will handle the node until it has determined the type of the target of the access. This problem is particularly severe during interpretation, since the late decision will involve evaluating part of the ASTAccess node and then possibly rolling-back to allow another component to process the node. If this component then re-evaluates the node, any side effects will occur twice (at least!).

The solution again uses environments. When a component supporting extensible syntax processes an AST node, it refers to any sub-expressions evaluated by name and stores the results in the run-time environment. The interpreter uses this to ensure that a named sub-expression is only evaluated once.

Putting a language together

A Vanilla language is defined as a collection of pods integrated within the framework. The system uses *language definition files* or LDFs to list of the components making up a language. These classes are the instantiated and integrated into the language framework described above to produce an interpreter. This integration may happen dynamically – using a shell to build an interpreter from an LDF on demand – or statically to construct a stand-alone interpreter for the language defined by the LDF. A designer may use the dynamic approach for development and then deploy a static version from the same components and definitions.

In advocating the component-based approach we have stressed pod re-use across languages as a major goal. For this position to be defensible we need both a suitable population of "standard" pods and a illustration of their power when re-combined. The intention is then to re-use as much language "boilerplate" as possible, allowing the designer to concentrate ore fully on the novel features of the language being explored. We have used Vanilla to implement a small number of "real" languages and language extensions including Pascal, O-2[2], and a number of "synthetic" languages illustrating particular features. We have now started exploring some domain-specific languages.

Our limited experiences to date indicate that Vanilla is a powerful tool for language design and exploration. The average complexity of new pods is sufficiently low that they require only minimal coding effort, and the vast majority of features are provided by default by other pods from our standard set. This allows the language designer to focus exclusively on the novelty of the language being explored.

The resulting interpreters show perfectly adequate performance, making them realistic propositions for fairly extensive experimentation. We have performed several analyses of the performance implications of different component designs within our composition pattern. A component is simply a large conditional ranging over the AST nodes which the it handles, with the interested components being selected using hashing. For large components the former is considerably slower than the latter, so fine-grained decomposition often actually improves the performance of the tool. While it is difficult to quantify exactly where the cross-over point occurs, it means that there is generally no penalty – and often considerable benefit – from designing small, orthogonal components, which in turn improves potential component re-use.

Related work

The idea of extending a language's abilities is probably most familiar through languages such as Lisp and Forth, which allow new control and data structures to be added easily. Both the languages are dynamically typed, and avoid the difficulties of providing compositional extensions to typing.

A number of other language construction tools appear in the literature, especially concentrating on grammars and parser definition. The most common of these tools (such as `lex`, `yacc` and `JavaCC`) focus on syntax and provide only minimal leverage for the language designer. More refined approaches use attribute grammars, for example the Eli toolkit[8]. Indeed, several research languages (such as Philips' Elegant language [1]) are completely implemented as attribute grammars. Such tools simplify design by using high-level specifications of language functionality, but do not of themselves encourage the construction and re-use of independent language fragments.

Several authors have observed that individual programming languages tend to support a single programming paradigm, which in turn constrains the solutions programmers may develop. Languages such as Leda[4] address this by supporting multiple paradigms. We believe that Vanilla provides the language designer with an excellent tool for exploring these issues of paradigm composition, which may expose interesting new embeddings of features within more-or-less familiar languages.

The functional language community has experimented extensively with monadic composition for building interpreters, for example [10][13]. These systems have tended to stay strictly within the type framework of the host language rather than allowing the designer free rein to modify or extend it. A similar comment applies to recent trends in meta-programming such as OpenJava[14] and JTS[3]. Vanilla takes a considerably more direct approach, seeking to provide for the open implementation of languages *ab initio* rather than by extending any particular base. As a consequence the system is lower-level, less amenable to mathematical analysis, but perhaps better able to integrate Java's ever-expanding feature set into languages in a controlled way.

Conclusions

Computer science will always need new languages, as new contexts change the rules for application development. In order to find the solutions we need, we must be able to experiment with new constructs quickly and easily, exploring how they interact when placed together with other existing constructs. This incremental approach is key to the rapid evolution of new programming languages, systems and methodologies.

Vanilla's approach to constructing languages from components is a promising route to simplifying the deployment of new language features, at least within the research community. It minimises the effort required in prototyping, and encourages a "differential" approach which focuses on the novel features of the new system. It radically simplifies the inclusion of advanced concepts within experimental or domain-specific languages (highlighted and encouraged by several authors, for example [12]), and is well-suited to use by students or domain experts who are not language designers and need not understand the full complexity of the tools or more advanced components in order to use them. It facilitates the rapid exchange of new features between researchers, in the form of Vanilla pods which may be integrated into a range of different experimental platforms. As a side benefit, it provides a useful vehicle for teaching language and compiler theory.

The ability to build a complete language dynamically means that languages may be downloaded from the web. We speculate that one might provide a system similar to Java "applets" in which a web page containing a program also links to a description of the language needed to execute it – whose components may then be downloaded to execute the program. Equally one might envision a language which is extended syntactically and semantically on-the-fly by downloading new components. These are areas for our future research.

Java's ubiquity makes it an obvious vehicle for presenting new language concepts. The Java compiler itself is far from easy to modify or extend, however, and we are currently implementing a version of Java in Vanilla to facilitate such experiments. Whilst it may seem slightly strange to implement Java using a system written in Java, this is an approach which has proven fruitful in the past, for example with the ML Kit.

Perhaps the most important lesson for language design is the large – and somewhat surprising – degree of orthogonality between individual programming constructs. We originally anticipated that there would be considerable overlap between components, leading to quite complex interdependencies; in reality we have discovered that there remarkably few necessary constraints on how features may be combined. Even very entwined concepts may often be separated quite easily. This lends credibility to the idea of building languages from largely independent components. More generally, it suggests that co-operative component systems will be most successful when they work uniformly with any other component. Dependencies on an *entire* sub-system are not a problem: complexity only arises when there are dependencies on *parts* of a sub-system. Those systems which can be decomposed in this way will be best suited to co-operative components.

Vanilla has been released as open source on the web at `http://www.vanilla.ie/`.

References

1. Elegant. http://www.research.philips.com/generalinfo/special/elegant/elegant.html.
2. Martín Abadi and Luca Cardelli. *A theory of objects.* Springer Verlag, 1996.
3. Don Batory, Bernie Lofaso, and Yannis Smaragdakis. JTS: tools for implementing domain-specific languages. In *Proceedings of the 5th International Conference on Software Reuse*, 1998.
4. Tim Budd. *Multiparadigm programming in Leda.* Addison-Wesley, 1995.

5. Luca Cardelli. Typeful programming. Technical Report Research report 45, Digital SRC, 1994.
6. Simon Dobson. Modular parsers. Technical Report TCD-CS-1998-19, Department of Computer Science, Trinity College Dublin, 1998.
7. David Gelernter and Suresh Jagannathan. *Programming linguistics*. MIT Press, 1990.
8. Robert Gray, Vincent Heuring, Steven Levi, Anthony Sloane, and William Waite. Eli: a complete, flexible compiler construction system. *Communications of the ACM*, 35(2):121–131, 1992.
9. Samuel Kamin. *Programming languages: an interpreter-based approach*. Addison Wesley, 1990.
10. Sheng Liang, Paul Hudak, and Mark Jones. Monad transformers and modular interpreters. In *Proceedings of the ACM Symposium on Principles of Programming Languages*, pages 333–343, 1995.
11. Robin Milner, Mads Tofte, and Robert Harper. *The definition of Standard ML*. MIT Press, 1990.
12. Charles Simonyi. Interviewed in *The Edge*, 1998.
13. Guy Steele. Building interpreters by composing monads. In *Proceedings of the ACM Symposium on Principles of Programming Languages*, pages 472–492, 1994.
14. Michiaki Tatsubori. An extension mechanism for the Java language. Master's thesis, Tsukuba University, 1999.

From Macros to Reusable Generative Programming*

Shriram Krishnamurthi[1], Matthias Felleisen[1], and Bruce F. Duba[2]

[1] Department of Computer Science
Rice University
Houston, TX 77005-1892, USA
[2] Department of Computer Science
Seattle University
Seattle, WA 98122-4460, USA

Abstract. Generative programming is widely used both to develop new programming languages and to extend existing ones with domain-specific sub-languages. This paper describes McMicMac, a framework for generative programming. McMicMac uses tree-transforming macros as language specifications, and enhances them with inherited and synthesized attributes. The enhanced transformers can describe general compilation tasks. Families of these specifications are grouped into mixin-like collections called vocabularies. Programmers can define new languages by composing these vocabularies. We have implemented McMicMac for Scheme and used it to build several systems, including the DrScheme programming environment. The principles of McMicMac carry over to other languages and environments.

1 Introduction

Generative programming is an old and good idea—write programs to write your programs for you. This idea has been applied widely, from compilation to creating domain-specific languages to the mass-production of components. It is gaining increasing prominence due to its potential economic impact, because it can both reduce manual labor and increase the efficiency and correctness of programs.

In this paper, we describe a general framework for generative programming in Scheme [21]. Concretely, we describe McMicMac, a framework developed at Rice University. McMicMac supports the production of extensible language components. A programmer can generate new languages by composing language components. Because the components are parameterized over the base language, McMicMac programmers can reuse the same language-defining components to build many different languages. The system thus greatly simplifies the design and implementation of domain-specific languages as extensions of base languages.

Our system plays a crucial role in the construction of a large programming environment, DrScheme [12]. Conversely, the process of building DrScheme has

* This work is partially supported by NSF grants CCR-9619756, CDA-9713032, and CCR-9708957, and a Texas ATP grant.

K. Czarnecki and U.W. Eisenecker (Eds.): GCSE'99, LNCS 1799, pp. 105–120, 2000.

helped us debug and refine the design of our system. McMicMac has also been used to build tools for languages other than Scheme. Starting with a type-checker and compiler for a parenthetical version of Java, it has been used to create language extensions representing design patterns [16] and other specifications [26].

The rest of this paper is organized as follows. Section 2 provides an extended example that illustrates some of the kinds of abstractions that generative programming makes possible. Section 3 describes the structure of McMicMac through a series of examples, and section 3.3 and section 4 refine this discussion. Section 5 summarizes the deployment of McMicMac. Section 6 discusses related efforts, and section 7 offers concluding remarks and suggests directions for future work.

2   An Illustrative Example

Suppose a programmer wanted to distribute a library that creates and executes finite-state automata. The library of types and procedures (or classes with methods) should hide the actual representation used for the automata, because there are at least two different automata representations: data structures and executable values. Data structures are useful for manipulating automata as data, e.g., for minimizing automata. They can also be run via an interpreter, though this can be inefficient. If the automata are being created solely for execution, then it is typically much more efficient to translate them directly into code, such as functions or labeled statements.

Hence, the library should offer programmers a way to specify in-line automata in a representation-independent, yet intuitive, manner. This would allow clients to write expressions such as that shown in figure 1. The example uses a new construct, **automaton**, to define an automaton that, starting in *1-state*, checks whether a stream of 0s and 1s begins with 0 and then alternates strictly between the two values.

The specification in figure 1 might translate into the Scheme code shown in figure 2. It represents automata as procedures that consume an input stream. The states are nested, mutually-recursive procedures. Each procedure represents one state's transition relation. All unexpected inputs generate an exception, *unexpected-input-exn*, so the empty transition relation represents an error state. If the automaton attempts to inspect past the end of a finite input stream, a different exception is raised, which a client can handle to observe successful completion. Because programming languages like Scheme optimize calls in tail position to jumps or "goto"s, the state transitions in the example are quick and accumulate no evaluation context (colloquially, "stack space") [7].

Unfortunately, the library programmer cannot define **automaton**, because it is not a procedure. The sub-terms of **automaton** are not expressions in Scheme, as procedure arguments must be; rather they are terms in a distinct, domain-specific language. Furthermore, **automaton** is a *binding* construct (as clarified by figure 2), which cannot be defined procedurally. Therefore, **automaton** cannot be defined in most traditional programming languages.

```
(automaton 1-state
  (0-state ((0 ⟶ error-state)
            (1 ⟶ 1-state))
  (1-state ((0 ⟶ 0-state)
            (1 ⟶ error-state)))
  (error-state)))
```

Fig. 1. An Automaton Description

```
(lambda (input-stream)
  (letrec
      ((0-state (lambda ()
                  (case (next-token input-stream)
                    ((0) (error-state))
                    ((1) (1-state))
                    (else (raise (make-object unexpected-input-exn))))))
       (1-state (lambda ()
                  (case (next-token input-stream)
                    ((0) (0-state))
                    ((1) (error-state))
                    (else (raise (make-object unexpected-input-exn))))))
       (error-state (lambda ()
                      (case (next-token input-stream)
                        (else (raise (make-object unexpected-input-exn)))))))
    (1-state)))
```

Fig. 2. Compiled Automaton Representation

The automaton library might contain other operations of this form. For instance, the library may provide a means for interleaving the execution of two automata. This would enable the client programmer to write

(run/alternating (*M1 stream-1*) (*M2 stream-2*))

which runs automaton *M1* on stream *stream-1* and *M2* on *stream-2* in strict alternation. In this case, even though both sub-terms of **run/alternating** are legal Scheme expressions, Scheme's call-by-value evaluation order would first run *M1* on *stream-1* until termination—which may never occur—before it begins to run *M2*. Thus **run/alternating** also cannot be a procedure in a call-by-value language.

Both constructs illustrate useful and important abstractions that help programmers write software effectively. These abstractions are not *procedural*, however. Instead they define notations that are not part of the language's syntax. In other cases, they require behavior that is different from what the language's semantics specifies. More generally, **automaton** and **run/alternating** are both *linguistic* abstractions, i.e., they create a little language within a larger language

```
(define-macro (automaton ⟶)
  (automaton start-state
             (state-name (input ⟶ new-state) ...) ...)
  ⟹ (syntax
       (lambda (input-stream)
         (letrec ((state-name
                    (lambda ()
                      (case (remove-token input-stream)
                        ((input) (new-state)) ...
                        (else (raise (make-object unexpected-input-exn)))))) ...)
           (start-state)))))
```

Fig. 3. Automaton Macro

to accomplish some specialized task. Generative programming frameworks must support such language construction.

3   The McMicMac Framework

McMicMac is a framework for creating languages such as that for automata. We explain McMicMac through a series of examples reflecting increasingly complex protocols. The examples are intentionally simplistic in flavor, but they correspond to some of the non-trivial uses we have encountered while building DrScheme.

3.1   Macros

Examples like **automaton** and **run/alternating** are expressible as McMicMac *macros*. The macros of McMicMac are descendants of those in Lisp and Scheme [21,33]. They transform tree-shaped data, rather than manipulating flat data like the string-processing macros in the C pre-processor [22]. In short, macros implement a simple form of extensible parsing.

A parser is conceptually a table of rules that map syntactic shapes to code. When the input matches a shape, called a *trigger*, the parser looks up the trigger's transformation rule, called the *elaborator*, and uses it to produce abstract syntax. The parsing table is traditionally fixed, thus limiting the input language a parser can recognize. Macro definitions add rules to a parser's table. Unlike traditional parse rules, though, macro rules do not directly generate abstract syntax. Instead, they generate terms in the source language. The parser then re-analyzes the generated term and continues this process until it obtains a canonical form.

In McMicMac, the programmer defines triggers using a pattern-matching notation originally due to Kohlbecker and Wand [24]. When an input term matches

```
(define-macro (automaton —→)
   (automaton start-state
                 (state-name (input —→ new-state) ...) ...)
   ⟹ (syntax
         (make-automaton-rep start-state
            (list (make-state-rep state-name
                      (make-transition-rep input new-state) ...)
               ...)))))
```

Fig. 4. Alternate Automaton Macro

a trigger, the matcher generates a pattern environment that maps pattern variables to the corresponding source terms in the input. It then invokes the elaborator to generate a source term. This term can be parameterized over sub-terms in the input. The elaborator extracts these input sub-terms from the pattern environment.

Figure 3 presents a concrete example: the macro for the **automaton** construct of section 2. The keyword **define-macro** is followed by a set of literals (here, **automaton** and —→) that may appear in the input. The literals are followed by the trigger. All symbols in the trigger that do not appear in the literal set are *pattern variables*. A pattern followed by ellipses (...) matches zero or more instances of the pattern. It binds each pattern variable to the sequence of sub-terms that correspond to the pattern variable's position in the matching instances. Ellipses can be nested arbitrarily deep.

The macro definition specifies an elaborator following the ⟹ keyword. The elaborator uses **syntax** to construct a new source term. The **syntax** form consumes a template and converts the template into a term in the source language by replacing all pattern variables with their bindings from the (implicit) pattern environment. Thus, in the output term, *start-state*, *state-name*, *input* and *new-state* are replaced with the corresponding source text in the input expression, while all other names are inserted literally.[1]

Macros of this sort have traditionally been put to four main uses:

- to affect the order of evaluation. For instance, **run/alternating** requires delayed evaluation in a call-by-value language. The macro can wrap the expressions in procedures that are invoked to control stepping.
- to create new binding constructs. The procedural translation of **automaton** turns the state-names into binding and bound occurrences of variables.
- to mask the creation of a data-structure. It is straightforward to implement an **automaton** macro that produces a traditional data structure representation of automata.
- to represent structural program properties, such as uses of design patterns.

---

[1] We have elided from our specification many McMicMac features that are useful in practice; e.g., the macro writer can specify guards on the structure of sub-terms.

```
(define-micro (if)               ;; for if's
  (if test then else) ⟹ (lambda ()
                         (make-if-IR
                          ((dispatch (syntax test)))
                          ((dispatch (syntax then)))
                          ((dispatch (syntax else)))))))
```

Fig. 5. A Micro Specification

As the **automaton** example illustrates, a single macro can serve several of these purposes simultaneously. This is especially likely to happen in the case of *data languages*, whose constructs are supposed to mask their representation of the data from the client programmer, since the same source can be used to generate either representation. Figure 4 presents an alternate compiled representation for automata: instead of creating procedures, it generates a data structure.

Different applications can choose alternate expansions (using the mechanism described in section 3.3) without any intervention from the user who specifies the automata. Linguistic extensions are especially important in this context, because they are often the only way to mask these concrete representations. In most languages, for instance, it is impossible to define a construct that elaborates into a procedure. This makes it extremely difficult, if not impossible, to write the **automaton** abstraction through any other means.

3.2   Beyond Conventional Macros

Though conventional macros can describe many interesting linguistic abstractions, they are not powerful enough for many other generative-programming tasks. McMicMac therefore generalizes macros in several ways. These generalized macros propagate information about the program to guide elaboration.

From Expansion to Parsing   Parsers have the type scheme

$$source \longrightarrow \text{IR}$$

where *source* is the type of source expressions and IR that of the intermediate representation. In many cases, McMicMac programmers writing language extensions need the power to generate terms of type IR directly. McMicMac thus allows programmers to create such elaborators, called *micros*.

In principle, micros have the type

$$source \longrightarrow \text{IR} ,$$

in contrast to macros, which denote source-to-source rewriting functions:

$$source \longrightarrow source .$$

```
(define-micro (if)              ;; for if's
  (if test then else) ⟹ (lambda (env)
                           (make-if-IR
                             ((dispatch (syntax test)) env)
                             ((dispatch (syntax then)) env)
                             ((dispatch (syntax else)) env))))

(define-micro (lambda)          ;; for lambda's
  (lambda vars body) ⟹ (lambda (env)
                           (make-lambda-IR vars
                             ((dispatch (syntax body)) (append vars env)))))
```

Fig. 6. Micros with Attributes

In practice, the parsing process described in section 3.1 has two parts: the elaborators that create IR and the dispatcher that does pattern matching and invokes an elaborator. The dispatcher, called *dispatch*, has type

$$source \longrightarrow micro \ ,$$

i.e., given a source term, it returns the corresponding micro. Micros are elaborators represented as procedures of no arguments that create IR, whose type we denote as

$$() \longrightarrow IR \ .$$

(The reason for this seemingly needless level of indirection will become clear in the following sections.) The output of micros, unlike that of macros, is not automatically expanded again. If it were automatically expanded, this could result in a type conflict. Therefore, a micro must invoke **dispatch** to reduce source terms to IR.

Figure 5 shows the micro definition for a simple conditional construct. Like **define-macro**, **define-micro** is followed by a list of literals and a trigger pattern. To the right of the ⟹ keyword is the specification of the micro's elaborator, a procedure of no arguments. The elaborator uses *make-if*-IR to construct the IR representation of **if** expressions. The invocation

```
((dispatch (syntax test)))
```

extracts the source term corresponding to *test* from the pattern environment, uses *dispatch* to obtain the corresponding micro, which is a procedure of no arguments, and invokes the micro to generate the IR value for *test*.

Attributes Suppose a programmer wants a simple value inspection facility. Specifically, the expression (**dump**) should print the names and values of all the variables bound in the lexical scope. Provided we have access to the names of all the variables in that lexical context, the transformation associated with (**dump**) is quite straightforward. McMicMac allows programmers to make this contextual information explicit by associating *attributes* with the dispatcher. Thus a programmer can declare the type of a micro to be

$$env \longrightarrow \text{IR}$$

where *env* is the type of the lexical environment. The micro can inspect this environment to determine the names of the bound variables.

This type generalizes to

$$attr \cdots \longrightarrow \text{IR}$$

to indicate that there can be several attributes. Every micro must accept all the attributes, and must propagate them to micro dispatches on sub-terms. Figure 6 presents the definition for **lambda** (which affects the set of lexical variables listed in *env*) and a revised definition of **if** (which doesn't).

To use McMicMac, an application must invoke **dispatch** on the source program while supplying appropriate values for all the attributes. The result of invoking **dispatch** is an IR value, which the program can use for subsequent processing. Some applications use the same type for the source and IR, i.e., they only exploit attributes, not the ability to transform representations.

Threaded Attributes One possible IR to choose may be the set of values in the language. In that case, the "parser" may convert programs to their final answers, i.e., it may really be an interpreter. We expect McMicMac to deal with such transformations too. They are useful for prototyping small embedded domain-specific languages, or for optimizing code-generators. Attributes can represent various aspects of the language's evaluation. In figure 6, for example, the environment maintains only a list of names bound in each context, but in an interpreter, the environment could map names to locations or values.

Non-trivial languages, though, have two kinds of attributes. Some attributes, e.g., environments, are *functional*, meaning they do not represent computational effects. Other attributes, however, are *threaded*. They are affected in the processing of sub-terms, and their order of propagation from the processing of one sub-term to another matters. A canonical example of such an attribute is the store. If the same store were passed to all sub-terms, then side-effects in the evaluation of one would not be visible in the other. Micros therefore return the updated values of threaded attributes along with the IR. Thus the type of a micro in the interpreter implementation can be

$$env \times store \longrightarrow \text{IR} \times store$$

or, in general, micros can have a type with the shape

$$funattr \cdots \times threadattr \cdots \longrightarrow \text{IR} \times threadattr \cdots .$$

Once again, it is the micro programmer's responsibility to invoke McMicMac, provide arguments for the attributes, accept the final IR value and the values of the threaded attributes, and process them.

```
(define-micro (set!)               ;; for set!'s
  (set! var val) ⟹ (lambda (env store)
                      (let/values (((val-value val-store)
                                    ((dispatch val) env store))
                        (values ;; the value:
                          (void-value)
                          ;; the new store:
                          (extend store var val-value)))))

(define-micro ()                   ;; for function applications—no literals
  (fun arg) ⟹ (lambda (env store)
                (let/values (((fun-value fun-store)
                              ((dispatch fun) env store))
                  (let/values (((arg-value arg-store)
                                ((dispatch arg) env fun-store))
                    ;; functions must return value/store pairs
                    (fun-value arg-value arg-store)))))
```

Fig. 7. Threaded Attributes

We illustrate this new form of micro with two definitions in figure 7 that implement a stateful language in a purely functional manner using the store-passing style technique from denotational semantics. (**set!** is Scheme's assignment statement.) The code uses Scheme's multiple-value facility to return the actual value and the potentially modified store.

3.3   Modular Specifications

We have thusfar discussed the kinds of transformations that programmers can express. In this section, we discuss how programmers can group these transformations into resuable units.

Vocabularies Most programming languages consist of several sub-languages: those of expressions, statements, types, argument lists, data, and so on. The programmer must therefore specify which sub-language a micro extends. McMicMac provides *vocabularies* for this purpose. A vocabulary is a grouping of related micros. All micros in a vocabulary must satisfy the same type signature. Figure 8 illustrates the revised declarations from earlier examples. Each micro declares membership in a vocabulary just before specifying its literal set.

The sum of declarations in a vocabulary specifies the syntax and the elaboration rules of a language. Put differently, a vocabulary describes the syntax table that is used by **dispatch**, and must therefore be a parameter to **dispatch**. We update the type of **dispatch** from section 3.2 to reflect this:

$$source \times vocab \longrightarrow micro \ .$$

```
(define scheme-exprs                    (define automata
  (make-vocabulary))                      (make-vocabulary))

(define-micro scheme-exprs (set!)       (define-micro automata
  (set! var val) ⟹                        (automaton ⟶)
    (lambda (this-vocab env store)        (automaton ···) ⟹
      ···))                                 (lambda (this-vocab) ···))

(define-micro scheme-exprs ()           (define-micro automata
  (fun arg) ⟹                             (run/alternating)
    (lambda (this-vocab env store)        (run/alternating ···) ⟹
      ···))                                 (lambda (this-vocab) ···))
```

Fig. 8. Vocabulary Specifications

```
(define compiler (make-vocabulary))     (define analysis
(define-micro compiler (let)              (make-vocabulary))
  (let ((var val) ...) body) ⟹          (define-micro analysis (let) ···)
    ···)                                 (define-micro analysis (letrec) ···)
(define-micro compiler (letrec)
  (letrec ((var val) ...) body) ⟹       (define analysis-language
    ···)                                   (extend-vocabulary scheme-exprs
                                                             analysis))
(define compiler-language
  (extend-vocabulary scheme-exprs
                     compiler))
```

Fig. 9. Tool-Dependent Expansions

The change in the type of **dispatch** forces us to update the programming pattern for micros. Each recursive call to **dispatch** must pass along a vocabulary, which the invoked micro must accept.

As we describe below, however, a micro may not always know which vocabulary it is in. Micros therefore take the vocabulary from which they were selected as an argument—in figure 8, each micro accepts a vocabulary, *this-vocab*, as its first argument—which they use to process sub-terms in the same language; alternatively, they can choose a different vocabulary for sub-terms in other languages. For instance, a function declaration may have some sub-terms in the expression language and others in the language of types. Micros therefore have the type scheme

$$vocab \times funattr \cdots \times threadattr \cdots \longrightarrow \text{IR} \times threadattr \cdots .$$

Composing Vocabularies McMicMac actually allows programmers to build vocabularies by extending and composing them. Thus programmers can divide a language into sets of related features, and compose these features to build a processor for the complete language. A programmer can also create an extension vocabulary that overrides some definitions in a base vocabulary with tool-specific constraints. This explains why a micro may not know which vocabulary it is in; after all, the non-overridden micros of the base are also in the new, composite vocabulary. This scenario is analogous to instance variables in an object-oriented language that reside both in a class and in its extensions.

With vocabularies, we can generate programs in various interesting ways:

– While traditional transformation techniques are limited in where they can be applied—macros and templates are usually restricted to the expression or statement languages—the McMicMac programmer can write transformations for any sub-language. For instance, we have used it to define abbreviations over types and to extend the language of procedural parameters.
– In realistic programming environments, different program-processing tools often have differing views of the underlying language. For example, a compiler might translate the binding construct **let** (which creates non-recursive local bindings) into a local function application while treating **letrec** (which introduces mutually-referential local bindings) as a primitive. In contrast, a polymorphic type inference engine might treat **let** as a core form, while it will transform **letrec** into a more primitive term. These distinctions are easy to express through vocabularies, as shown in figure 9. The function *extend-vocabulary* extends the language of its first argument with the triggers and elaborators of the second, overriding clashes in favor of the second.
– Some languages allow programmers to write lexically-scoped macros [21]. This is easy to define in McMicMac. The micro for a lexical macro construct creates a temporary vocabulary, populates it with the local macro, and extends the current language with the new macro. Because these are local, not global, changes, the language extension disappears when the body has been parsed, so terms outside this lexical context are unaffected.
– A programmer can use vocabularies to organize several traversals over the program. Typically, earlier passes synthesize information for later passes. For example, a programmer may want to add first-class closures to an object-oriented language like Java 1.0. The translator that implements this transformation would need (1) to determine the free variables of the closure's body; (2) to create a class to represent the closure and move its definition to the top-level, as required in many languages; and, (3) to rewrite the creation and uses of the closure.
A series of vocabularies solves this problem elegantly. The first maintains the lexical environment while traversing code (figure 6); when it encounters an instance of the closure construct, it traverses the body with a vocabulary that computes the set of free variables. This list of free variables is the IR of this vocabulary. It can then generate the class definition. A threaded attribute accumulates top-level definitions created in internal contexts and propagates them outward. Finally, another vocabulary rewrites the creation and use expressions. Determining uses can be done either from type information or through a dynamic check, depending on the target language.

- If a larger language is constructed by composing smaller language layers, programmers can define restricted versions of the larger language by leaving out some layers. We have found this ability especially useful in the DrScheme programming environment [12], which presents the Scheme programming language as a sequence of increasingly complex sub-languages. This hides the complexity of the complete language from the student; in particular, it flags terms that are errors in the linguistic subset but that might be legal—though often not what the student expected—in the full language. This provides much better feedback than an environment for just the complete language would provide, and considerably improves the learning experience.

4   Extensibility and Validation

To implement a system like McMicMac in other languages, programmers must resolve the tension between extensibility and validation:

Extensibility There are two main sources of extensibility in McMicMac, both related to vocabularies:
- Vocabularies resemble classes with inheritance; since they have variable parent vocabularies, they are essentially mixins, which enhance reuse by allowing the same class-extensions to be applied to multiple classes.
- The pattern of passing the vocabulary as an argument accomplishes the effect of the **this** keyword found in many object-oriented languages. It ensures that micros can be reused without having to know about all future extensions. Using this style, programmers can also experiment with interesting language extensions, such as the lexical macros described in section 3.3.

Validation Information is communicated through the attributes; the threaded attributes are fundamentally denotational, or monadic [31,35], in nature. The problems associated with composing vocabularies are thus the same as those with composing arbitrary programming languages.

There are some efforts to design sound type systems for mixins [15], but these are still preliminary. There are unfortunately few type systems that type mixins in their own right and also support the traditional functional types that have been used to represent monadic information. Some of issues that arise from the interplay of types and extensibility are discussed in greater detail by Krishnamurthi, et al. [27].

We have purposely restricted our attention to Scheme, which has no native static type discipline. While the lack of a type system has obvious disadvantages, it has also had its benefits. Because there are no candidate type systems that can cleanly capture the properties we are interested in, restricting ourselves to any one type system would have complicated the design of McMicMac. We were instead interested in first studying the programs that generative programmers write, and can now focus on constructing a type system that supports such programs.

5   Implementation Experience

Over the past five years, we have implemented several generations of McMicMac. The current implementation consists of over 10,000 lines of Scheme. It includes a "standard system", which consists of parsing vocabularies for different parts of Rice's version [14] of the Scheme programming language, including the functional core, side-effecting features, modules and signatures, and the class system. The implementation is efficient enough for daily use as the core of a widely-used programming environment, DrScheme [12], and as a pre-processor by various tools including a stepper, static debugger [13] and compiler. We have also exploited McMicMac's attributes to build processors for typed languages, notably for a parenthesized representation of CLASSICJAVA [15].

Our implementation provides source-object correlation [10] and transformation tracking [26], which is extremely useful for interactive programming environments. It eliminates most of the feedback comprehension problems present in traditional macro and template systems. All the tools in DrScheme use this information to provide source-level feedback to the user. This also greatly facilitates linguistic prototyping for features that can be translated, sometimes quite elaborately, into existing ones. The translation ensures that we can reuse existing tools such as the static debugger, and the source correlation hides the complexity of the translation from the user.

6   Related Work

The ideas behind generative programming have a long history. Macros appear to have originally been proposed by McIlroy [29], and a symposium in 1969 [5] consolidated progress on extensible languages. Macros have also had a long history of use in various versions of Lisp, and are incorporated into Common Lisp [33], Scheme [21] and others.

C++ has recently added support for a limited form of generative programming called templates. These are intimately connected with the type system of the language, and are thus useful for describing type-based transformations. They have been especially successful at generating families of related components [8].

The Scheme programming language has offered some of the most innovative macro systems. Kohlbecker and others [23–25] introduced both pattern-based rewriting and hygiene for macros. Dybvig, et al. [9] describe a macro system that offers some of the flexibility of micros, but without the structure. Dybvig, et al. [10] present the first source-correlating macro system. Taha and Sheard [34] have designed a macro-like system for ML that lets programmers nest metaprogramming annotations to arbitrary depth, and ensures that the resulting generated code is type-correct. We achieve a similar effect using the static debugger MrSpidey [13] in conjunction with source-correlation.

McMicMac is also related to parser generators such as Yacc [19]. Several researchers have extended these works to adaptable grammars [6]. Some of the most recent work has been done by Cardelli et al. [4], which shows how similar systems can be constructed for non-parenthesized syntaxes. While this system can be used to restrict and extend syntax, it offers no support for organizing elaborator specifications analogous to McMicMac's attributes, and does not present languages as modular layers.

Our extensibility protocol is based on mixins, which are a programming pattern used in Common Lisp [33], and were first formalized by Bracha [3]. The use of mixins in McMicMac lead to a formalized model of mixins for a Java-like language [15]. Our protocol is closely related to that of Smaragdakis and Batory [32], which is a successor to the model of Batory and O'Malley [2]. The work most similar to McMicMac appears to be Batory, et al.'s JTS [1]. JTS shares many common characteristics, including the presentation of languages as layers. The emphases of the two systems appear to be slightly different. JTS is concerned primarily with the construction of component systems, while McMicMac concentrates on the programming forms that simplify specifications.

Some researchers have proposed using languages like Haskell [18] and ML [30] for embedding domain-specific languages, employing higher-order functions, the language's ability to define new infix operators, and (in Haskell's case) laziness to define new notations [11, 17]. These features are, however, not enough to construct abstractions like **automaton** (figure 1). Kamin and Hyatt [20] describe the problem of lifting existing operators to deal with domain-specific constraints; this can also be addressed by generative programming. Finally, Kamin and Hyatt's language reflects a common problem when language extensions cannot define new binding forms. Even though ML already has lexical environments, they must create their own methods and conventions for managing these, thereby inhibiting reuse.

7   Conclusions and Future Work

We have described McMicMac, a generative programming system for Scheme. McMicMac extends traditional macro-based generative programming techniques in several ways. First, it lets programmers attach attributes to specifications, which provides a way to propagate information during elaboration, and to guide elaboration itself. Second, it provides a structuring construct called *vocabularies*. Vocabularies are analogous to mixins in object-oriented languages, and permit programmers to define language fragments as components that can be composed. We have used McMicMac to build several tools, including the widely-used DrScheme programming environment [12].

There are two main areas for future work. First, McMicMac is concerned with generative programming in general, and is independent of any notion of components. It has been used in the absence of components, within components, and to generate components. Because linguistic abstractions are different from traditional, procedural abstractions, the integration of components with generative programming can lead to unexpected consequences that should be studied carefully.

Second, the programming style in McMicMac is very much like that used with the Visitor pattern in object-oriented programming [16]. Though we do not show it in this paper, McMicMac allows programmers to separate the specification of triggers from that of the elaborators, so that the elaborator specifications more closely resemble traditional object-oriented programs. Some McMicMac specifications could benefit from higher-level specifications such as adaptive programming [28]. The traditional presentation of adaptive programming, however, does not integrate smoothly with the typed style of specification in McMicMac.

Acknowledgements

We thank Robby Findler, Cormac Flanagan and Matthew Flatt for their feedback on McMicMac. We also thank the referees for their comments.

References

1. Batory, D., B. Lofaso and Y. Smaragdakis. JTS: Tools for implementing domain-specific languages. In *International Conference on Software Reuse*, June 1998.
2. Batory, D. and S. O'Malley. The design and implementation of hierarchical software systems with reusable components. *ACM Transactions on Software Engineering and Methodology*, 1(4):355–398, October 1992.
3. Bracha, G. *The Programming Language Jigsaw: Mixins, Modularity and Multiple Inheritance*. PhD thesis, University of Utah, March 1992.
4. Cardelli, L., F. Matthes and M. Abadi. Extensible syntax with lexical scoping. Research Report 121, Digital SRC, 1994.
5. Christensen, C. and C. J. Shaw, editors. *Proceedings of the Extensible Languages Symposium*. Association for Computing Machinery, 1969. Appeared as *SIGPLAN Notices*, 4(8):1–62, August 1969.
6. Christiansen, H. A survey of adaptable grammars. *ACM SIGPLAN Notices*, 25(11):35–44, November 1990.
7. Clinger, W. D. Proper tail recursion and space efficiency. In *ACM SIGPLAN Conference on Programming Language Design and Implementation*, pages 174–185, June 1998.
8. Czarnecki, K. and U. Eisenecker. *Generative Programming: Methods, Techniques, and Applications*. Addison-Wesley, 1999.
9. Dybvig, R. K., D. P. Friedman and C. T. Haynes. Expansion-passing style: A general macro mechanism. *Lisp and Symbolic Computation*, 1(1):53–75, January 1988.
10. Dybvig, R. K., R. Hieb and C. Bruggeman. Syntactic abstraction in Scheme. *Lisp and Symbolic Computation*, 5(4):295–326, December 1993.
11. Fairbairn, J. Making form follow function: An exercise in functional programming style. *Software—Practice and Experience*, 17(6):379–386, June 1987.
12. Findler, R. B., C. Flanagan, M. Flatt, S. Krishnamurthi and M. Felleisen. DrScheme: A pedagogic programming environment for Scheme. In *Ninth International Symposium on Programming Languages, Implementations, Logics, and Programs*, pages 369–388, 1997.
13. Flanagan, C., M. Flatt, S. Krishnamurthi, S. Weirich and M. Felleisen. Catching bugs in the web of program invariants. In *ACM SIGPLAN Conference on Programming Language Design and Implementation*, pages 23–32, May 1996.

14. Flatt, M. PLT MzScheme: Language manual. Technical Report TR97-280, Rice University, 1997.
15. Flatt, M., S. Krishnamurthi and M. Felleisen. Classes and mixins. In *Symposium on Principles of Programming Languages*, pages 171–183, January 1998.
16. Gamma, E., R. Helm, R. Johnson and J. Vlissides. *Design Patterns: Elements of Reusable Object-Oriented Software*. Addison-Wesley Personal Computing Series. Addison-Wesley, Reading, MA, 1995.
17. Hudak, P. Modular domain specific languages and tools. In *International Conference on Software Reuse*, 1998.
18. Hudak, P., S. Peyton Jones and P. Wadler. Report on the programming language Haskell: a non-strict, purely functional language. *ACM SIGPLAN Notices*, 27(5), May 1992. Version 1.2.
19. Johnson, S. C. YACC — yet another compiler compiler. Computing Science Technical Report 32, AT&T Bell Laboratories, Murray Hill, NJ, USA, 1975.
20. Kamin, S. and D. Hyatt. A special-purpose language for picture-drawing. In *USENIX Conference on Domain-Specific Languages*, 1997.
21. Kelsey, R., W. Clinger and J. Rees. Revised[5] report on the algorithmic language Scheme. *ACM SIGPLAN Notices*, 33(9), October 1998.
22. Kernighan, B. W. and D. M. Ritchie. *The C Programming Language*. Prentice-Hall, 1988.
23. Kohlbecker, E. E., D. P. Friedman, M. Felleisen and B. F. Duba. Hygienic macro expansion. In *ACM Symposium on Lisp and Functional Programming*, pages 151–161, 1986.
24. Kohlbecker, E. E. and M. Wand. Macros-by-example: Deriving syntactic transformations from their specifications. In *Symposium on Principles of Programming Languages*, pages 77–84, 1987.
25. Kohlbecker Jr, E. E. *Syntactic Extensions in the Programming Language Lisp*. PhD thesis, Indiana University, August 1986.
26. Krishnamurthi, S., Y.-D. Erlich and M. Felleisen. Expressing structural properties as language constructs. In *European Symposium on Programming*, March 1999.
27. Krishnamurthi, S., M. Felleisen and D. P. Friedman. Synthesizing object-oriented and functional design to promote re-use. In *European Conference on Object-Oriented Programming*, pages 91–113, July 1998.
28. Lieberherr, K. J. *Adaptive Object-Oriented Programming*. PWS Publishing, Boston, MA, USA, 1996.
29. McIlroy, M. D. Macro instruction extensions of compiler languages. *Communications of the ACM*, 3(4):214–220, 1960.
30. Milner, R., M. Tofte and R. Harper. *The Definition of Standard ML*. MIT Press, Cambridge, MA, 1990.
31. Moggi, E. An abstract view of programming languages. Technical Report ECS-LFCS-90-113, Laboratory for Foundations of Computer Science, University of Edinburgh, Edinburgh, Scotland, 1990.
32. Smaragdakis, Y. and D. Batory. Implementing layered designs and mixin layers. In *European Conference on Object-Oriented Programming*, pages 550–570, July 1998.
33. Steele, G. L., Jr., editor. *Common Lisp: the Language*. Digital Press, Bedford, MA, second edition, 1990.
34. Taha, W. and T. Sheard. Multi-stage programming with explicit annotations. In *ACM SIGPLAN Symposium on Partial Evaluation and Semantics-Based Program Manipulation*, pages 203–217, 1997.
35. Wadler, P. The essence of functional programming. In *Symposium on Principles of Programming Languages*, pages 1–14, January 1992.

Aspect-Oriented Compilers

Oege de Moor[1], Simon Peyton-Jones[2], and Eric Van Wyk[1]

[1] Oxford University Computing Laboratory
[2] Microsoft Research, Cambridge

Abstract. Aspect-oriented programming provides the programmer with means to *cross-cut* conventional program structures, in particular the class hierarchies of object-oriented programming. This paper studies the use of aspect orientation in structuring syntax directed compilers implemented as attribute grammars. Specifically, it describes a method for specifying definitions of related attributes as 'aspects' and treating them as first-class objects, that can be stored, manipulated and combined. It is hoped that this embedding of an aspect-oriented programming style in Haskell provides a stepping stone towards a more general study of the semantics of aspect-oriented programming.

1 Introduction

Compilers are often structured by recursion over the abstract syntax of the source language. For each production in the abstract syntax, one defines a function that specifies how a construct is to be translated. The method of structuring compilers in this syntax–directed manner underlies the formalism of *attribute grammars* [2, 14,18]. These provide a convenient notation for specifying the functions that deal with each of the production rules in the abstract syntax. The compiler writer need not concern himself with partitioning the compiler into a number of passes: the order of computation is derived automatically. One way of achieving that ordering is to compute the attribute values in a demand-driven fashion. Indeed, attribute grammars can be viewed as a particular style of writing lazy functional programs [11,19].

Unfortunately, however, compilers written as attribute grammars suffer from a lack of modularity [16]. In their pure form, the only way in which attribute grammars are decomposed is by *production*. It is not possible to separate out a single semantic *aspect* (such as the 'environment') across all productions, and then add that as a separate entity to the code already written. The compiler writer is thus forced to consider all semantic aspects simultaneously, without the option of separating his concerns. Many specialised attribute grammar systems offer decomposition by aspect, but only at a *syntactic* level, not at a *semantic* one. In particular, aspects cannot be parameterised, and the compiler writer cannot define new ways of combining old aspects into new. For the purpose of this paper, let us define an *aspect* as a set of definitions of one or more related attributes. This paper proposes an implementation of aspects that makes

K. Czarnecki and U.W. Eisenecker (Eds.): GCSE'99, LNCS 1799, pp. 121–133, 2000.
© Springer-Verlag Berlin Heidelberg 2000

them independent semantic units, that can be parameterised, manipulated and compiled independently.

Our proposed compiler aspects are implemented in a variant of the programming language Haskell, augmented with extensible records. It is this highly flexible type system which allows us to give a type to each aspect. In particular, it ensures that each attribute is defined precisely once — an important feature when attribute grammars are composed from multiple components. It is assumed that the reader is familiar with programming in Haskell [5]. The concepts are not dependent on the Haskell language and they could be presented in a abstract, language independent form. However, we hope that an concrete implementation (available on the web [6]) will encourage others to explore aspect-oriented compilers. The LaTeX source of this paper is itself an executable Haskell program. The lines preceded by the > symbol are the Haskell program that is this paper. Note however, that some unenlightening portions of the program code appear in LaTeX comments and are thus not visible in the printed version.

2   A Polymorphic Type System for Extensible Records

We shall use the *Trex* extension of Haskell, which provides a rich set of record operations [9]. In this variant of Haskell, a record with three fields called x, y, and z may be written (x=0, y='a', z="abc"). The type of this expression is Rec(x :: Int, y :: Char, z :: String). For each field name, there is a *selection function*, named by prefixing with a #. We thus have, for example, that #y (x=0, y='a', z= "abc") evaluates to 'a'. Records can be extended with new fields. The function

```
f r = (z = "abc" | r)
```

adds a new field named z to its argument. The type of f reflects that this function should not be applied to a record that already has a field named z:

```
f :: r\z => Rec r -> Rec (z :: String | r)
```

That is, for each *row* r of fields that *lacks* z, f maps a record with fields r to a record that has one more field, namely z, whose value is a string.

Since a record can be extended, it is natural to consider a starting point for such extensions, namely the empty record, which is written EmptyRec, and whose type is Rec EmptyRow.

3   Motivating Example: Algol 60 Scope Rules

In contrast to a good many of its successors, Algol 60 has very clear and uniform scope rules. A simplification of these scope rules is a favourite example to illustrate the use of attribute grammars [16]. A definition of an identifier x is visible in the smallest enclosing block with the exception of inner blocks that also contain a definition of x. Here we shall study these scope rules via a toy language that has the following example program and abstract syntax:

```
>example = [Use "x", Use "y",
>           Local [Dec "y", Use "y", Use "x"],
>           Dec "x", Use "x", Dec "y"]

>type Prog  = Block
>type Block = [Stat]
>data Stat  = Use String | Dec String | Local Block
```

We aim to translate programs to a sequence of instructions for a typical stack machine. The type of instructions is

```
>data Instr = Enter Int Int |  Exit Int  | Ref (Int,Int)
```

Each block entry and exit is marked with its lexical level. Each entry is also marked by the number of local variables declared in that block. Each applied occurrence of an identifier is mapped to a (level, displacement) pair, consisting of the lexical level where the identifier was declared, and the displacement, which is the number of declarations preceding it at that level. To wit, we wish to program a function `trans :: Prog -> [Instr]` so that, for instance, we have

```
trans example = [Enter 0 2, Ref (0,0), Ref (0,1),
                 Enter 1 1, Ref (1,0), Ref (0,0), Exit 1,
                 Ref (0,0), Exit 0]
```

4   A Traditional Compiler

We now proceed to write a program for `trans`, in the traditional attribute grammar style, especially as suggested in [4,11,19,26,28]. This means that we will not be concerned with slicing the computations into a minimal number of passes over the abstract syntax; such a division into passes comes for free by virtue of lazy evaluation. While this section only reviews existing techniques for writing attribute grammars, we write `trans` using the extensible record notation to set the stage for Section 5, where extensible records are a key component of our new modular approach to defining attribute grammars.

First we provide the context–free grammar for the source language:

```
Program: Prog  -> Block    List:  Block -> SList    Use: Stat -> String
SList0:  SList ->           Local: Stat  -> Block    Dec: Stat -> String
SList1:  SList -> Stat SList
```

This context–free grammar is close to the type definitions we stated earlier. Roughly speaking, types correspond to nonterminals, and constructors correspond to production rules. Note, however, that we have explicitly written out productions for statement lists, although these productions are not explicit in the type definitions.

The standard strategy for writing an attribute grammar consists of three steps, namely the definition of *semantic domains*, *semantic functions*, and *translators*.

4.1   Semantic Domains

For each nonterminal symbol S we define a corresponding *semantic domain* S'. The compiler will map values of type S to values of type S'. These types will likely include the generated code, as in `type Prog' = Rec (code :: [Instr])`, and will be defined via record types where the fields represent various aspects of the semantics. For other grammar symbols, however, a mere record type will not suffice, because their semantics depends on the context in which they occur. That motivates semantic domains that are functions between record types: the input record describes attributes of the context – these are called *inherited* attributes, and the output record describes resulting attributes of the grammar symbol itself – these are called *synthesized* attributes. For example, we have

```
>type SList'  = Rec (level :: Int, env :: Envir) ->
>                   Rec (code :: [Instr], locs :: [String])
```

That is, given the lexical level and environment (which maps identifiers to (level,displacement) pairs), a statement list will yield code, which is a list of instructions and a list of local variable names, called locs.

It remains to define a semantic domain for blocks and for statements themselves, which happens to be the same as for statement lists:

```
>type Block' = Rec (level::Int, env::Envir) -> Rec (code::[Instr])
>type Stat'  = SList'
```

4.2   Semantic Functions

Before we can define the semantic functions that make up the compiler, we first need some primitive operations for manipulating environments. An environment is an association list from identifiers to (level,displacement) pairs, and we shall write `Envir` for the type of environments. The two operations `apply` and `add` are defined on environments and have the types `apply :: Envir -> String -> (Int,Int)` and `add :: Int -> [String] -> Envir -> Envir`. The function `apply e x` finds the first occurrence of x in e, and returns the corresponding (level,displacement) pair. We shall build up the environment by adding all local definitions at a given lexical level. This is the purpose of the function `add`: it takes a level, a list of local definitions, and an environment, and it adds the local definitions to the environment.

We are now in a position to define the semantic functions. For each production P: X -> Y Z, we define a *semantic function* p: Y' -> Z' -> X' that combines semantic values of the appropriate type. For example, we define the binary semantic function `slist1 :: Stat' -> SList' -> SList'` that takes the translations of a statement and a statement list, and produces the translation of the composite statement list. The two arguments, and the result appear in reverse order, when compared to the production SList1. The type of `list` is also obtained by reversing sides of the corresponding production rule to yield

```
>list :: SList' -> Block'
>list slist blockIn
> = (code = [Enter (#level blockIn) (length (#locs slistOut))]
>              ++ #code slistOut ++   [Exit (#level blockIn)])
>    where slistIn = (level = #level blockIn,
>                     env = add (#level blockIn) (#locs slistOut)
>                                (#env blockIn))
>           slistOut = slist slistIn
```

It is worthwhile to note the seeming circularity in the argument and result of
slist. Such definitions are only acceptable because of lazy evaluation. If we
programmed the same computation in a strict language, we would have to remove
such pseudo-circularities by introducing multiple passes over the abstract syntax.

The above definition of list illustrates how in the traditional approach to
writing attribute grammars, different aspects must all be defined in a single
location. The aspects cannot be split apart, forcing the compiler writer to consider all the semantic aspects simultaneously. It is this deficiency that we aim to
remedy below.

The definitions of the other semantic functions are similar and we omit details. To avoid confusion, we mention that our notion of 'semantic function' is
different from that in the attribute grammar literature. There, a semantic function is understood to be the right-hand side of the definition of a single attribute,
and what we call a semantic function is simply termed a 'production'.

4.3   Translators

For each nonterminal S, we define a *translator* of type transS :: S -> S' that
maps values of type S to the corresponding semantic domain S'. For example, the
function that translates programs has type transProg :: Prog -> Prog' and
the translator for statement lists has type transSList :: SList -> SList'.
Assuming the existence of a semantic function for each production, we can define
a translator for each type in the abstract syntax by:

```
>transProg p         = program (transBlock p)
>transBlock b         = list (transSList b)
>transSList []        = slist0
>transSList (s:ss)    = slist1 (transStat s) (transSList ss)
>transStat (Use x)    = use x
>transStat (Dec x)    = dec x
>transStat (Local b)  = local (transBlock b)
```

5   An Aspect-Oriented Compiler

We now aim to embed the attribute definition language as a combinator library into Haskell. To some extent, we already did that in the previous section,

but to obtain a truly modular design, we propose making nonterminals, attribute definition rules, semantic functions and aspects first-class objects. We then use polymorphic operations on extensible records to give types to these objects and the combining forms for these objects. As we shall see below, the trickiest problem is to find an appropriate type of attribute definition rules.

As in the traditional approach above, we define a translator `trans'` with type `trans' :: Prog -> [Instr]` so that `trans' example` evaluates to the same result as `trans example` above. As in Section 4.3, `trans'` is defined using a collection of translators, one for each production in the abstract syntax. The semantic functions used in these translators are not the named semantic functions `program`, `list`, etc. used in the traditional approach, but are extracted from the fields of an attribute grammar named `ag ()`. For example, the translator function `transProg'` for production `program` is defined as `transProg' p = #program (ag ()) (transBlock' p)`. Thus, `ag ()` is a record with a field for each abstract syntax production which contains its semantic function. The fields of this record have the same names and types used for the semantic functions in the traditional approach. The important distinction is that the semantic functions in `ag ()` are built using an aspect-oriented approach. That is, they are constructed by grouping attribute definitions by aspect instead of by production. (The dummy argument () to `ag` and other constructs is required because of a technicality in Haskell's type system, known as the monomorphism restriction.)

5.1   Combining Aspects

In our example, the aspects are named `levels`, `envs`, `locss` and `codes` and define, respectively, the attributes lexical level, environment, local variables, and target code. Given these aspects, we combine them into an attribute grammar `ag ()` in the following way:

```
>ag () = knit (levels() `cat` envs() `cat` locss() `cat` codes())
```

Here, `knit` and `cat` are functions for combining aspects into attribute grammars and are defined below. Given this framework, it is clear that we can write new aspects and add them into our attribute grammar using these combinators.

5.2   Aspect Definitions

The semantic function of a production P must define each of the *synthesised* attributes of the parent of P, and each of the *inherited* attributes of P's children (Section 4.2). Together we refer to these attributes as P's *output* attributes. To produce the output attributes, the semantic function takes as arguments all of P's *input* attributes, that is the synthesised attributes of P's children, and the inherited attributes of P's parent. The trouble with the traditional approach is that we are forced to define all P's output attributes simultaneously — just look at the definition of `list` in Section 4.2. Our new, modular approach is to express each semantic function as a composition of one or more rules. Each rule for a production P defines a subset of P's output attributes and is implemented as a function which takes the input attributes from the parent and children of P.

Given a context–free grammar, a *rule grammar* is a record whose fields consist of rules, one for each production. Because of the monomorphism restriction mentioned above, we define an *aspect* as a function taking the dummy argument () and returning a rule grammar. Many aspects involve only a tiny subset of the productions. Think, for example, of operator priorities: these only affect productions for expressions. A rule grammar involves all productions, by definition. Therefore, definitions of aspects are written so that only the rules being defined by an aspect are explicitly written and default rules are provided for the rest.

Our first concrete example of an aspect is *lexical level*. The level attribute is inherited, and it is explicitly defined in two productions, namely program and local:

```
>levels ()=(program=(\b p -> ((level = 0 | #i b), #s p)),
>            local=(\b p -> ((level = #level (#i p) +1 | (nolevel(#i b))),
>                     #s p))        | grammar)
>       where nolevel (level=_ | r) = r
>             (program=_, local=_ | grammar) = none ()
```

As we will see, the default behaviour for rules for inherited attributes is to copy the parent's attribute value to the children. Thus, we don't write explicit rules for the other productions. This is accomplished by the phrase (program=_, local=_ | grammar) = none() which first fills the fields in grammar (all those except program and local) with the default copy rules pulled from the identity rule grammar, named none(). These defaults are added to the definitions of rules for program and local to create a complete rule grammar. The given rules are written using lambda expressions (the \ above can be read as λ); these functions take the input attributes, held in the child argument b and parent argument p, and return a tuple which adds the attribute level to the inherited attributes of the child b, and adds no new synthesized attributes to the parent p. These parameters pair up the inherited and synthesized attributes of each symbol in a type of nonterminal: >type NT ai as = Rec (i :: Rec ai, s :: Rec as) Note that both arguments to this type definition, ai and as, are row variables. The fields in these rows are the attributes themselves.

The record generated by a rule keeps track of the attribute definitions made so far; above, we are adding the level attribute definition to the attribute definitions already made to the block b. In the definition of the rule for local we override the default definition of level, by removing it with the function nolevel, and then adding a fresh level field. Apart from the fact that the above definition of levels is re-usable, we also find it easier to read: the flow of the level computation over the abstract syntax tree is clear at a glance, especially because the default copy rules allow us to leave out all irrelevant detail.

The *local variables* aspect of the compiler records the local variables declared at each lexical level. The locs attribute is synthesised, and it is adjoined to five rules. Because `locs` is synthesised, we cannot rely on default copy rules, so this aspect is somewhat more complex than the previous one, which dealt with inherited attributes.

```
>locss ()=(slist0 = (\p      ->(locs= []  | #s p)),
>          slist1 = (\a as p ->(#i a, #i as,
>                    (locs= #locs (#s a) 'union' #locs (#s as) | #s p))),
>          use    = \a -> (\p->(locs= []  | #s p)),
>          dec    = \a -> (\p->(locs= [a] | #s p)),
>          local  = (\b p ->(#i b, (locs= []  | #s p)))   | grammar)
>          where (slist0=_,slist1=_,use=_,dec=_,local=_|grammar) = none()
```

Here we see that `use` and `dec` are special: they are functions that take a string and yield a rule of arity 0. This is the usual way of dealing with grammar symbols (such as identifiers) that fall outside an attribute grammar.

5.3   Attribute Definition Rules

We now show the development of the rules used to compose semantic functions. The type of a rule has been alluded to above as a function which maps a subset of a productions input attributes to a subset of its output attributes. In this section we provide a precise definition of rules. We build a semantic function by composing rules. When we compose rules, the type system will ensure that no attribute is defined twice; when we assert that a composition of rules defines a complete semantic function, the type system will ensure that every attribute that is used is also defined.

For example, we will be able to construct the `list` semantic function of Section 4.2 thus:

```
list=knit1(list_level 'cat1' list_env 'cat1' list_locs 'cat1' list_code)
```

Here `list_level` etc. are rules, `cat1` composes rules, and `knit1` transforms a composed rule into a semantic function. The "1" suffixes refer to the fact that the `List` production has just one child; we have to define variants of `knit` and `cat` for productions with a different number of children.

We seek a mechanism of composing rules into semantic functions which allows the use of default rules, since we have seen that they shorten and clarify aspect definitions. Also, there is no record concatenation operator in type systems for polymorphic extensible records. For these two reasons, we do not concatenate the records generated by rules, but rather use a solution suggested by Rémy [23, 24] to compose the functions that build up those records.

To apply Rémy's technique in the particular example of attribution rules, a rule also takes as input the existing output attributes which are passed to the rule in the nonterminal symbols. A rule does not return fixed records of defined attributes; instead it transforms existing definitions by adding new fields for new attribute definitions or by replacing field values with new values. The latter is done to overwrite the default rules. For example, consider the rule `list_level`:

```
list_level = \c p -> ( (level = level p | (nolevel (#i c))), #s p)
```

This rule overwrites the definition of `level` of the inherited attributes of the
child and leave the synthesised attributes of the parent unchanged. The type of
such a unary rule is

```
>type  Rule1 child parent childInh parentSyn
>    =  child ->  parent ->  (Rec childInh, Rec parentSyn)
```

Here `child` and `parent` are understood to be nonterminals, whereas `childInh`
and `parentSyn` are row variables. The type of `list_level` is thus

```
list_level :: (childInh\level,parentInh\level) =>
              Rule1 (NT (level :: Int | childInh)  childSyn)
                    (NT (level :: Int | parentInh) parentSyn)
                    (level :: Int | childInh)  parentSyn
```

With this definition of rules, it is straightforward to define the concatenation
operator as suggested by Rémy's work:

```
>cat1 :: Rule1  (NT ci   cs)  (NT pi ps)   ci'  ps'  ->
>          Rule1  (NT ci'  cs)  (NT pi ps')  ci'' ps'' ->
>          Rule1  (NT ci   cs)  (NT pi ps)   ci'' ps''
>cat1 f g c p = g (i=ci', s= #s c) (i= #i p, s=ps') where (ci',ps')=f c p
```

This definition encodes the sequential composition of rule `f` followed by `g`. The
lifted version of this combinator, named `cat` takes two rule grammars (records
with a rule for each production), and it concatenates their corresponding fields.
The concatenation operator does of course have an identity element, namely the
rule that leaves all attribute definitions unchanged:

```
>none1 :: Rule1 (NT ci cs) (NT pi ps) ci ps
>none1 c p = (#i c, #s p)
```

The lifted version, `none()`, is similar to `cat` and is a record with fields for each
production which contains the identity rule of the appropriate arity.

5.4   Semantic Functions

Once we have defined all the requisite attribute values by composing rules, we
can turn the composite rule into a *semantic function*. In effect, this conversion
involves connecting attribute definitions to attribute applications. We shall call
the conversion *knitting*. The type of semantic functions of arity 1 is

```
>type Semfun1   childInh  childSyn parentInh parentSyn
> = (Rec childInh -> Rec childSyn) -> (Rec parentInh -> Rec parentSyn)
```

The operation knit1 takes a rule, and it yields a semantic function. The function that results from knit1 takes the semantics of child c (which is of type Rec ci -> Rec cs) as well as the inherited attributes for parent p (a value of type Rec pi). It has to produce the synthesised attributes of p. This is achieved by applying the rule, which builds up the synthesised attributes of p starting from the empty record and builds up the inherited attributes of c starting from the inherited attributes of p. This implies that inherited attributes of p are copied to c, unless otherwise specified. There is no such default behaviour, however, for synthesised attributes.

```
>knit1 :: Rule1 (NT pi cs) (NT pi EmptyRow) ci ps -> Semfun1 ci cs pi ps
>knit1 rule c pi = ps    where (ci,ps) = rule (i=pi,s=cs)(i=pi,s=EmptyRec)
>                              cs       = c ci
```

The type of knit1 shows that the rule is required to yield the synthesised attributes ps, starting from the empty record. Furthermore, the rule must transform the inherited attributes pi into the inherited attributes ci of the child. It also shows that the child's and parent's inherited attributes given as input to the rule have the same type, namely pi. The definition shows that the parent's inherited attributes, pi, are given as the default values of the child's inherited attributes in the application of rule. Thus, if a rule does not redefine a child's inherited attributes, the default behavior is to copy them from the parent. When the resulting semantic function is applied to the semantics of the child c, and to the inherited attributes of the parent, pi, it returns the synthesised attributes ps. The inherited attributes ci of the child, and the synthesised attributes ps are the joint result of applying rule.

This completes the set of basic combinators for manipulating rules and semantic functions of arity 1. There are similar combinators for other arities, and we omit the details.

6   Discussion

6.1   Aspect-Oriented Programming (AOP)

The inability to separate aspects is not exclusive to the area of compiler writing, and it has received considerable attention in other areas of programming. Gregor Kiczales and his team at Xerox have initiated the study of *aspect-oriented programming* in general terms [17], and the notion of *adaptive object-oriented programming* of Karl Lieberherr *et al.* shares many of these goals [21]. Don Batory and his team at UTA have studied ways to describe aspects in software generators that cut across traditional object class boundaries [3]. The present paper is a modest contribution to these developments, by showing how compilers can be structured in an aspect-oriented style. We are hopeful that the techniques we have employed here can be applied to writing aspect-oriented programs in other problem domains as well.

It is worthwhile to point out some deviations from Kiczales' original notion of AOP. The notion of aspect in this paper is highly restrictive, and only covers those examples where the "weaving" of aspects into existing code is purely name-based, and not dependent on sophisticated program analyses. For example, in Kiczales' framework, one might have an aspect that maintains an invariant relationship between variables x and y. Whenever either of these is updated, the invariant must be restored by making an appropriate change to the other variable. To weave the aspect into existing code, we have to find places where either x or y is changed: the techniques in this paper have nothing to say about such sophisticated aspects. In fact, to avoid all forms of program analysis, we require that the original attribute grammar is written as a rule grammar, and not in its knitted form.

Another seeming difference is one of style. In AOP, the traditional method of composing programs is not replaced, but is complemented by the introduction of aspects. The example we used in this paper is misleading, because we took an extreme approach, and sliced up the original attribute grammar completely in terms of aspects, thus abandoning the primary composition method. That was done purely for expository purposes, and there is no reason why one could not write a rule grammar in the traditional style, and then add one or two aspects later. Indeed, that is likely to be the norm when writing larger attribute grammars. Therefore, we do not suggest that the 'production' method of composition be replaced by the aspect, but simply augmented by it. Aspects are a useful tool for creating attribute grammars that in many instances is superior to composition by production.

In summary, we expect that the techniques of this paper are relevant to other applications of aspect-oriented programming, in other problem domains, but only those where the weaving is purely name-based. Because our definitions are in a simple functional programming language, one could also view our contribution as a first step towards a semantics of aspects.

6.2   Attribute Grammar Systems

An obvious objection to the work presented here is that many attribute grammar based compiler generators offer the factorisation we seek, but at a purely syntactic level [7,25,28]. The programmer can present attribution rules in any order, and a preprocessor rearranges them to group the rules by production. The situation is akin to the dichotomy between macros and procedures: while many applications of procedures can be coded using macros, the concept of a procedure is still useful and important. In contrast to macros, procedures offer sound type checking, and they are independent entities that can be stored, compiled and manipulated by a program. The benefits deriving from having aspects as explicit, first-class entities in a programming language are the same. Adams [1] proposes a similar decomposition method, but lacks the type checking of aspects possible here.

Ganzinger and Giegerich [8] also modularize attribute grammars but by decomposing the translation process into phases. This is a coarser decomposition than our proposed method, which could be used to decompose the specifications of their phases by aspect instead of by production.

The type system guarantees that all attributes are defined, and that they are defined only once. These guarantees are of course also ensured in specialised attribute grammar systems. Such systems usually also test for cycles in attribute definitions [12,18]. In moving from a dedicated attribute definition language to a general programming language, this analysis is a feature one has to give up. Cycle checks are only an approximation, however, so they inevitably rule out attribute grammars that can be evaluated without problems.

Although we are still investigating if additional advanced features found in other systems [10,13,15,25,20] can be mimicked in our setting, a companion [6] to this paper presents a substantial case study that shows how our technique admits concepts such as *local attributes* and *higher-order attribute grammars* in a natural manner. An attribute grammar for a production language's complete semantics has not been completed; however, we are confident (but not yet certain) that this method will scale to handle these larger attribute grammars.

The ultimate aim of this work is to provide a suitable meta-language for rapid prototyping of domain-specific languages in the *Intentional Programming* system under development at Microsoft Research [27] which, although different from attribute grammar systems, faces many of the same issues of modularity, evaluation schemes, and specification language choice.

References

1. S. R. Adams. *Modular Grammars for Programming Language Prototyping.* PhD thesis, Department of Electronics and Computer Science, University of Southampton, UK, 1993.
2. A. V. Aho, R. Sethi, and J. D. Ullman. *Compilers: Principles, Techniques, and Tools.* Addison-Wesley, 1986.
3. D. Batory, V. Singhal, J. Thomas, S. Dasari, B. Geraci, and M. Sirkin. The GenVoca model of software-system generators. *IEEE Software*, 11(5):89–94, 1994.
4. R. S. Bird. A formal development of an efficient supercombinator compiler. *Science of Computer Programming*, 8(2):113–137, 1987.
5. R. S Bird. *Introduction to Functional Programming in Haskell.* International Series in Computer Science. Prentice Hall, 1998.
6. O. De Moor. First-class attribute grammars. 1999. Draft paper available from URL http://www.comlab.ox.ac.uk/oucl/users/oege.demoor/homepage.htm
7. P. Deransart, M. Jourdan, and B. Lorho. *Attribute grammars — Definitions, systems and bibliography*, volume 322 of *LCNS*. Springer Verlag, 1988.
8. H. Ganzinger and R. Giegerich. Attribute Coupled Grammars. In *Proceedings of the ACM Symposium on Compiler Construction*, 157–170, 1984. Published as *ACM SIGPLAN Notices*, 19(6).
9. B. R. Gaster and M. P. Jones. A polymorphic type system for extensible records and variants. Technical report NOTTCS-TR-96-3, Department of Computer Science, University of Nottingham, UK, 1996. Available from URL http://www.cs.nott.ac.uk/Department/Staff/mpj/polyrec.html.
10. R. W. Gray, V. P. Heuring, S. P. Levi, A. M. Sloane, and W. M. Waite. Eli: A complete, flexible compiler construction system. *CACM*, 35:121–131, 1992.

11. T. Johnsson. Attribute grammars as a functional programming paradigm. In G. Kahn, editor, *Functional Programming Languages and Computer Architecture*, volume 274 of *LNCS*, pages 154–173. Springer-Verlag, 1987.

12. M. Jourdan. Strongly non-circular attribute grammars and their recursive evaluation. *SIGPLAN Notices*, 19:81–93, 1984.

13. M. Jourdan, D. Parigot, C. Julié, O. Durin, and C. Le Bellec. Design, implementation and evaluation of the FNC-2 attribute grammar system. In *Conference on Programming Languages Design and Implementation*, pages 209–222, 1990. Published as *ACM SIGPLAN Notices*, 25(6).

14. U. Kastens. Attribute grammars in a compiler construction environment. In *Proceedings of the International Summer School on Attribute Grammars, Applications and Systems*, volume 545 of *LNCS*, pages 380–400, 1991.

15. U. Kastens, B. Hutt, and E. Zimmermann. *GAG: A Practical Compiler Generator*, volume 141 of *LNCS*. Springer Verlag, 1982.

16. U. Kastens and W. M. Waite. Modularity and reusability in attribute grammars. *Acta Informatica*, 31:601–627, 1994.

17. G. Kiczales. Aspect-oriented programming. *ACM Computing Surveys*, 28A(4), 1996. See also: http://www.parc.xerox.com/spl/projects/aop.

18. D. E. Knuth. Semantics of context-free languages. *Mathematical Systems Theory*, 2:127–146, 1968.

19. M. Kuiper and S. D. Swierstra. Using attribute grammars to derive efficient functional programs. In *Computing Science in the Netherlands CSN '87*, 1987. See: ftp://ftp.cs.ruu.nl/pub/RUU/CS/techreps/CS-1986/1986-16.ps.gz.

20. M. Kuiper and J. Saraiva. LRC — A Generator for Incremental Language-Oriented Tools. In K. Koskimies, editor, *7th International Conference on Compiler Construction*, pages 298-301. volume 1383 of *LNCS*. Springer Verlag, 1998.

21. K. J. Lieberherr. *Adaptive Object-Oriented Software: The Demeter Method with Propagation Patterns*. PWS Publishing Company, 1996.

22. A. Ohori. A polymorphic record calculus and its compilation. *ACM Transactions on Programming Languages and Systems*, 17(6):844–895, 1995.

23. D. Rémy. Typechecking records and variants in a natural extension of ML. In *Proceedings of the ACM Symposium on Principles of Programming Languages (POPL '89)*, pages 77–88. ACM Press, 1989.

24. D. Rémy. Typing record concatenation for free. In C. A. Gunter and J. C. Mitchell, editors, *Theoretical Aspects of Object-Oriented Programming: Types, Semantics and Language Design*, Foundations of Computing Series. MIT Press, 1994.

25. T. W. Reps and T. Teitelbaum. *The Synthesizer Generator: A system for constructing language-based editors*. Springer-Verlag, 1989.

26. D. Rushall. *An attribute evaluator in Haskell*. Technical report, Manchester University, 1992. See URL: http://www-rocq.inria.fr/oscar/www/fnc2/AG.html.

27. C. Simonyi. Intentional programming: Innovation in the legacy age. Presented at IFIP Working group 2.1, 1996. Available from URL http://www.research.microsoft.com/research/ip/.

28. S.D. Swierstra, P. Azero and J. Saraiva. Designing and implementing combinator languages. In S. D. Swierstra, editor, *3rd International Summer School on Advanced Functional Programming*, volume 1608 of *LNCS*. Springer Verlag, 1999. See also URL http://www.cs.uu.nl/groups/ST/Software/index.html.

29. M. Wand. Type inference for record concatenation and multiple inheritance. *Information and Computation*, 93:1–15, 1991.

Dynamic Component Gluing

Linda Seiter[1], Mira Mezini[2], and Karl Lieberherr[3]

[1] College of Engineering, Santa Clara University, Santa Clara, CA, USA.
lseiter@scu.edu
[2] College of Engineering and Computer Science, University of Siegen, Germany.
mira@informatik.uni-siegen.de
[3] College of Computer Science, Northeastern University, Boston, MA, USA.
lieber@ccs.neu.edu

Abstract. Frameworks elevate encapsulation and reuse to the level of large-grained components, namely groups of collaborating classes. The abstract collaboration defined in a framework is easily customized by an application through static subclassing. However, this implies non-independent development of the application and framework models and excludes the possibility of *dynamically* deploying the framework. We propose the *dynamic composite adapter* design pattern, which employs the use of Java inner classes to achieve dynamic, modular, non-invasive, component adaptation. We also present a new scoping construct for succinctly defining dynamic adaptation of Java components.

1 Introduction

Component software is becoming an increasingly popular choice for system development, its goal being the development of highly reusable, customizable software components. In this paper we focus on a type of component design referred to as *collaboration-based* design [7,8]. A collaboration may be viewed as a slice of a class model, specifying the structural and behavioral relations required to accomplish a specific task. A collaboration can be implemented as a white-box framework, i.e. a set of abstract classes (representing roles in the collaboration) along with their structural relations, a set of abstract primitive operations, and a set of concrete template methods that define the collaboration skeleton by invoking the primitive operations. The framework's abstract model is easily customized through static subclassing. This works well when the assignment of framework roles to application classes is statically fixed prior to runtime. However, it is often desirable for an application to dynamically customize a framework, especially with Java's runtime architecture in which classes are dynamically loaded. A running application may wish to apply a newly loaded collaboration scheme to a set of previously loaded classes. Static subclassing will not support such customization. Even if the customization is known to be static, it is not feasible to require that the application be "written" to the framework. Component-oriented programming emphasizes the gluing of pre-existing binary components; hence, it is natural to assume that the application model and the collaborative designs

K. Czarnecki and U.W. Eisenecker (Eds.): GCSE'99, LNCS 1799, pp. 134–146, 2000.

that model business processes are independently developed by different component vendors, and are then "glued together" at the customer site. Thus, we outline several requirements for dynamic component adaptation:

- *Framework/Application independence:* the framework and application components should be independent of each other, allowing the framework to be reused by many applications, and an application to dynamically deploy many frameworks.
- *Adapter independence:* framework deployment must be *non-invasive*, in that the existing framework and application classes need not be modified.
- *Tolerance to interface incompatibility:* an application interface may not correspond to a framework interface due to conflicts in name, argument type and cardinality. Additional control flow may be required when gluing together the application and the framework. Thus, a simple mapping among method names (parameterization) may not be sufficient.

To manage these requirements, we introduce the *dynamic composite adapter* design pattern. The technique is described in general terms in Section 2 and illustrated with an example in Section 3. Related work is discussed in Section 4, followed by a brief summary of the paper in Section 5.

2   The Dynamic Composite Adapter Design Pattern

Consider the *Framework* package in Fig. 1, defining the abstract classes *FrameworkRoot* and *FrameworkChild*. The composite structure between parent and child is modeled through the structure mapping method *frameworkChild()* rather than through an aggregation relation. This allows the abstract framework structure to be subsequently implemented in terms of a concrete application structure. The template methods define the collaboration skeleton, invoking abstract primitive operations that will be customized by individual applications. As the primitive operations may unexpectedly modify the structure of the application composite object, it is important that template methods always use structure mapping methods to reference the elements of the composite. Thus, framework methods should not maintain local references to the elements of the composite structure. However, it is acceptable for a framework method to define a local variable to reference an object that is not part of the current composite object, for example an object that results from a computation.

Fig. 1 also defines an application model in the *Application* package, consisting of the composite class structure *AppRoot* and *AppChild*. Assume we wish to deploy the framework using the application, with *AppRoot* playing the *FrameworkRoot* role and *AppChild* playing the *FrameworkChild* role. The dashed enclosures in Fig. 1 represent *dynamic class extensions*. Each depicts how an application class needs to be extended to fulfill a framework role, with the abstract framework methods implemented in terms of the concrete application methods.

Our goal is to utilize the framework's collaboration scheme within the application without "physically" extending the application classes. Rather, we make

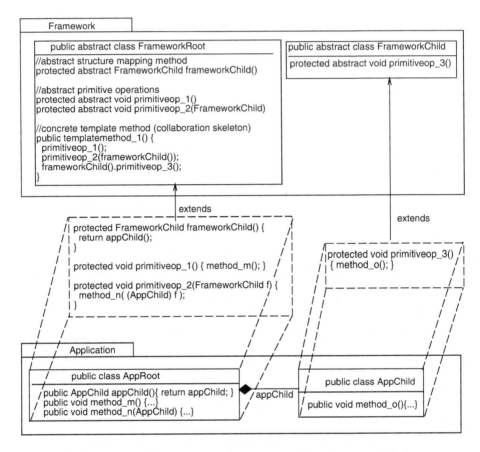

Fig. 1. Extension of Application Class Model to Framework Roles

the application objects appear to acquire the types encoded by the dynamic class extensions of Fig. 1. That is, given the root of an application object *o: AppRoot* on which we want to apply the framework's collaboration scheme, we need to:

1. Wrap the object *o* with the code in the *AppRoot* dynamic class extension.
2. While executing the code defined in a dynamic class extension, application objects may come into scope as the result of either (a) invoking an application operation that returns an object, or (b) directly instantiating an application class. Each such application object will be wrapped with the dynamic extension of its class.
3. A wrapped application object should be unwrapped before it can leave the scope of a dynamic class extension. This occurs when an application object (a) is passed as a parameter into an application operation, or (b) has an application operation invoked on it.

This is exactly what the *dynamic composite adapter* design pattern does. The structure of the pattern is shown in Fig. 2. The toplevel adapter class

AR_to_FR implements the framework deployment, defining two inner adapter classes to simulate each dynamic class extension: *AppRoot_FrameworkRoot* and *AppChild_FrameworkChild*. Each inner class serves as both an *application object wrapper* and a *framework role implementor*. It is important to reuse the same adapter once an application object is wrapped, as the framework may add local state to the application object. Each inner class implements a framework role interface by explicitly delegating to the wrapped application object.

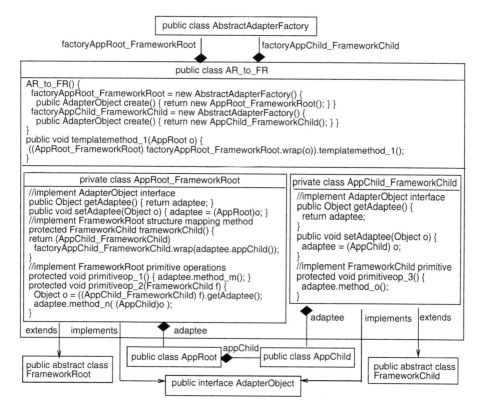

Fig. 2. Dynamic Composite Adapter - Java Inner Class Implementation

The pattern relies on the adapter utility package shown in Fig. 3. The *AbstractAdapterFactory* class serves to generate adapter objects that will wrap application objects in order to dynamically extend them, while the *AdapterObject* interface will be implemented to maintain a reference to the wrapped application object. The *wrap* method maintains a hashtable for the mapping between an application object and the adapter that wraps it. The abstract *create* method is implemented in the *AR_to_FR* constructor to generate a specific adapter class instance. The toplevel class *AR_to_FR* will define one *AbstractAdapterFactory* class instance per inner class.

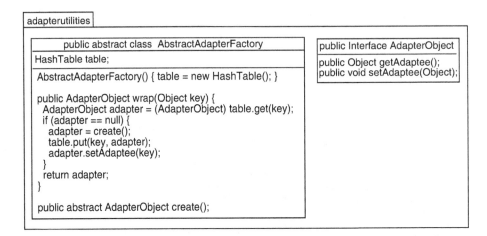

Fig. 3. Adapter Package

Clients can then invoke the public template method *templatemethod_1()* on an *AR_to_FR* object, passing the root of the application composite along as a parameter. This is where the root of the application composite gets wrapped with the corresponding *AppRoot_FrameworkRoot* adapter. Each application object that comes into scope, either through direct instantiation or as the result of invoking an application operation, is wrapped by the dynamic extension of its class. For example, in the *frameworkChild()* method the application object returned from the *appChild()* method is wrapped by a *AppChild_FrameworkChild* adapter. Subsequent framework method invocations are sent to the adapter. The resulting structure of an *AR_to_FR* adapter object is shown in Fig. 4. Conversely, an application object is unwrapped before it can be passed into an application method, such as the parameter to *primitive_op2* that is passed to *method_n()*.

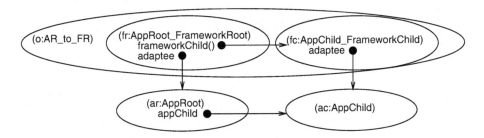

Fig. 4. Composite Object Structure

Fig. 2 shows that no modification of the framework or application is required and that all gluing code is encapsulated within the adapter class, including code for traversing the application composite (e.g. the invocation of *adaptee.appChild()* within *frameworkChild()*) as well as code for mapping types from one domain to the other due to incompatible signatures (wrap/unwrap plus the necessary type casts). New adaptations can be dynamically added because adapters are implemented as separate objects.

There are two main drawbacks of the technique. First, the delegation model requires additional method invocations for each invocation of a framework method. However, the source of this problem is the attempt to simulate dynamic modification of object behavior in a static language like Java. The second drawback is the complexity of the technique, especially when several frameworks are deployed within an application. Our experience with using the technique shows that it is best suited for code generators that would implement high-level language constructs such as *Adaptive Plug and Play Components*, (*AP&PCs*) [7].

2.1   Succinct Specification of Dynamic Component Adaptation

```
adapter AR_TO_FR {
  adapter AppRoot_FrameworkRoot adapts AppRoot extends FrameworkRoot {
    protected FrameworkChild frameworkChild() { return appChild(); }
    protected void primitiveop_1() { method_m(); }
    protected void primitiveop_2(FrameworkChild f)
    { method_n( (AppChild) f ); }
  }
  adapter AppChild_FrameworkChild adapts AppChild extends FrameworkChild{
    protected void primitiveop_3() { method_o(); }
  }
}
//example main program that applies the adapter to an application object
public class Client {
 static public void main(String[] args) {
  ((AR_to_FR) new AppRoot()).templatemethod_1();
}
```

Fig. 5. Dynamic Component Adaptation - Succinct Specification

Fig. 5 defines the framework deployment using a dedicated scoping construct called a *pluggable composite adapter* for succinctly specifying dynamic composite adaptation. The composite adapter defines a set of nested class adapters, each representing the dynamic extension of an application class to a framework role. Note that the method bodies within the nested class adapters are simply written as if the application class was a static subclass of the framework role.

The adapter class of Fig. 2 can be generated from this specification. For each nested class adapter, an inner class is generated based on the ternary relation between the application class (aggregation), framework role (extends), and *AdapterObject* interface (implements). A hashtable is also generated per dynamic class extension. Following the Hollywood principle of framework design (*don't call us, we'll call you*), the generated code in the primitive operations simply delegates to the application object. An application object that comes into scope is automatically wrapped by an instantiation of its nested class adapter, using the appropriate hash table. Conversely, application objects that are passed into application class methods are automatically unwrapped. Finally, the *AR_to_FR* cast in the main method in Fig. 5 is replaced by the invocation of the template method on a new adapter class instance.

3   Modeling Collaboration-Based Designs

We now demonstrate the technique with an example, namely the *Pricing* component described by Holland [4]. The component is part of a framework for order entry systems developed at IBM, which is subsequently customized in different applications to customer-specific pricing schemes.

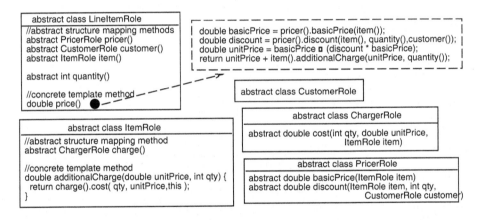

Fig. 6. Pricing Framework Class Model

Fig. 6 contains the pricing framework model. *LineItemRole* is responsible for calculating the price of a line item purchased by a customer. *PricerRole* provides price and discount information for a given item and customer. *ItemRole* is responsible for calculating additional charges, defined in *ChargerRole*. Fig. 6 defines the collaboration required to compute the price of a line item. The *price* and *additionalCharge* methods are template methods that define the message and data flow of the collaboration. The primitive operations (*basicPrice, discount, etc.*) are abstract, to be filled in with an application-specific implementation.

The class model of an example application domain, a product package, is shown in Fig. 7. Assume we wish to deploy the pricing component with the product application according to three pricing schemes. Each scheme requires the application model to conform to the framework model in a different way.

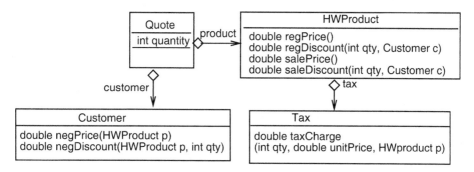

Fig. 7. Product Application Class Model

- *Regular Pricing*: Each product has a base price that may be discounted based on quantity ordered. *Quote* plays the *LineItemRole*. *HWProduct* plays the *ItemRole* and *PricerRole*, implementing *basicPrice, discount* for regular pricing. *Tax* plays the *ChargerRole*, implementing the *cost* method. Finally, *Customer* maintains the customer role.
- *Negotiated Pricing*: A customer may have negotiated certain item prices and discounts. *Quote* plays the *LineItemRole*. *Customer* plays the *PricerRole*, implementing *basicPrice, discount* for negotiated pricing. *HWProduct* plays the *ItemRole*. Customer maintains its role. Finally, *Tax* plays the *ChargerRole*.
- *Sale Pricing*: Each product has a designated sale price and no discounting is allowed. *Quote, HWProduct, Tax* and *Customer* play the same roles as they do with the regular pricing scheme. However, *HWProduct* will implement *basicPrice* and *discount* for sales pricing rather than regular pricing.

The traditional framework deployment technique uses static inheritance to model *plays-the-role-of* mappings. For example, the regular pricing scheme would require *Quote* to be redefined as a subclass of *LineItemRole*, *HWProduct* to be redefined as a subclass of both *ItemRole* and *PricerRole*, etc. Note that each of the three pricing schemes requires multiple inheritance. As Java does not support multiple inheritance, some of the mappings would be established indirectly using e.g., the original adapter design pattern [3]. Framework deployment using static inheritance has three drawbacks. First, it is invasive in that it requires modification of the application classes to encode the customization and the inheritance relationships. Second, it does not encapsulate the multiple roles into a single construct, as the roles would be spread out among the various application classes. Third, it is static in that it restricts the product application to a particular pricing implementation at the point of *Quote* class instantiation.

Trying to accommodate all three pricing schemes and allow dynamic switching between them, e.g., by exploiting the strategy pattern [3], results in a proliferation of classes and spurious relations in which the original design gets lost. Our main concern is that deployment of the pricing functionality with the product application requires the modification of the application classes. Reuse of

```
abstract class AbstractPricingScheme {
  protected AbstractAdapterFactory factoryQuote_LineItemRole,
    factoryCustomer_CustomerRole, factoryHWProduct_ItemRole,
    factoryTax_ChargerRole;
  AbstractPricingScheme() {
    factoryCustomer_CustomerRole = new AbstractAdapterFactory() {
        AdapterObject create() { return new Customer_CustomerRole();}};
    // instantiate factoryHWProduct_ItemRole and factoryTax_ChargerRole
    ...
  }

  public abstract class Quote_LineItemRole
  extends LineItemRole implements AdapterObject {
    protected Quote adaptee;
    public void setAdaptee(Object o) { adaptee = (Quote)o; }
    public Object getAdaptee() { return adaptee; }
    protected ItemRole item() { return (HWProduct_ItemRole)
        factoryHWProduct_ItemRole.wrap(adaptee.product()); }
    protected CustomerRole customer() { return (Customer_CustomerRole)
        factoryCustomer_CustomerRole.wrap(adaptee.customer()); }
    //concrete pricing schemes will implement pricer()
    protected int quantity() { return adaptee.quantity(); }
  }

  public class Customer_CustomerRole
  extends CustomerRole implements AdapterObject {
    protected Customer adaptee;
    public void setAdaptee(Object o) { adaptee = (Customer)o; }
    public Object getAdaptee() { return adaptee; }
  }

  public class HWProduct_ItemRole
  extends ItemRole implements AdapterObject {
    protected HWProduct adaptee;
    public void setAdaptee(Object o) { adaptee = (HWProduct)o; }
    public Object getAdaptee() {return adaptee;}
    protected ChargerRole charge() { return (Tax_ChargerRole)
      factoryTax_ChargerRole.wrap(adaptee.tax()); }
  }

  public class Tax_ChargerRole
  extends ChargerRole implements AdapterObject {
    protected Tax adaptee;
    public void setAdaptee(Object o) { adaptee = (Tax)o; }
    public Object getAdaptee() { return adaptee; }
    public double cost(int qty, double unitPr, ItemRole item) {
      HWProduct o = (HWProduct) ((AdapterObject)item).getAdaptee();
      return adaptee.taxCharge(qty, unitPr, o); }
  }
}
```

Fig. 8. Abstract Pricing Adapter

the original application class model becomes impossible and the resulting tangled code is very hard to maintain. This is especially true in a real-life scenario where many business objects and processes are involved. Hence, we conclude that traditional object-oriented frameworks do not properly support component technology. The core of the problem is that there is no direct way to establish some kind of "plays-the-role-of" wiring relationship between classes in different components independently of the component implementations.

3.1 Dynamic, Non-invasive Framework Deployment

Let us now model the same example using the dynamic composite adapter technique. Each pricing scheme is defined in a separate adapter class, which serves to dynamically augment an *existing* quote object with a new pricing scheme by mapping each object accessible from the quote object to the appropriate pricing framework roles. Fig. 8 shows the non-invasive deployment of the application to the framework. *AbstractPricingScheme* defines that part of the deployment that is shared by all three pricing schemes; concrete adapter classes for each individual pricing scheme will subclass it. *AbstractPricingScheme* contains an inner class for each role in the pricing framework. Each inner class implements the abstract framework methods based on a specific pricing scheme, and also maps a part of the application composite object to the appropriate framework role. Note that *AbstractPricingScheme* does not define an inner class for the *PricerRole* role. The deployment for this role is specific for concrete schemes and will be provided by concrete subclasses *RegPricingScheme*, *NegPricingScheme*, and *SalesPricingScheme*. *RegPricingScheme* is given in Fig. 9 for illustration. Note that in Figs. 8 and 9 it is not obvious how the application classes fulfill the framework roles, as much of the code is related to the *dynamic composite adapter* implementation technique. Fig. 10 on the other hand clearly captures the essence of the pricing framework deployment, using the adapter construct.

4 Related Work

VanHilst and Notkin propose an approach for modeling collaborations based on templates and mixins as an alternative to using frameworks [11]. However, this approach may result in complex parameterizations and scalability problems. Smaragdakis and Batory solve this by elevating the concept of a mixin to multiple class granularity, using C++ parameterized nested classes [8]. However, their approach does not address the issue of dynamic customizations as described by Holland [4]. A *Contract* [4] allows multiple, potentially conflicting component customizations to exist in a single application. However, contracts do not allow conflicting customizations to be simultaneously active. Thus, it is not possible to allow different instances of a class to follow different collaboration schemes.

Seiter et al. proposed a *context relation* to link the static and dynamic aspects of a class [9]. While supporting multiple dynamic collaboration schemes, the approach is based on dynamically altering a class definition for the duration of a method invocation, thus affecting all class instances. Multiple dynamic variations of an object's behavior are also supported in the RONDO model [6]. However, RONDO does not provide explicit support for collaborations. In this paper we propose a model for scoping the different collaboration schemes, thus we can be selective as to which objects are affected.

```
class RegPricingScheme extends AbstractPricingScheme {
  protected AbstractAdapterFactory factoryHWProduct_PricerRole;
  RegPricingScheme() {   super();
    factoryQuote_LineItemRole = new AbstractAdapterFactory() {
        AdapterObject create() {return new Quote_LineItemRole();} };
    factoryHWProduct_PricerRole = new AbstractAdapterFactory() {
        AdapterObject create() {return new HWProduct_PricerRole();} };
  }
  public double price(Quote q) {   return ((Quote_LineItemRole)
      factoryQuote_LineItemRole.wrap(q)).price();   }
  public class Quote_LineItemRole
    extends AbstractPricingScheme.Quote_LineItemRole {
      protected PricerRole pricer() { return (HWProduct_PricerRole)
        factoryHWProduct_PricerRole.wrap(adaptee.product()); }
  }
  public class HWProduct_PricerRole
  extends PricerRole implements AdapterObject {
    protected HWProduct adaptee;
    public void setAdaptee(Object o) { adaptee = (HWProduct)o; }
    public Object getAdaptee() { return adaptee; }
    public double basicPrice(ItemRole item) {
      HWProduct o = (HWProduct) ((AdapterObject)item).getAdaptee();
      return o.regPrice();
    }
    public double discount(ItemRole item, int qty, CustomerRole cust) {
      HWProduct o1 = (HWProduct) ((AdapterObject)item).getAdaptee();
      Customer o2 = (Customer) ((AdapterObject)cust).getAdaptee();
      return o1.regDiscount( qty, o2 );
    }
  }
}
```

Fig. 9. Regular Pricing Adapter

Batory proposed the *GenVoca* architecture for parameterized, plug-compatible, interchangeable and interoperable components [1]. The *GenVoca* model is based on the notion of *realm, interface, component* and *layer*. Layers represent encapsulations of composite-object decorators, which could be dynamically composed. The inner class technique we have presented can be used as an elegant

Java implementation for *GenVoca* layers. Einarson and Hedin also suggest the use of inner classes as alternative implementations of several design patterns [2].

```
abstract adapter AbstractPricingScheme {
  abstract adapter Quote_LineItemRole adapts Quote extends LineItemRole {
    protected ItemRole item () { return product(); }
    protected CustomerRole customer() { return customer(); }
    protected int quantity() { return Quote.this.quantity(); }
  }
  adapter Customer_CustomerRole adapts Customer extends CustomerRole {}
  adapter HWProduct_ItemRole adapts HWProduct extends ItemRole {
    protected ChargerRole charge() { return tax(); }
  }
  adapter Tax_ChargerRole adapts Tax extends ChargerRole {
    public double cost(int qty, double unitPrice, ItemRole item)
    { return taxCharge(qty, unitPrice, (HWProduct) item); }
  }
}

adapter RegPricingScheme extends AbstractPricingScheme {
  adapter RegPricingScheme.Quote_LineItemRole
  extends AbstractPricingScheme.Quote_LineItemRole {
    protected PricerRole pricer () { return product(); }
  }
  adapter HWProduct_PricerRole adapts HWProduct extends PricerRole {
    public double basicPrice(ItemRole item)
    { return ( (HWProduct)item ).regPrice(); }
    public double discount(ItemRole item, int qty, CustomerRole cust)
    { return ( (HWProduct)item ).regDiscount( (Customer)cust ); }
  }
}
//example main program that applies the adapter to an application object
public class Client {
 static public void main(String[] args) {
  Quote q = new Quote();
  System.out.println(((RegPricingScheme)q).price());
}
```

Fig. 10. Pricing Component Adapter - Succinct Specification

An underlying theme of the work described in this paper is separation of concerns to avoid software tangling. This is also the motivation behind both *Aspect-Oriented Programming* [12] and *HyperSpaces* (a new model of subject-oriented programming) [10]. AspectJ [12] is an extension of Java that allows one to program different aspects separately. Mezini and Lieberherr proposed *Adaptive Plug and Play Components*, or AP&PCs, which define a slice of behavior for a set of classes, and can be parameterized to allow reuse with different class models. An enhanced form of AP&PCs that decreases tangling of connectors and aspects in AspectJ is described in [5]. This improved form of AP&PC uses similar techniques as described in this paper, along with tool support.

Summary

This paper studied traditional framework customization techniques and concluded that they are inappropriate for component-based programming since they lack support for non-invasive, encapsulated, dynamic customization. We proposed an implementation technique for dynamic framework customization, based on Java inner classes. The technique allows the separation of customization code from application and framework implementations, thus supporting the gluing of pre-existing components by third-parties.

Acknowledgements

This work has been partially sponsored by the National Science Foundation under grant number CDA-972057, by the Defense Advanced Research Projects Agency (DARPA) and Rome Laboratory, under agreement number F30602-96-2-0239.

References

1. D. Batory, The GenVoca Model of Software-System Generators. in *IEEE Software*, September 1994.
2. D. Einarson, G. Hedin, Using Inner Classes in Design Patterns, Code examples available at <http://www.dna.lth.se/home/daniel/patterns_inner_classes.html>.
3. E. Gamma, R. Helm, R. Johnson, and J. Vlissides, *Design Patterns: Elements of Reusable Object-Oriented Software*. Addison-Wesley, 1994.
4. I. Holland, The design and representation of object-oriented components, Ph.D. Dissertation, Northeastern University, Computer Science, 1993.
5. K. Lieberherr, Lorenz, and M. Mezini, Aspect-Oriented Components, College of Computer Science, Northeastern University, Technical Report, Boston, MA, 1999.
6. M. Mezini. Variational Object-Oriented Programming Beyond Classes and Inheritance. Kluwer Academic Publishers, 1998.
7. M. Mezini and K. Lieberherr, Adaptive Plug and Play Components for Evolutionary Software Development. Proc. OOPSLA, October 1998. ACM Press.
8. Y. Smaragdakis and D. Batory, Implementing Layered Designs with Mixin Layers, in *Proc. ECOOP'98*, 550-570. Springer Verlag, Lecture Notes in Computer Science.
9. L. Seiter, J. Palsberg, and K. Lieberherr, Evolution of Object Behavior using Context Relations, in *IEEE Transactions on Software Engineering*, January 1998.
10. P. Tarr, H. Ossher, W. Harrison, S. Sutton Jr., *N* Degrees of Separation: Multi-Dimensional Separation of Concerns, In *ICSE'99*. May 1999.
11. M. VanHilst and D. Notkin, Using Role Components to Implement Collaboration-Based Designs, In *OOPLSA'96*. ACM Press.
12. Xerox PARC AspectJ Team, AspectJ, Xerox PARC Technical Report, January 1999, http://www.parc.xerox.com/spl/projects/aop/

Recursive Types and Pattern-Matching in Java

Rémi Forax and Gilles Roussel
http://vodka.univ-mlv.fr/~forax
http://monge.univ-mlv.fr/~roussel

Institut Gaspard Monge,
Université de Marne-la-Vallée

Abstract. *Recursive types definitions* and *pattern-matching* are two useful built-in features of functional languages. There is no such mechanism in the Java language. In this article, we investigate different implementations to support these features in Java. First, we review methods to define recursive types. Then, we expose several approaches allowing to simulate pattern-matching on structures of these types. Finally, we present re-use techniques for algorithms featuring this mechanism.

1 Introduction

Describing algorithms on recursive structures is among the fundamental concepts of computer science. Strongly typed functional languages propose type-constructors and pattern-matching mechanisms which make easier the expression of such algorithms. These constructions are not classical idioms of object-oriented languages. As a matter of fact, these notions are often opposed to the object notion, but we promote that they are complementary [12,1].

In this article, we review different implementations to support these features in Java.

First, we study different implementations for recursive types definition. These types, allow to type-check algorithms over recursive data structures.

Then, we review different techniques which allow to specify algorithms over recursive structures, just as if a pattern matching was featured in the language. More or less, these solutions simulate CLOS multi-methods [2] or Dylan functions [8] late binding according to method arguments types.

Finally, we study the specification of algorithms, loosely coupled with the data structure, in order to ease their re-use.

This work brought us to propose :

- a definition for recursive types based on inner interfaces.
- a `PatternMatcher` generic component to implement late binding according to method arguments.
- two main techniques to implement loosely coupled algorithms :
  - one based on interface adapter

K. Czarnecki and U.W. Eisenecker (Eds.): GCSE'99, LNCS 1799, pp. 147–164, 2000.
© Springer-Verlag Berlin Heidelberg 2000

- another based on default traversal mechanism whose most general implementation is the new *Codec Pattern*

In section 2, we study a classical object-oriented way to implement recursive types and algorithms on recursive data structures. In section 3, we present an implementation of recursive types based on inner interfaces and review methods to simulate pattern-matching. In section 4, we use previous results to implement loosely coupled algorithms.

2   Concrete Recursive Types

A classical way [12] to represent recursive types in an object-oriented language such as Java is drawn from the functional languages type constructors. The type is implemented by a *base class* A, and each constructor of the type is represented by a *constructor class* B that inherits from the base class A.

Thanks to the sub-typing mechanism, the reference to objects of constructor classes (B) can be used wherever a A-typed reference is expected.

In order to illustrate this method we will use a simple example of recursive type: a chained list of integers. For a typed functional language, the definition of the recursive type List is something like:

```
List int = Nil | Cons of int * List int;
```
which means: a list of integers is either, an empty list of name Nil, or an pair of name Cons which includes an integer and a list of integers.

In an object-oriented language, the product '*' can be implemented by fields in the constructor classes and the alternative '|' by the inheritance mechanism, with several sub-classes which inherit from a single class. Therefore, the type List is translated into the three following Java classes.

```
abstract class List { }
class Nil extends List { }
class Cons extends List {
  int value;
  List tail;
  public Cons(int value,List tail) {
    this.value=value;
    this.tail=tail;
  }
}
```

The class List is the base class and variable of this type can contain references to instances of the Nil and Cons constructor classes.

Nevertheless, this interpretation of functional type constructors in Java allows the type to be extended by adding new classes inheriting from (or implementing) base class List. For instance, one could add a ConsDouble class containing a double instead of an int and inheriting form List. Then, a variable of type List could contain a reference to an heterogeneous list. It constitutes a major difference with the functional approach where the type is not extensible [5] and homogeneous.

2.1   Algorithms on Recursive Structures

Now that we have seen how recursive types are classically described with classes, we study how specify algorithms on recursive structures (instances of these classes).

A first approach consists in declaring an abstract function (algorithm) in the base class and then to implement its behavior in each constructor sub-class.

Using this approach, let us consider the implementation of a function sum computing the sum of integers contained in a list. The base class List will, now comprise an abstract sum() method which will be defined in each constructor class.

```
abstract class List {
  public abstract int sum();
}
class Nil extends List {
  public final int sum() {
    return 0;
  }
}
class Cons extends List {
  int value;
  List tail;
  public Cons(int value,List tail) {
    this.value=value;
    this.tail=tail;
  }
  public final int sum() {
    return value+tail.sum();
  }
}
```

With this method, it is easy to add (resp. remove) other constructor classes: the algorithm parts specific to each constructor are independent one from the other.

On the other hand, this implementation is not exactly suitable for adding (resp. removing) a new algorithm within this structure, as it would be then necessary to alter each class. This forbids separate compilation of each different algorithm.

3   Abstract Recursive Types

In the Java language, when a class is declared, in fact, two features are mixed: a type declaration and a object "skeleton" definition. The type declared is not the type of objects of that class but the one of references to object of that class.

This type determines the members (fields or methods) that can be accessed via a reference of that type. In other words, it defines an interface[1].

This is why we argue that recursive types should not be implemented as classes but as a set of Java `interface`. Since a Java `interface` does not allow non-constant field declaration, type fields are represented by methods.

In this approach, the list type is constituted of three interfaces, a *base interface* and two *constructor interfaces*. We chose to define the interfaces `Nil` and `Cons` as inner-interface of the `List` one to encapsulate the type definition into a unique interface and to constrain names of list sub-classes. Classes implementing that type must implement the `List.Nil` or the `List.Cons` interface.

```
interface List {
  interface Nil extends List { }
  interface Cons extends List {
    public abstract int getValue();
    public abstract List getTail();
  }
}
```

With this approach constructor interfaces of a recursive type could be found by reflection [10] with the method `getDeclaredClasses()` of class `Class`. Then it is possible in some implementation to verify that the list type has not been extended by `List` sub-interfaces.

It is obvious to create concrete classes, implementing these interfaces, similar the one of section 2.

One should notice that the use of access methods relaxes the type implementation: methods can either be implemented by static fields access or by dynamic computations of the field. This allow to reuse methods working on recursive types, with a large set recursive structures as argument. For example, the argument of a method `void m(List)` can either be a classical list of integers or a lazily defined list of all the integers, as defined below.

```
class LazyCons implements List.Cons {
  List tail;
  int value;
  public LazyCons(int value) {
    this.value=value;
  }
  public List getTail() {
    if (tail==null)
      tail=new LazyCons(value+1);
    return tail;
  }
  public int getValue() {
    return value;
  }
```

---

[1] Here, the term interface is used in a more general sense than Java keyword `interface`.

}

More generally, developers should never use classes to define types but always define the corresponding interfaces to ease reusability. Unfortunately, the use of interfaces slows down execution and multiplies the number of files to maintain. Therefore, an automated way to move from one specification to the other should be investigated.

3.1   Algorithms on Recursive Structures

Inheritance is not well suited to specify algorithms on abstract recursive types. For instance, the sum() method cannot be added simply to the previous List interface using inheritance because, in the Cons class, this method is called on the getTail() return value which is of a static type List. It is therefore necessary to modify the List interface or to use type cast and multiple implementation of interfaces as proposed below.

```
interface SumList extends List {
  public abstract int sum();
}
abstract class Cons implements List.Cons, SumList {
  public final int sum() {
    // return getValue()+getTail().sum();   error!!
    return getValue()+((SumList)getTail()).sum();
  }
}
abstract class Nil implements List.Nil, SumList {
  public final int sum() {
    return 0;
  }
}
```

The cast is needed because the Java language does not provide a way to specify contravariant return type for the method getTail(). In the above example, a SumList getTail() method cannot overwrite the List getTail() method defined in the List class.

3.2   Functional Approach

In this section we investigate an alternative to inheritance that we call the functional approach. It avoids to modify multiple classes to specify a new algorithm since the whole algorithm is encapsulated within a single class. We no longer view algorithms as methods of objects but rather as objects. Since algorithms studied in this article share a common behavior – i.e. they do pattern matching – objects representing them should inherit from a common PatternMatcher class implementing the pattern matching. To maintain the modularity, the algorithm is broken down along each interface constituting the type (List). The algorithm part associated to one constructor interface is specified within a method `match()` taking this constructor interface as parameter. For the `List` type, this class should look like:

```
class PatternMatcher {
  public final Object match(List.Nil n)  { ... }
  public final Object match(List.Cons c) { ... }
}
```

In order to simulate the pattern matching, a mechanism must be available to search for the appropriate `match()` method according to the actual argument type, like CLOS multi-methods do [2]. A late binding of method has to be performed according to the type of the first argument. The idea is to write the `match(List.Cons)` and `match(List.Nil)` methods and to be able to call the `match()` method with a reference statically typed as `List`; the choice of the method being dynamic.

However, it cannot be done in the Java language because the method binding is established from the statically determined types of the argument. Late binding of methods is only performed according to the type of the target object[2].

Now we will describe two different ways to simulate this late binding.

3.3   Visitor Pattern

A first general solution to solve this problem is known as the *Visitor Pattern* [6]. This pattern is very close to the functional approach and we present it for the list example.

First, the recursive type must be defined. Each of its classes must implement an `void accept(Visitor)` method. Thus, the type list can no longer be specified using interfaces. A way to specify algorithms over interfaces is proposed in a following section.

```
abstract class List {
  public void accept(Visitor v);
}
class Nil extends List {
  public void accept(Visitor v) {
    v.visit(this);
  }
}
class Cons extends List {
  int value;
  List tail;
  public Cons(int value,List tail) {
    this.value=value;
    this.tail=tail;
  }
  public void accept(Visitor v) {
    v.visit(this);
```

---
[2] We call this late binding: classical late binding.

```
    }
}
```

Then, an algorithm on the recursive structure is now specified within a single `SumVisitor` class implementing the interface `Visitor`. For each `List` subclass, there is a method `visit()`, i.e. `visit(Cons)` and `visit(Nil)`.

```
interface Visitor {
  public void visit(Cons c);
  public void visit(Nil n);
}
class SumVisitor implements Visitor {
  int sum=0;
  public final void visit(Nil n) { }
  public final void visit(Cons c) {
    sum+=c.value;
    c.tail.accept(this);
  }
}
```

In order to invoke the appropriate method according to the dynamic type of the first argument, the standard Java late binding mechanism (according to the target object) is used. More precisely, method overwriting, here of the `accept(Visitor)` method, is used. When `target.accept(v)` is executed, the virtual machine selects dynamically the appropriate `accept()` method according to the target object type (standard late binding). As each `accept()` method knows statically the object class in which it is defined, then it can call the appropriate `visit()` method by taking `this` (statically typed) as its argument.

This exchange between target object and argument object is not very natural. It forces the user to call the `accept()` method on the list, rather than the `visit()` method as shown in the next example.

```
public final static void main(String[] argv) {
  List l=new Cons(2,new Cons(3,new Nil()));
  SumVisitor visitor=new SumVisitor();
  l.accept(visitor);
  System.out.println("sum :"+visitor.sum);
}
```

3.4   A Reflection Mechanism

In the previous approach, the method overwriting of `accept()` allows to match a corresponding `visit()` method to the actual type of an object. We introduce here another construction which saves the need for implementing `accept()` methods in recursive types.

A similar approach is described in the article *The Essence of the Visitor Pattern* [15] although in that case it was limited to one argument and mixed with a default traversal feature (see in section 4.2).

The main idea of the construction we propose is to use a `match(List)` method which dynamically invokes the appropriate `match()` method according to the dynamic type of its argument thanks to the standard reflection mechanism of Java. The `getClass()` method of `java.lang.Class` allows to determine the actual type of the argument. Then the `getMethod()` method finds the appropriate `match()` method. Eventually, the resulting `match()` method is invoked with the `invoke()` method.

As a matter of fact, we adopt a general method where late binding can be performed on several arguments (passed as an object array). The key part of this approach is the `PatternMatcher` class. It is a generic component which performs the pattern matching whatever is the parameter type used.

The inheritance of this component ease the specification of algorithms that use pattern-matching on a recursive structure. Unlike *Visitor Pattern*, this method does not make mandatory, for each type, the writing of an interface containing a method for each constructor class.

The following code is a naive implementation for the generic `PatternMatcher` component. A more generic class could take as argument the name of the matching method and the `Class` instance in which the method should be looked for.

```java
class PatternMatcher {
  public final Object match(Object[] l) {
    Class lClass[]=new Class[l.length];
    for(int i=0;i<l.length;i++)
      lClass[i]=l[i].getClass();
    return match(l,lClass);
  }
  public final Object match(Object[] l,Class[] c) {
    try {
      Method m=getClass().getMethod("match",c);
      return m.invoke(this,l);
    }
    catch(Exception e){
      throw new NoMatchingMethodException(e.getMessage());
    }
  }
}
```

In this class, we have defined two `match()` methods. The first one identifies argument types with argument classes. In the general case this is not true since arguments of primitive type are wrapped into objects. Thus, the second method provide a way to pass arguments as objects together with their type.

To illustrate the use of this generic component, we present the `Merger` algorithm. It performs a pattern-matching on its two arguments in order to merge two lists alternately. Specifying the algorithm computing the sum of the list integers would have been as simple.

```
class Merger extends PatternMatcher {
  public final List match(Nil n,Cons c) {
    return c;
  }
  public final List match(Nil n1,Nil n2) {
    return n1;
  }
  public final List match(Cons c,Nil n) {
    return c;
  }
  public final List match(Cons c,Cons c2) {
    List tail=c.getTail();
    c.setTail(c2);
    c2.setTail(match(tail,c2.getTail()));
    return c;
  }
  public final List match(List l1,List l2) {
    return (List)match(new Object[]{l1,l2});
  }
}
```

The last `match()` method specializes the generic `PatternMatcher` for the specific type `List`.

3.5   Algorithm Optimization

The main problem with this implementation, also observed by *Palsberg & Jay*, is its speed. In fact, for each class, the algorithm has to process a method search. One possible optimization consists in calculating in advance the set of classes for which a `visit()` method is available save this information in an hash-table.

The benchmark chosen to validate this implementation, is the one described in the article *The Essence of the Visitor Pattern* [15]. The aim is to calculate the sum of the list integers. The list is composed of 2000 links. The test was made on a 64 Megabytes SPARCstation 10. The compiler and the run-time engine were taken from the jdk1.1.6.

Implementation	processing time
redefining method	0.02 min
Visitor Pattern	0.03 min
`PaternMatcher`	1.18 min
Optimized `PaternMatcher`	0.15 min

Optimizing the `PaternMatcher` implementation allows to significantly boost its speed. We estimate that more thorough optimizations should lower its execution time to that of the *Visitor Pattern* since optimizations performed to boost the classical late binding [11] could be applied for parameter late binding. As a corollary, the reflection mechanism implemented in the *JVM* could be improved if including these optimizations.

3.6   Extending the Reflection Search Method

The dynamic method search mechanism searches for the methods according to its exact profile. In the previous example, the `PatternMatcher` performs the method search according to the concrete class rather than its interface. That is to say that the Java dynamic reflection method search does not perform dynamically type unification as it is done at compile time for method matching.

In fact, the `PatternMatcher` and the *Visitor Pattern* do not follow the same semantics. The `PatternMatcher` implementation does not work with a recursive type defined using interfaces as advocated.

We propose a new implementation of the `java.lang.Class.getMethod()` which performs a dynamic type unification. We think this method should be included in Java reflection API.

```
public Method getBestMethod(String name,Class types[])
  throws NoSuchMethodException, SecurityException {
  Method methods[]=getMatchMethods(name,types);
  Method bestMethod=methods[0];
  Class bestMethodTypes[]=bestMethod.getParameterTypes();
  for(int i=1;i<methods.length;i++) {
    int j=0;
    int value=0;
    Class pTypes[]=methods[i].getParameterTypes();
    for(;j<pTypes.length;j++) {
      int diff=(bestMethodTypes[j].isAssignableFrom
      (pTypes[j]))?1:
        (pTypes[j].isAssignableFrom(bestMethodTypes[j]))?-1:0;
      if (diff==0 || (value!=diff && value!=0))
        throw new TwoMethodMatchException(
          "two methods "+name+" match parameters");
      value=diff;
    }
    if (value==1) {
      bestMethod=methods[i];
      bestMethodTypes=pTypes;
    }
  }
  return bestMethod;
}
private Method[] getMatchMethods(String name,Class types[])
  throws NoSuchMethodException, SecurityException {
  Vector vector=new Vector();
  Method methods[]=getMethods();
  for(int i=0;i<methods.length;i++)
  if (methods[i].getName().equals(name)) {
    Class pTypes[]=methods[i].getParameterTypes();
    if (types.length==pTypes.length) {
```

```
      int j=0;
      for(;j<types.length && pTypes[j].isAssignableFrom
      (types[j]);j++);
      if (j==types.length)
        vector.add(methods[i]);
    }
  }
  if (vector.size()==0)
    throw new NoSuchMethodException("method "+name+" not
    found");
  return (Method[])vector.toArray(new Method[vector.size()]);
}
```

The getMatchMethods() method constructs the array of methods well typed according to arguments. Then, the getBestMethod() method looks for the most precise method. It performs this search dynamically with the same algorithm used by Java compilers statically. Moreover, the Java compilers use argument static types whereas the getBestMethod() method uses their real dynamic types to allow late binding.

In the ambiguous cases the getBestMethod() method throws a TwoMethod-MatchException.A simpler but less general method search, used by parasitic multi-methods [13], consists in choosing the first matching method.

If no method matches argument types a NoSuchMethodException is thrown by the getMatchMethods(). This feature is not desirable in a strongly typed language. Implementing a default behavior [15] (see. section 4) solves this problem.

Default parameter
This version allows the List base interface to be used as a parameter type. It behaves as a default parameter type (the functional '_'). Writing a Merger becomes even simpler since it is not necessary to write a method match() for each combination of constructor interfaces.

```
class Merger extends PatternMatcher {
  public final List match(Nil n, List l) {
    return l;
  }
  public final List match(Cons c,Nil n) {
    return c;
  }
  public final List match(Cons c,Cons c2) {
    return new Cons(c.getValue(),new Cons(c2.getValue(),
      match(c.getTail(),c2.getTail())));
  }
  public final List match(List l1,List l2) {
    return (List)match(new Object[]{l1,l2});
  }
}
```

4   Loosely Coupled Algorithms

The aim of this section is to investigate several techniques allowing to describe
"translation" between two similar, but non isomorphic, recursive types, so that
algorithms specified for one type can be applied on the other one. Then, algorithms can be specified on their natural recursive type and reuse everywhere
they make sense.

4.1   Interface Adapter

We saw in section 2 that using interfaces allows to abstract the structure from
its internal representation. Moreover, they also allow to achieve loosely coupling
of algorithms. To do so, an adapter class performs the type "translation". We
believe that implementation of such adapter should use the `PatternMatcher`
generic component since it needs to perform pattern matching on the input
recursive structure.

To illustrate this technique, we present an example where objects of class
`BiList` are considered as objects of class `List`. A `BiList` is a list where each
link contains two values.

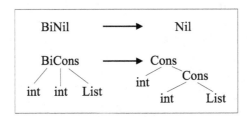

The idea of our implementation is to(lazily) construct the `List` step by step
using a pattern matching over the `BiList`. A `BiCons(a,b,tail)` is translated
into `Cons1(a,Cons2(b,tail))` and `BiNil` into `Nil`. Classes `Cons1` and `Cons2`
implements `List.Cons`, `Nil` implements `List.Nil`. To reuse a algorithm specified for a `List` one should call:

```
    Algo.match(BiListToListAdapter.match(biList))
class BiListToListAdapter extends PatternMatcher {
  public final List match(BiList l) {
   return (List)match(new Object[]{l});
  }
  public final List match(BiList.BiCons bicons) {
    return new Cons1(bicons);
  }
  public final List match(BiList.BiNil binil) {
    return new Nil();
  }
  static class Nil implements List.Nil { }
```

```
class Cons1 implements List.Cons {
  public Cons1(BiList.BiCons bc) {
    this.bc=bc;
  }
  public final int getValue() {
    return bc.getValue1();
  }
  public final List getTail() {
    if (cons2==null)
      cons2=new Cons2(bc);
    return cons2;
  }
  Cons2 cons2;
  BiList.BiCons bc;
}

class Cons2 implements List.Cons {
  public Cons2(BiList.BiCons bc) {
    this.bc=bc;
  }
  public final int getValue() {
    return bc.getValue2();
  }
  public final List getTail() {
    if (list==null)
      list=match(bc.getTail());
    return list;
  }
  List list;
  BiList.BiCons bc;
}
}
```

It is not easy to implement such adapters by hand. We are investigating the automatic generation of adapter classes inspired from other languages approaches [7,4]. The common idea of these techniques is to deduce from type definitions a mapping between types.

Moreover, the use of an adapter generates a intermediate data structure that could be discard. We hope to adapt functional deforestation methods [3,14] to statically eliminate the adapter implementation.

4.2   Default Traversal

Another approach, introduced by Lieberherr [9], as *adaptive programming* introduced the notion of default traversals on every structure subtypes which do not have a specified visit method. The writing is therefore more independent from

the algorithm and the structure, as the structure is modified, the description of
the algorithm remains the same.

The version proposed by Lieberherr is a static version in which all classes are
available when traversals are defined. We study here two methods which use the
Java reflection mechanism to introduce the default traversal.

4.3   Walkabout Pattern

A first method proposed by *J. Palsberg & C.B. Jay* for defining this default
traversal i.e. unspecified `match()`, consists in executing a visit in all the fields of
non-primitive type of the class.

In the chained list example, only the visit in the `Cons` class has to be written
because the traversal of `Nil` is the default one. In fact, the *Walkabout Pattern*
will not visit the `Nil` as it does not contain fields.

```
class Sum extends Walkabout {
  int sum=0;
  public final void match(Cons c) {
    sum+=c.getValue();
    visit(c.getTail());
  }
}

class Walkabout extends PatternMatcher {
  public final void match(Object l) {
    if (l!=null) {
      try {
        match(new Object[]{l});
      }
      catch(NoMatchingMethodException e) {
        Field fields[]=l.getClass().getFields();
        for(int i=0;i<fields.length;i++)
          if (!(fields[i].getType().isPrimitive()))
            try {
              match(fields[i].get(l));
            }
            catch(IllegalAccessException e2) {
            }
      }
    }
  }
}
```

4.4   Codec Pattern

The *Walkabout* takes advantages of the `PatternMatcher` dynamic method search
according to the classes and interfaces of the hierarchy. A natural continuation

to the *Walkabout Pattern* consists in using the inheritance tree, not only for dynamic method search, but also to specify the traversal on the structure.

The basic idea of the *Codec Pattern*, is to enable the specification of algorithm fractions, not only for terminal (final) classes of the inheritance hierarchy, but also for all internal classes of the hierarchy. This implies to extends the *Walkabout Pattern* default traversal with a traversal of the inheritance hierarchy.

The traversal of the inheritance tree visits each class twice: once in the direction of the inheritance, and once in the opposite direction. Two *wrappers* (`match()` methods) can be specified for each class, `prefix()` called when going down in the tree and `suffix()` called when going up. These wrappers overwrite default `prefix()` and `suffix()` methods. The default `prefix()` method does nothing. The default `suffix()` method traverses fields declared (not inherited) in the class like *Walkabout Pattern*[3].

The implementation of the *Codec Pattern* is much more complex and space consumer than the others, this is why we only present an example using this component.

To illustrate the use of this component, we slightly modify the implementation of the list by inserting an abstract class `Item` between the interface `List` and the `Cons` links in order to add a `Link` link.

The figure 1 shows, for a `Link` object, the call flow of wrappers in the *Codec Pattern*.

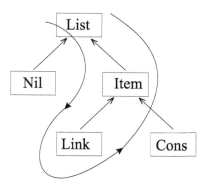

Fig. 1. Traversal

The above example describes a *PrintVisitor* class which traverse a list and displays the content of each link by using the `Codec` component. The example `RevPrintVisitor` produces the reversed list in relation to the `PrintVisitor`.

```
class PrintVisitor extends Codec {
  public final void prefix(Cons c) {
```

---

[3] It has to be noted that the fields traversal order is not, *a priori*, the same than the *Walkabout Pattern*.

```
    System.err.println(
      "Cons.value "+c.getValue());
  }
  public final void prefix(Link l) {
    System.err.println(
      "Link.color "+l.getColor());
  }
  public final void prefix(Nil n) {
    System.err.println("Nil");
  }
  // public final void suffix(Item i) {
  //    visit(i.list);
  // }
}
class RevPrintVisitor extends Codec {
  public final void suffix(Cons c) {
    System.err.println(
      "Cons.value "+c.getValue());
  }
  public final void suffix(Link l) {
    System.err.println(
      "Link.color "+l.getColor());
  }
  public final void suffix(Nil n) {
    System.err.println("Nil");
  }
  public final void prefix(Item i) {
    visit(i.getTail());
  }
}
```

The traversal executed by the *Codec Pattern* is quite close to the one executed by the *tree-traversal* of Lieberherr [9]. The propagation during the visit is executed in a similar way. However, the *Codec Pattern* stays blind as for the direction it has to take regarding the *tree-traversal* which benefits a static analysis of the class graph.

Our actual implementation turns out to be much more complex than the simple version of the `PatternMatcher` and its performances regarding size and speed are unattractive. We estimate that thorough optimizations shall allow to obtain acceptable performances.

5   Conclusions

In this article, we propose several implementations, featuring a reflection mechanism, which ease the use of recursive types in Java. These implementations cover recursive type definition, pattern matching and re-use of algorithms by mimicking features of typed functional languages.

The main difference between these two approaches (functional and object-oriented) remains the type-check. In the case of Java, the type-check is performed dynamically and may throw exceptions at running time, which can be qualified of "heretic" for strongly typed languages. This loosely type-check is issued from the intensive use of the Java reflection mechanism.

In addition to the technical aspect of implementing pattern-matching in Java, this article shows that reflection allows to define new mechanisms, in that case, the late binding of the method according to the arguments type, without altering the language. This track is quite interesting, as it could lead to a language whose base mechanisms would be extremely poor (do not contain idiomatic constructions) and easy to master, and where programmers would add in a very simple way other mechanisms according to their needs, thanks to generic components, using the reflection mechanism.

Acknowledgments

We would like to thank Didier Parigot and Loïc Correnson for our discussions, and also Etienne Duris and Marc Dalesme for their help regarding the writing of this article.

References

1. Luca Cardelli, Peter Wegner *On Understanding Types, Data Abstraction, and Polymorphism* Computing Surveys, Vol 17 n. 4, pp 471-522, December 1985.
2. L. G. DeMichiel, R. P. Gabriel. *Common lisp object system overview* ECOOP'87, LNCS 276 pp 151-170, 1987.
3. Philip Wadler. *Deforestation: Transforming Programs to Eliminate Trees* In Harald Ganzinger, editor, European Symposium on Programming (ESOP '88), LNCS 300 , pages 344-358, Nancy, March 1988. Springer-Verlag.
4. Carole Le Bellec, Martin Jourdan, Didier Parigot and Gilles Roussel. *Specification and Implementation of Grammar Coupling Using Attribute Grammars* In Proceedings of Programming Language Implementation and Logic Programming (PLILP '93), LNCS 714, pages 123-136, Tallinn, August 1993.
5. Pascal André et Jean-Claude Royer. *La modélisation des listes en programmation par objets.* Dans JFLA'94, P. Cointe, C. Queinnec et B. Serpette (éditeurs), Collection Didactique de l'INRIA, pages 259-285, Noirmoutier, Janvier 1994.
6. Erich Gamma, Richard Helm, Ralph Johnson, and John Vlissides. *Design Patterns: Elements of Reusable Object-Oriented Software* Addison Wesley, 1995.
7. Johann Jeuring. *Polytypic pattern matching* Conference Record of FPCA '95, SIGPLAN-SIGARCH-WG2.8 Conference on Functional Programming and Computer Architecture, pages 238–248, San Diego 1995.
8. Andrew Shalit *The Dylan Reference Manual* Addison-Wesley, September 1996
9. Karl J. Lieberherr. *Adaptive Object-Oriented Software: The Demeter Method with Propagation Patterns* PWS Publishing Company, Boston, 1996.

10. James Gosling, Bill Joy, Guy Steele. *The Java Language Specification* The Java Series, Addison Wesley, 1996.
11. Tim Lindholm, Franck Yellin. *The Java Virtual Machine Specification* The Java Series, Addison Wesley, 1996.
12. Martin Odersky and Philip Wadler. *Pizza into Java: Translating theory into practice* 24th ACM Symp. on Principles of Programming Languages, 1997.
13. John Boyland and Giuseppe Castagna *Parasitic Methods: An Implementation of Multi-Methods for Java.* OOPSLA '97 Atlanta, ACM 0-89791-000-0/97 USA 1997.
14. Loïc Correnson, Etienne Duris, Didier Parigot et Gilles Roussel. *Symbolic Composition* JFLA. Come, Italie, feb 1998.
15. Jens Palsberg and C. Barry Jay. *The Essence of the Visitor Pattern* In Proceedings of COMPSAC'98, 22nd Annual International Computer Software and Applications Conference, pages 9-15, Vienna, Austria, August 1998.

C++ Function Object Binders Made Easy

Jaakko Järvi*

Turku Centre for Computer Science
Lemminkäisenkatu 14 A, FIN-20520 Turku, Finland
jaakko.jarvi@cs.utu.fi

Abstract. A novel argument binding mechanism that can be used with STL algorithm invocations is proposed. Without using any adaptors, binding can be applied directly to pointers to nonmember functions, pointers to const and nonconst member functions and STL function objects. The types and number of arguments in the functions to be bound can be practically arbitrary; argument list lengths up to few dozens of elements can be supported.

The unbound arguments are expressed as special placeholders in the argument list; they can appear for any argument position. Hence, binding sites preserve the resemblance to the function prototype of the underlying function, leading to simple and intuitive syntax.

Binding can be applied recursively. This results in a versatile function composition mechanism. The binding mechanism is efficient in the sense that it induces very little or no runtime cost.

1 Introduction

The Standard Template Library (STL) [1], now part of the C++ standard library [2], is a generic container and algorithm library. STL algorithms are function templates operating on container elements via iterators and *function objects*. Any C++ construct which can be called with the ordinary function call syntax is a function object. This includes pointers and references to nonmember functions and static member functions, and class objects with a function call operator. Nonstatic member functions are not function objects, but the STL includes a set of *function adaptors* for creating function objects from member functions.

Adaptable function objects are a subset of function objects. They are class objects which, in addition to the function call operator, define a certain set of types. New adaptable function objects can be created from adaptable function objects using function adaptors. For example, function objects can be projected by binding one argument to a constant. Some STL implementations [3] add function composition objects and other adaptor extensions to the standard. Superficially,

---

* This work has been supported by the Academy of Finland, grant 37178. The author is grateful to Harri Hakonen and Daveed Vandevoorde for their valuable comments on the manuscript of this paper.

K. Czarnecki and U.W. Eisenecker (Eds.): GCSE'99, LNCS 1799, pp. 165–177, 2000.

this seems to provide a great amount of flexibility for adapting functions to satisfy commonly encountered needs. However, a closer look reveals that this is not the case.

The function objects accepted by STL algorithms are either *nullary*[1], *unary* or *binary*. Standard adaptors accept only unary or binary function objects. Consequently, all functions with more than two parameters, and all member functions having more than one parameter, cannot be passed as function objects to STL algorithms. To be able to pass such functions to STL algorithms, explicit function object classes must be written. Often this results in considerable programming overhead—especially when only a simple operation or algorithm needs to be supported. This inconvenience in turn discourages the use of an otherwise compact and intuitive functional programming style, and not infrequently the STL invocation is expanded by hand.

For example, consider the following two functions for computing values of exponential and Gaussian distributions:

```
double exponential(double x, double lambda);
double gaussian(double x, double mean, double standard_deviation);
```

The computation of the values of the exponential distribution for a set of points (in vector x) can be programmed as follows:

```
vector<double> x, result;    double lambda;
        . . .
transform(x.begin(), x.end(), result.begin(),
          bind2nd(ptr_fun(exponential), lambda));
```

The ptr_fun wrapper creates an adaptable binary function object from the exponential function and bind2nd binds the second argument to lambda. The transform algorithm calls this unary function object for each element in x and places the result in result.

We should expect the code for computing Gaussian distribution values to be analogous. However, it turns out that an explicit function object class is needed:

```
vector<double> x, result;    double mean, std;
        . . .
class gaussian_caller {
  double mean_, std_;
public:
  gaussian_caller(double mean, double std) : mean(mean_), std(std_) {};
  double operator()(double x) const { return gaussian(x, mean, std); }
}
transform(x.begin(), x.end(), result.begin(), gaussian_caller(mean, std));
```

This is a consequence of the ptr_fun adaptor only being defined for functions taking fewer than three arguments. To overcome this limitation, it is possible

---

[1] A function with no arguments.

to define more ptr_fun templates to cover functions with longer argument lists. Unfortunately, this is not enough, since the binder adaptors are defined for binary function objects only. Hence, n binders (bind1st–bindNth) would be needed for each argument list of length n. Even with all these $k^2/2$ templates, k being the longest allowed argument list length, the outcome is not particularly intuitive. It becomes difficult to see how the gaussian function is actually called:

```
transform(x.begin(), x.end(), result.begin(),
          bind2nd(bind3rd(ptr_fun(gaussian),std),mean));
```

This article proposes a more general binding mechanism. Instead of specifying the index of the argument to bind, special *placeholder* objects are used in the argument list. For example, the previous example becomes:

```
transform(x.begin(), x.end(), result.begin(), bind(gaussian, free1, mean, std));
```

The role of the placeholder free1 is to specify the varying argument to be left unbound. Other arguments are bound to the values given. The binder invocation syntax preserves a direct resemblance to the original function prototype, revealing instantly which parameters are bound. This mechanism bears similarities to the built-in binding mechanism of the programming language Theta [4], as well as with *agents*, a recently proposed extension to Eiffel [5]. The technique is also related to *currying*, the partial function application mechanism in the functional programming domain.

This article describes the functionality and design of the generic *Binder Library*, BL in the sequel. The BL allows argument binding in the above style for (almost) any C++ function. The library can be downloaded from the address *www.cs.utu.fi/BL*.

2   Binder Library Functionality

Binding is an operation which creates a k-argument function object, a *binder object*, from an n-argument *bindable function object*, such that $k \leq n$. Some of the arguments of the original function object are bound to fixed values, the remaining unbound arguments are called *free*.

2.1   Bindable Function Objects

Binding can be applied to nonmember functions and to static member functions, as well as to pointers to such entities. Pointers to const and nonconst member functions are bindable as well. Other function objects, i.e., class objects with a function call member operator, are bindable if they contain a specific set of member typedefs. For smooth integration with the STL, function objects adhering to the adaptable function object requirements of the STL are bindable. Constructors are not bindable.

The STL has special wrapper templates for creating adaptable function objects from nonmember function (ptr_fun) and member function (mem_fun, mem_fun_ref) pointers. They provide a uniform call syntax for different types of functions: a wrapped n argument member function can be called with $n + 1$ arguments, where the first argument is a reference or pointer to the object whose member is called. In the BL such wrappers are not needed. (A similar mechanism is used but it is hidden from the client.) Hence, binding can be applied directly to pointers to member and nonmember functions.

2.2   Function Argument List Length

As explained in section 1, STL style binders cannot easily be applied to functions with more than two arguments. The binding mechanism using placeholders, in turn, does not have this restriction. However, the implementation requires a set of template definitions for each supported argument list length. This imposes a predefined upper limit for the number of allowed arguments. The limit is not particularly restrictive, since argument lists up to a few dozen elements can be supported—the size of the library grows linearly with the supported argument list length.

2.3   Argument Binding

A binder object is created with a call to an overloaded generic bind function. The first argument in this call is the bindable function object, henceforth called the *target function*. The remaining arguments correspond to the argument list of the target function.

The argument list can contain free arguments, which are specified with placeholder objects. Since there are no STL algorithms accepting function objects with more than two arguments, the BL defines just two placeholder objects. These are called free1 and free2 and refer to the first and second argument of the function call operator in the resulting function object. Depending on which placeholders are used, this function call operator is either nullary, unary or binary.

Consider the following examples, where Op is a four-argument bindable function object callable with arguments of some types A, B, C and D. Further assume that a, b, c and d are variables of these types, respectively.

```
bind(Op, a, b, c, d);
bind(Op, a, free1, c, d);
bind(Op, free1, b, c, free2);
bind(Op, free2, free2, free1, free1);
```

The first line creates a nullary function object fixing all arguments. The second invocation of bind creates a unary function object taking one argument of type B. The third line results in a binary function object with the first argument of type A and second of type D. The last use of bind illustrates how several free arguments can be unified. In this case A and B as well as C and D must be compatible types. The call results in a function object taking two variables. The first is of type C, second of type A. An invocation with, say, c and a, results in a call Op(a, a, c, c) of the original function object. Therefore, a must be implicitly convertible to B and c to D.

To summarise, the argument list can contain an arbitrary number of both types of placeholders, but if it contains one or more free2 placeholders, it must contain at least one free1 placeholder. A violation of this rule leads to a compile time error. This is reasonable, since the omission of free1, while free2 is present, would result in a function object having the second argument but not the first.

2.4   Argument Types

The parameter types of target functions can be arbitrary[2]. However, references to nonconst objects and to objects which cannot be copied require special treatment.

Arguments to bind functions are passed as reference to const. Thus, if a parameter of type reference to nonconst object is bound, the actual argument must be wrapped inside a special object, which creates a temporary const disguise for the argument. This is achieved with a simple function call. For example:

```
void up_and_down(int& i, int& j) { i++; j−−;}
list<int> a_list;    int counter = 0;
    . . .
for_each(a_list.begin(), a_list.end(), bind(up_and_down, ref(counter), free1));
```

The example decrements each element of a_list by one and increments counter by one n times, n being the number of elements in a_list. Since counter is bound to the nonconst reference parameter i, it is wrapped using the generic ref function. Although the parameter corresponding to the free argument is a reference to a nonconst type as well, it need not be wrapped. The wrapping mechanism is safe with respect to constness: a const reference cannot be wrapped.

The original motivation for requiring the use of the ref wrapper was the desire to avoid combinatorial explosion of template definitions. However, it is semantically beneficial as well. As the example above demonstrates, side effects in bound arguments quickly lead to code that is hard to comprehend. Wrapping forces the programmer to explicitly state that an argument is susceptible to side effects.

By default, the binder object stores copies of the bound arguments. If an argument is of a type which cannot be copied, another wrapper is needed: cref instructs the binder object to store a reference to the argument instead of a copy. Array types are exceptions. Although they can not be copied, wrapping is not necessary: a reference to const array type is stored by default. This ensures that string literals can be used directly as bound arguments. The cref wrapper is used similarly to the ref wrapper.

---

[2] Volatile qualified types are not supported in the current version of the BL.

2.5   Member Functions

When binding member functions, the object for which the member function is to be called, is the first argument after the target function. This *object argument* can be a reference or pointer to the object; the BL supports both cases with a uniform interface. Similarly, if the object argument is free, the sequence can contain either pointers or references. For instance:

```
bool A::f(int); A a;
vector<int> ints;    vector<A> refs;    vector<A*> pointers;
        . . .
find_if(ints.begin(), ints.end(), bind(&A::f, a, free1));
find_if(ints.begin(), ints.end(), bind(&A::f, &a, free1));
        . . .
find_if(refs.befin(), refs.end(), bind(&A::f, free1, 1));
find_if(pointers.begin(), pointers.end(), bind(&A::f, free1, 1));
```

The first two calls to find_if are equivalent. In the first one, A::f is called using the .* -operator, whereas in the second the same member is called through the ->* -operator. The latter two find_if invocations both find the first A for which A::f returns true. The .* -operator is used in both cases, the library automatically dereferences object arguments of pointer types.

The call mechanism is safe with respect to constness. A nonconst member function can only be called via a reference or pointer to a nonconst object. This holds whether the object argument is bound or free. Note that the ref wrapper is not needed for the object argument. This is a deliberate design choice. It is understood that the object's state may be changed when a nonconst member function is called—there is no need to explicitly state it.

2.6   Function Composition with Binders

Binding can be applied recursively, thereby enabling function composition. Consider the following example:

```
void canvas::point(double x, double y, colour c);
canvas* canv;    vector<double> x, y;
for_each(x.begin(), x.end(), y.begin(),
         bind(&canvas::point, canv, free1, free2, black));
```

point is a function for drawing points on a canvas using some colour. The for_each invocation draws the points given by the coordinates in vectors x and y. Note that this two-sequence for_each algorithm is not part of the C++ standard library, it is however straightforward to write [6, p. 532].

Now, to represent the y coordinates in logarithmic scale, the standard library function double log(double) can be bound as follows:

```
for_each(x.begin(), x.end(), y.begin(),
         bind(&canvas::point, canv, free1, bind(log, free2), black));
```

The resulting binder object invokes canv–>point(*iter1, log(*iter2), black) at each
iteration, where iter1 and iter2 are the iterators provided by for_each: they point
to the elements of x and y. Hence, a nested binder object defers the target
function call and acts as the inner function in a function decomposition.

The number of nested recursive bindings can be arbitrary. With respect to
placeholders, the argument lists of all nested binders are treated as one concatenated list. This means that the requirements stated at the end of section 2.3
must hold for the concatenated argument list, not for any of the individual lists.

2.7   Nullary Functions

For completeness, nullary functions can be bound as well. This may seem super-
fluous, but with function composition, it is a powerful feature. For instance, the
following code creates a vector of 100 random number pairs:

```
vector<pair<int, int> > pvec;
generate_n(back_inserter(pvec), 100,
          bind(&make_pair<int, int>, bind(rand), bind(rand)));
```

3   Library Design

This section describes the general library design and discusses the key programming techniques used in its implementation. Certain technical details have been
omitted from the presented code for clarity.

To begin with, some parts of the binder library cannot be written generically
with respect to the length of the target function parameter list. A set of templates
are repeated with slight modifications for each supported argument list length.
A great deal of this repetition can be avoided using *tuples.*

3.1   Tuples

The binder library uses a set of templates comprising a tuple abstraction [7].
These template definitions are rather intricate and not presented here. Nevertheless, their usage is intuitive.

The tuple template is basically a generalisation of the pair template in the
standard library. It can be instantiated to contain an arbitrary number (up to
some predefined limit) of elements of arbitrary types. E.g., tuple<int, string, A>
is a valid tuple type, corresponding to a class having three member variables of
types int, string and A. As is the case of standard pairs, tuples can be constructed
directly or using make_tuple (cf. make_pair) helper templates:

```
tuple<int, string, A>(1, string("foo"), A());
make_tuple(1, string("foo"), A());
```

The elements can be accessed in a generic fashion with the syntax get<N>(x), where x is some tuple and N is an integral constant stating the index of the element. The get function template is a *template metaprogram* [8], which resolves a reference to the given element of a tuple at compile time.

The types of the tuple elements can be expressed generically as well: the expression tuple_element<N, Y>::type gives the type of the Nth element of a tuple type Y. This expression is a kind of a *type function* from the constant N and type Y to the element type.

The implementation is based on compile time lists [9,10], which are recursively instantiated templates. Consider, for example, how the pair instantiation pair<int, pair<string, pair<A, nil> > > could represent the preceding tuple. The compile time lists in the BL are structurally similar, but they are not based on the pair template.

3.2 The Bind Function Templates

The bind function templates define the binding interface. They are repeated for each argument list length. For example, the four-argument bind function is defined as:

```
template <class Target, class A1, class A2, class A3>
inline binder<Target, 3, tuple<A1, A2, A3> >
bind(Target fun, const A1& a1, const A2& a2, const A3& a3) {
    return binder<Target, 3, tuple<A1, A2, A3> >
        (fun, make_tuple(a1, a2, a3));
};
```

These functions group the actual arguments to the target function into a tuple and create a binder object. There are two overloaded bind function templates for each argument list length because nonconst target member functions must be handled differently.

3.3 Binder Objects

An important goal in the design of the BL was to minimise the code repetition. This has considerably impacted the structure of the binder classes. Binder objects are instances of class types that fit in the four-level class hierarchy illustrated in Fig. 1. Each level in the hierarchy encapsulates some task orthogonal to the tasks in the other levels. This reduces the amount of partial specialisations, since only one property must be taken into consideration at a time. It also avoids the need to repeat the member and type definitions which are generic with respect to the argument list length.

Target function The base class target_function is a generalisation of the STL templates unary_function and binary_function:

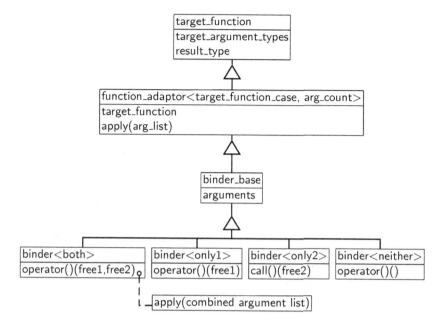

Fig. 1. Binder class hierarchy. The binder template arguments represent the intuitive interpretation of the specialisation criteria. The combined argument list in the call to the inherited apply function refers to the merged argument list where the placeholders have been substituted with the parameters of the function call operator.

```
template<class Args, class Result> struct target_function {
    typedef Args target_argument_types;
    typedef Result result_type;
};
```

It contains type definitions which specify the argument types and the result type of the target function. These type definitions are necessary in various type functions presented below. The same template covers all target function argument lengths, since the template is instantiated with Args substituted by a tuple type.

Function adaptors The purpose of the function adaptors is to unify the function invocation syntax for different types of functions. For each argument length, there are four specialisations of the function_adaptor template. They cover const and nonconst member functions, nonmember functions and other function objects.

Each specialisation contains an appropriately typed data member for storing the target function object and defines the apply function, which provides the uniform call syntax. Another task of the function adaptor templates is to decompose the type of the target function and forward the result and argument types to the target_function template.

For example, the primary template and the function adaptor for pointers to three-argument nonmember functions are defined as follows:

```
template <class Target, int ArgsCount> class function_adaptor;
         ...
template <class A1, class A2, class A3, class Result>
class function_adaptor<Result (*)(A1, A2, A3), 3>
  : public target_function<tuple<A1, A2, A3>, Result> {
  Result (*ptr)(A1, A2, A3);
public:
  explicit function_adaptor(Result (*x)(A1, A2, A3)) : ptr(x) {}
  Result apply(A1 a1, A2 a2, A3 a3) const { return (*ptr)(a1, a2, a3); }
};
```

Binder base The binder_base template has one member variable: the tuple containing the actual arguments of the bind call. This is the sole purpose of binder_base. One generic definition suffices for all argument lengths.

Binders The classes described in the preceding presentation are for internal use in the library, whereas the binder template provides the function call operator to be called from client code. For each target function argument list length, there are four bind specialisations. Which specialisation is instantiated depends on the composition of placeholders in the actuals of the bind invocation. For example, if free1 and free2 are both present, a specialisation defining a binary function call operator is instantiated.

The variables free1 and free2 are defined by the library and are of types placeholder<1> and placeholder<2> respectively. The objects themselves are not important but their types are. These types serve as tags that can be localised from the parameter lists using type functions.

The primary binder template is defined as follows:

```
template<class Target, unsigned int N, class Args,
        bool Free1 = find_free<1, Args>::value,
        bool Free2 = find_free<2, Args>::value>
class binder;
```

The first parameter is the target function type, the second the number of arguments in the target function and the third a tuple type representing the actual argument types deduced in the bind function template. The values of the two bool template parameters Free1 and Free2 indicate whether placeholder<1> or placeholder<2> types are present in Args. These values are deduced with the find_free type functions specified as default arguments.[3]

---

[3] In general, such use of default template arguments is a convenient technique. It can be used to specialise templates with respect to some property (of template arguments) that is not directly usable as a specialisation criterion.

One particular binder specialisation, for the case of a three-argument parameter list including both types of placeholders, is defined as follows:

```
template<class Target, class Args>
class binder<Target, 3, Args, true, true>
  : public binder_base<Target, 3, Args> {
public:
    typedef binder_base<Target, 3, Args> inherited;
    typedef typename inherited::target_argument_types TA;
    typedef typename deduce_free<1, TA, Args>::type first_argument_type;
    typedef typename deduce_free<2, TA, Args>::type second_argument_type;
    explicit binder(const Target& fun, const Args& a) : inherited(fun,a) {}
    typename inherited::result_type operator()
      (first_argument_type a, second_argument_type b) const {
        return apply( choose(get<1>(args), a, b),
                      choose(get<2>(args), a, b),
                      choose(get<3>(args), a, b));
    }
};
```

This covers the case where Free1 and Free2 template parameters both evaluate to true and thus the specialisation defines a binary function call operator. The result type of this function is the result type of the target function, which is defined in the inherited instantiation of target_function.

The argument types are more intricate because they must be deduced by comparing the types in the actual argument type tuple Args and the parameter types of the target function (inherited::target_argument_types). The type function deduce_free<N, Tuple1, Tuple2>::type defines these deductions. Slightly simplified, the first argument type is resolved by locating a placeholder<1> type from Tuple1 and then selecting the corresponding element in Tuple2. The second argument type is deduced in a similar way. These type definitions provide a function call operation with the correct prototype—the correct functionality is achieved with the choose function templates. Their task is to provide the right arguments to the inherited apply function, which invokes the target function. The args tuple contains the actual arguments—some of which are placeholders—of the bind call. Within each argument position, the choose templates select which argument is redirected to apply. For placeholders, a or b is chosen. Otherwise the bound argument, an element of the args tuple, is used.

The choose functions merely return one of their arguments. The types of the arguments determine which argument is returned. The code below shows the definitions of two particular choose function templates.

```
template<class T1, class T2, class T3>
inline T1& choose(T1& a, T2&, T3&) { return a; }

template<class T2, class T3>
inline T2& choose(const placeholder<1>& a, T2& b, T3&) { return b; }
```

3.4   Library Design Summary

In the interest of brevity, several important issues were omitted from the preceding description. The implementation of reference wrapping and of recursive binding was not described. The type functions were not shown in detail. How to achieve compatibility with STL function objects or ensure correct usage of free arguments were not addressed either. Crucial techniques for avoiding reference to reference situations in binder instantiations were not explained. Nevertheless, the library contains solutions to these technical aspects and provides the functionality described in section 2.

The library consists entirely of template definitions. It has a fixed as well as variable size part. The fixed size part is approximately 700 lines of code. The variable size part grows linearly with the maximum argument list length supported for target functions. Each supported argument list length requires approximately 100 lines of code and that code can be generated mechanically.

4   Performance Considerations

An important goal in the design of the STL was to provide a high level of abstraction without sacrificing efficiency [1]. The BL is compatible with this objective. The functions in the BL only redirect arguments and function calls. Every function in the library is inlined so that commercial-grade compilers can eliminate any overhead arising from these redirections.

In various tests performed with the gcc C++ compiler (version 2.95)[11], the performance of STL algorithms using BL style binder objects was nearly identical to algorithms using standard STL binders. Furthermore, compared with code where the algorithms had been expanded manually to call the target functions directly, the performance was essentially the same. However, due to the extensive template instantiations, the compilation of code using the BL requires more resources than corresponding code that does not use the BL.

5   Conclusions

Using STL algorithms and function objects is a step towards adopting a functional programming style. However, only a subset of C++ function objects can be used with STL algorithms. Function object adaptors and binders in the STL provide some means to adapt functions for STL algorithms, but the solution is insufficient.

This article proposed a novel argument binding mechanism and a generic binder library based on this mechanism. Unbound arguments are specified directly in the argument lists as opposed to an index within the function name of the binder. This allows much greater flexibility in bind expressions. Arguments of nonmember functions, const and nonconst member functions, as well as STL function objects can be bound. The types and number of the arguments can be arbitrary.

The binding syntax is very simple and intuitive. In particular, no adaptors (cf. ptr_fun or mem_fun in STL) are required prior to binding. Moreover, the library supports recursive binding, which provides a versatile function composition mechanism.

The library is type safe. Type errors in bind invocations result in compile time errors. As a downside, these error messages are sometimes lengthy and difficult to interpret. The proposed binding mechanism does not induce any performance degradation, it is as efficient as the standard STL binding mechanism.

References

1. Stepanov, A. A., Lee, M.: The Standard Template Library. Hewlett-Packard Laboratories Technical Report HPL-94-34(R.1) (1994) www.hpl.hp.com/techreports.
2. International Standard, Programming Languages – C++. ISO/IEC:14882 (1998).
3. The SGI Standard Template Library. Silicon Graphics Computer Systems Inc. www.sgi.com/Technology/STL.
4. Liskov, B., Curtis, D., Day, M., Ghemawat S., Gruber R., Johnson, P., Myers A. C.: Theta Reference Manual, Preliminary version. Programming Methodology Group Memo 88 1995, MIT Lab. for Computer Science www.pmg.lcs.mit.edu/Theta.html.
5. Agents, iterators and introspection. Interactive Software Engineering Inc. Technology paper www.eiffel.com.
6. Stroustrup, B.: The C++ Programming Language - Third Edition. Addison-Wesley, Reading, Massachusetts 1997.
7. Järvi J.: Tuples and multiple return values in C++. submitted for publication, see TUCS Technical Report 249 (1999) www.tucs.fi/publications.
8. Veldhuizen, T.: Using C++ Template Metaprograms. C++ Report **7** (1995) 36–43.
9. Järvi J.: Compile Time Recursive Objects in C++. Proceedings of the TOOLS 27 conference (Beijing Sept. 1998) 66–77. IEEE Computer Society Press.
10. Czarnecki, K.: Generative Programming: Principles and Techniques of Software Engineering Based on Automated Configuration and Fragment-Based Component Models. Ph.D. Thesis, Technische Universität Ilmenau, Germany 1998.
11. The GNU Compiler Collection. www.gnu.org/software/gcc/gcc.html.

Customizable Domain Analysis

Joachim Bayer, Dirk Muthig, Tanya Widen

Fraunhofer Institute for Experimental Software Engineering (IESE),
Sauerwiesen 6, D-67661 Kaiserslautern, Germany
+49 (0) 6301 707 251   {bayer, muthig, widen}@iese.fhg.de

Abstract. Generative and Component-Based Software Engineering are approaches to reuse. Within both approaches the scope of reuse can vary between general purpose and application specific. We argue for scoping the reusable assets based on a product line.

Domain analysis methods provide processes for determining the common and varying requirements for a product line. However, we experienced that existing methods have problems concerning applicability and instantiation support. Therefore, we have developed the Customizable Domain Analysis (CDA) method.

CDA is customizable to the project context where it will be applied. This ensures that the method and workproducts used for modeling are appropriate for the specific needs. CDA also provides full instantiation support for specifying systems in the product line.

Keywords: Domain Analysis, Domain Engineering, Product Line Software Engineering

1   Introduction

Generative and Component-Based Software Engineering are approaches to make software engineering more efficient through reuse.

Generative techniques require developing a high level language for specifying systems that is then used to generate the individual products. The more specific the language, the tighter it fits to the problems being solved (e.g., domain specific languages). Yet, one language can only be used for a particular class of problems. The more general the language, the more applicable it is (e.g., the object-oriented language Java or the functional language Haskel). The trade-off is that the language may contain much that is not needed in a particular situation. Additionally, it does not necessarily contain specifics for the problem (e.g., concepts or terminology). Therefore, general languages are more difficult to use than specialized languages.

Component-Based Software Engineering approaches, on the other hand, advocate building reusable components that can be plugged together to create new systems. The trade-off here is again generality versus specialization. General components can be used in many applications, but may be much more than needed. Specific components, on the other hand, are appropriate for the situation, but then there may be many specific components that you have to search through to find the one that exactly meets your needs, or the components may need to be adapted to the particular situation.

K. Czarnecki and U.W. Eisenecker (Eds.): GCSE'99, LNCS 1799, pp. 178–194, 2000.
© Springer-Verlag Berlin Heidelberg 2000

Product line engineering is an approach to reuse that can be used as both the generative approach and the component-based approach to reuse. It is a middle ground between specific assets (one time use) and general assets (applicable anywhere). The idea is to define a product line, which captures the intended scope of reuse. The products included in a product line are determined to have sufficiently common characteristics to make it more efficient to study the commonalities and variabilities once for all products of the product line and to build reusable assets, than to study and build all the products separately. Product line engineering approaches define how to leverage the commonalities and create reusable assets that increase the efficiency of developing the products.

Domain analysis is one part of product line engineering. Domain analysis methods provide processes for eliciting and structuring the requirements of a domain, or product line. The results are captured in a domain model. A domain model must capture both the common characteristics of the products and their variations. The domain model is the basis for creating other reusable assets like a domain specific language or a component-based architecture.

Many domain analysis methods have been proposed. However, we have identified two major problems in trying to use them: applicability and instantiation support.

For a method to be applicable, it must be appropriate and it must provide enough guidance so that it can be carried out. As in other areas of software development, the context for each domain analysis application varies, and methods that are appropriate in one context will not be in others. This fact is especially important for domain analysis because of the compound effects of inappropriate models over multiple products. Therefore, a generally applicable domain analysis method must be customizable to the context of the application.

Unfortunately, most existing domain analysis methods do not provide customization capabilities, and those that do, do not provide adequate support for customizing it and using the results.

Another requirement for domain analysis methods that is often not even addressed is the instantiation of the domain model for application development. Instantiating the domain model provides the requirements for the single system to be developed. Some approaches support making decisions for each variability in the domain model during instantiation. However, additional instantiation support is necessary because variations in the product line are related and selecting one alternative often has consequences on which other alternatives can be chosen during instantiation. These relations should be determined during domain analysis.

1.1   Approach and Context

In this paper, the Customizable Domain Analysis (CDA) method is presented. CDA is the domain analysis component of the PuLSE[TM] (Product Line Software Engineering)[1] methodology [4]. An overview of PuLSE is given in Section 2.

---

1. PuLSE is a registered trademark of the Fraunhofer Institute for Experimental Software Engineering

PuLSE-CDA was developed to be adaptable to the project needs, so that the most appropriate models can be used. In addition, the method provides enough guidance to make it can systematically applicable. Finally, the products of PuLSE-CDA support the processes that will use them, namely architecture development and instantiation.

The PuLSE-CDA method has been developed based on a study of existing domain analysis methods, which helped us determine the main variation points that customization will be based on. Additionally our experience trying to apply some of these methods provided insight into which context factors most affect customization of domain analysis.

PuLSE-CDA's support for instantiation is an expansion of the decision model from Synthesis [16]. The decision model concept is expanded with constraints/relationships to model the dependencies among variabilities.

1.2   Outline

The remainder of this paper is structured as follows: Section 2 provides an overview of the PuLSE approach. Section 3 presents the PuLSE-CDA method in detail and explains the domain decision model and customization of the method. Section 4 follows with an analysis of the PuLSE-CDA approach based on our experience so far. Section 6 discusses the related work. Section 6 concludes the paper.

2   PuLSE

PuLSE is a method for enabling the conception and deployment of software product lines within a large variety of enterprise contexts. This is achieved via a product-centric focus throughout its phases, customizability of its components, an incremental introduction capability, a maturity scale for structured evolution, and adaptions to a few main product development situations.

Figure Figure 1 shows an overview of PuLSE.

PuLSE is centered around three main elements: the deployment phases, the technical components, and the support components.

The *deployment phases* are logical stages of the product line life cycle. They describe activities performed to set up, use, and evolve product lines. The deployment phases are:

- PuLSE initialization: PuLSE is customized to the context of its application. The principle dimensions of adaption are the nature of the domain, the project structure, the organizational context, and the reuse aims.
- Product line infrastructure construction: The product line infrastructure is set up. This is done by scoping, modeling, and architecting the product line.
- Product line infrastructure usage: The product line infrastructure is used to create a single product line member. This is done by instantiating the product line model and architecture.

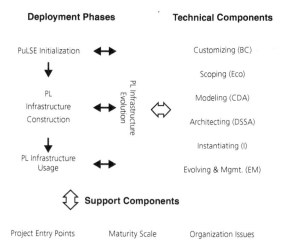

Figure 1. PuLSE Overview

- Product line infrastructure evolution: Concepts within the domain or other requirements on the product line may change over time. The evolution of the product line is handled in this phase.

The *technical components* provide the technical know-how needed to operationalize the product line development. They are used throughout the deployment phases. The technical components are:

- Baselining and Customization (PuLSE-BC): Baseline the enterprise and customize PuLSE. The result is an instance of PuLSE — that is instances of the other technical components — tailored to the specific application context.

- Economic scoping (PuLSE-Eco): Identify, describe, and bound the product line. This is done by determining the products that constitute the product line.

- Customizable Domain Analysis (PuLSE-CDA): Elicit the requirements for a domain and document them in a domain model (a.k.a. product line model).

- Domain Specific Software Architecture development (PuLSE-DSSA): Develop a reference (or domain specific) architecture based on the product line model.

- Instantiation (PuLSE-I): Specify, construct and validate one member of the product line. This encompasses the instantiation of the product line model and the reference architecture, the creation and/or reuse of assets that constitute the instance, and the validation of the resulting product.

- Evolution and Management (PuLSE-EM): Guide and support the application of PuLSE throughout the deployment phases initialization, construction, usage, and evolution.

The *support components* are guidelines that support the other components. They are:

- Project entry points: Project entry points are guidelines to customize PuLSE for a set of standard situations. For example, in reengineering driven PuLSE projects, legacy assets are a major source of information and guidelines on how to integrate them are given in the respective entry point.

- Maturity scale: This scale provides an integration and evolution path for product line adoption using PuLSE. The levels on the scale are: initial, full, controlled, and optimizing.

- Organization issues: For PuLSE to be most effective, an organization structure has to be set up and maintained that supports the development and management of product lines. Guidelines on how to do that are given here.

3   PuLSE-CDA

The purpose of PuLSE-CDA is to develop a domain — or product line — model that captures the requirements of a product line, and to enable the instantiation of this product line model for single systems that are members of the product line. In this section, different aspects of PuLSE-CDA are described. Section 3.1 starts with a high level process description.

A domain model consists of multiple workproducts that capture different views of a domain. Each view focuses on particular information types and relations among them. In the workproducts, common and distinguishing aspects of the domain are modeled. Workproducts are presented in more detail in section 3.2.

Each workproduct that captures variability has a decision model. Variability and decision models are discussed in section 3.3.

It is not possible to consider all possible future requirements on a product line. Therefore, evolution of the reusable assets and products that are built from them is a key concern. Section 3.4 describes evolutionary aspects for PuLSE-CDA.

The workproducts that are used to capture information in different domains vary. Additionally, processes to capture and document the information in the different workproducts vary. These customization aspects of PuLSE-CDA are discussed in section 3.5.

Due to the amount of information that makes up a domain model and the interrelations among the information, domain analysis requires tool support. In section 3.6, Diversity/CDA, a tool to support PuLSE-CDA is presented.

3.1   Process Description

In this section the PuLSE-CDA process is described. The process is illustrated in Figure Figure 2. It consists of three steps: refine scope definition, elicit raw domain knowledge, and model domain knowledge. These are described below.

The inputs to PuLSE-CDA are the product characteristics information and scope definition from PuLSE-Eco. The scope definition identifies the range of characteristics that systems in the product line cover. The characteristics themselves are listed and described in the product characteristics information. These inputs describe the contents of the product line.

In the first step of PuLSE-CDA, *refine scope definition*, the boundary of the product line is determined. Based on the scope definition that is focused on the contents of the

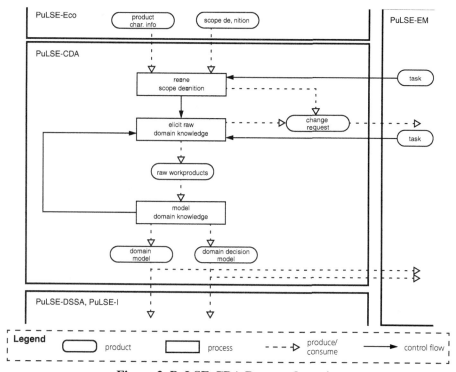

Figure 2. PuLSE-CDA Process Overview

product line, the boundary definition is created that focuses on the interfaces of the product line. Both views are used in the following process steps; the scope definition provides an initial structure for the domain information and the boundary definition limits the area to be analyzed.

In the second process step, *elicit raw domain knowledge*, information is gathered from various sources. Sources may include books and other literature, human sources like domain experts, expected system users, and application engineers, or existing systems.

At this point the information is considered raw, because it is not necessarily well structured. Information may describe single systems separately, or it may be at the wrong level of abstraction and detail. The raw information is captured explicitly in the workproducts.

As information is elicited and captured in the domain model workproducts, links are created to the source of the respective information. This supports evolution and maintenance.

In the final step of PuLSE-CDA, *model domain knowledge*, the elicited knowledge is modeled. This is done using the same workproducts that were used to capture the knowledge in the elicitation step.

The outputs of this step are the domain model — composed of the generic work-products — which describe the product line as a whole as opposed to single systems, and the domain decision model, which is used to extract single system descriptions from the generic workproducts.

There are five interrelated activities that are performed to model domain knowledge:

- Abstraction: Higher level models are built to connect low level models that may have been produced during elicitation. Within this activity, the completeness and consistency of the models is also checked.
- Restructuring: Existing abstractions are replaced with better ones (i.e., simpler, clearer, or more appropriate ones) that capture the same information.
- Building generic models: The systems in the product line are integrated through the explicit modeling of variability.
- Consolidation of variability: On top of the different decision models for the different workproducts, a domain decision model is built that combines them.
- Providing traceability: Links are established that explicitly model interrelationships among information in the different workproducts.

Elicitation and modeling are tightly coupled and there is no best way to combine them. Information may be directly elicited and modeled at the same time. On the other hand, during modeling the elicitation step can be revisited when information is not yet complete or considered inconsistent.

The outputs of PuLSE-CDA — the domain model and the domain decision model — are used in PuLSE-DSSA to guide the reference architecture construction and in PuLSE-I to create product specifications for the product line members. Additionally, the product line model can be used to introduce people to the product line.

Whenever, during the scope refinement or elicitation steps, the scope definition is determined to be insufficient, a change request is sent to PuLSE-EM that handles such requests and distributes them to the responsible PuLSE components.

On the other hand, the product line model can be subject to change. The scope of the product line or the product characteristics can change over time. Another reason for changes is inadequately or insufficiently modeled workproducts that have to be improved. In these cases tasks are passed from PuLSE-EM to PuLSE-CDA.

The evolution aspects of PuLSE-CDA are described in more detail in section 3.4.

3.2   Domain Model

The domain model, a set of workproducts, captures the requirements for all systems of a product line. There are two types of requirements: requirements that are common to all systems of the product line (commonalities), and requirements that vary from system to system (variabilities).

Commonalities are not different from requirements for a particular single system except that they hold for all members of a product family. Variabilities are requirements that may differ between members of the product family. There are three types of varying requirements:

- Optional requirements: requirements that do hold for a particular system or do not hold,

- Alternative requirements: a set of requirements of which only one or a subset holds for a particular system, and

- Range requirements: requirements that specify the potential range for a numerical value, which is supported by the domain model, instead of the specific value as required by a single system.

One goal of PuLSE-CDA is to be customizable to different environments (see section 3.5) and to minimize the necessary changes while introducing the product line approach. From a domain model point of view, this means that the workproducts to document requirements for the product line should be as similar as possible to the already established workproducts that have been used for documenting requirements for single systems.

To adopt the established workproducts for the product line approach, it must be decided which workproducts are supposed to capture variabilities and which workproducts capture only information that is valid independent of the particular instance. Additionally, there are workproducts that capture general domain information (e. g., a glossary to define domain-specific terms), but only parts of them are relevant for particular instances (e. g., only the terms that are really used in the instantiated workproducts are integrated into the domain model instance). Therefore, and to document constraints and relationships among information of the domain model, a means to link elements of (different) workproducts must be available.

Because there is no significant difference between commonalities and specific system requirements, the notations for documenting the latter can be adopted to document commonalities. But most of the notations used in practice do not consider variabilities. Hence, notations of generic workproducts (i. e., instantiatable workproducts that capture variant requirements) must be extended in a natural way. This is done by introducing meta elements that indicate points of variation and enable the instantiation of the workproducts.

For each generic workproduct and for each of the three types of variant requirements, meta elements are defined and integrated. They consist of three parts.

- The representation part defines the notation, that is the syntactic integration of variabilities into a workproduct. This includes the definition of representations within the instantiated workproduct dependent on the context of the particular product line instance.

- The transformation logic maps each possible instantiation of a variability to a useful and understandable representation. A simple example is the omission of a textual optional requirement when it is not valid for an instance.

- The decision model interface connects the meta element with a simple decision in the domain decision model. It controls the transformation logic with respect to the current resolution of the connected simple decision.

3.3   Domain Decision Model

The variabilities are connected to decisions that, when completely resolved, specify (via instantiating the domain model) a particular system, a member of the product line. The decisions are at different levels of abstraction and are hierarchically structured based on constraints among them. This decision hierarchy is the domain decision model. There are two types of constraints: exclusion and (partial) resolution.

Exclusion means that the resolution of a decision becomes irrelevant for the specification of a particular system because another decision has been resolved. For example, decisions concerning variabilities within the specification of an optional requirement are excluded when the option is not chosen.

(Partial) resolution means that the number of possible resolutions for a particular decision is reduced because of the resolution of another decision. When only one possible resolution is left, the constrained decision is also resolved.

There are different types of decisions. For each type of variability described in section 3.2, there exists an analogous decision type. A decision can constrain other decisions independent of its own and the other types. Its possible resolutions are mapped by constraints concerning the possible resolution sets of the constrained decisions.

At the lowest level of the decision hierarchy, there are simple decisions. Each simple decision is directly connected to a meta element, which is part of a domain model workproduct.

A single workproduct is instantiated when all simple decisions that correspond to one of the workproduct's meta elements are resolved. The decision hierarchy reduces the number of decisions that must be made and supports the intellectual control of constraints and dependencies.

The subhierarchy of decisions that is built only upon simple decisions of one workproduct (i. e., no decision concerning a different workproduct is constrained) is called the workproduct decision model. Decisions at the next higher level of abstraction with respect to the top level of a workproduct decision model consolidate variabilities modeled in different workproducts.

The domain model must be completely instantiated to specify a particular system. Therefore, all simple decisions that are not excluded must be resolved. The instance of the domain model is generated by passing resolution by resolution of simple decisions to the connected meta element, which instantiates its corresponding part of the domain model.

3.4   Evolution

PuLSE-CDA expects that the domain model will never be stable. This is founded on a basic idea of PuLSE to scope the domain dependent on products planned to be developed. Additional systems in the future will probably require a scope expansion. Therefore, PuLSE-CDA is designed for handling changes of the scope, as well as of the model. In general, there are three cases in which an evolution of the domain model is necessary:

- Workproducts of the domain model are modeled inadequately or insufficiently, so that it is not possible to construct an acceptable reference architecture. Therefore, PuLSE-DSSA, the technical component for constructing the reference architecture, sends a change request to the product line management. The management, PuLSE-EM, forwards the request as well-defined task to PuLSE-CDA.

- During the lifetime of a product line, the domain is continuously observed to recognize changes and new concepts. This is necessary to also cover anticipated requirements of potential future systems by the product line. The product line management decides whether observed changes and/or new concepts are integrated into the product line. In the case of integration, the scope definition is changed first. Then, the domain model and the domain decision model must be adapted accordingly.

- During the development of systems in the domain (i. e., members of the product line), requirements often arise that are not in the scope of the product line. Hence, the scope of the product line must be either expanded or system-specific assets must be developed.

In all cases, an effective and efficient identification of the domain model parts that are affected by the planned changes is required. For that purpose, traceability within the domain model is needed. First, information units are chosen that are affected by a change. This should be easily possible because the workproducts are customized for capturing concepts of the domain. Following the links starting at the chosen information units, related and hence further affected parts of the domain model can be identified. All affected parts of the domain model are modified according to the change.

One benefit of the product line approach is the idea that all members of the product line are based on a single set of assets. Thereby, the maintenance effort is reduced to this single asset base. Hence, existing products must always follow the evolution of the asset base. This means, existing products must be 'redeveloped' after changing the product line models when necessary. This is done by instantiating the changed domain model while reusing the existing resolution of the domain decision model.

The decisions abstract, as far as possible, from the concrete assets, which are the workproducts of the domain model. This means, the resolution of the domain decision model must be adapted only with respect to simple decisions that are connected to changed workproduct parts, higher level decisions related to changed decisions, as well as decisions that constrain changed decisions. Hence, necessary adaptations can be easily localized and performed. The domain model, the domain decision model, and all specifications of existing products have been adapted to the required evolution.

3.5 Customization

Customization of PuLSE-CDA to the context where it will be applied ensures that the process and products are appropriate. PuLSE-BC defines the customization process used for tailoring the other technical components. Through tailoring the technical components, a customized version of the construction, usage, and evolution phases of PuLSE is created.

The customization process is built upon variation points identified for each technical component. These points are called customization decisions.

Each customization decision has a number of factors that impact its resolution. Factors contain information about the context of application that influence the resolution of a decision. There are two types of factors: customization factors and intermediate decisions.

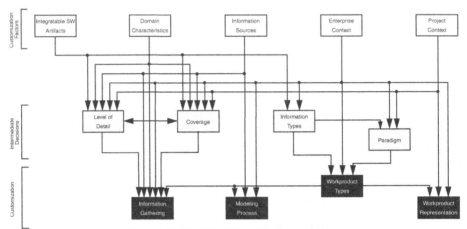

Figure 3. PuLSE-CDA Decision Graph

Customization factors define information about the context that can be directly collected from the enterprise. Intermediate decisions, on the other hand, define information about the context that cannot be collected directly. Rather, they are either (partially) based on subjective judgements or they are influenced by other factors, or both.

Each customization factor, intermediate decision, and customization decision has guidelines associated with it that provides strategies for collecting the information or resolving the decisions.

The goal of a PuLSE-BC application is the derivation of appropriate values for the different decisions and the integration of the adapted components into a coherent process for product line engineering. The assignment of values to the decisions is done using decision graphs and the strategies mentioned above. Figure 3 shows the (simplified) decision graph for PuLSE-CDA. Decision graphs relate the customization decisions that have to be resolved in order to customize a technical component to the customization factors that influence those decisions.

To simplify information gathering, the customization factors are categorized into:

- Domain characteristics: Factors that relate to the domain itself and are independent of implementation aspects.
- For PuLSE-CDA these are: complexity, size, maturity, and stability of the domain, as well as the business area abstractions and the predominant application types.
- Information sources: Factors that relate to the availability of information about the domain.
- For PuLSE-CDA these are: Available books, papers, and standards, as well as accessible users, domain experts, and application engineers.
- Implementation characteristics: Factors that influence implementations in the domain.
- These factors do not have an impact on PuLSE-CDA.

- Integratable software artifacts: Factors that relate to artifacts that can be integrated in a new product line.
- For PuLSE-CDA these are existing systems.
- Project context: Factors relating to the specific project that is planned.
- For PuLSE-CDA these are: resources (in terms of money, time, and personnel), project skills, and the reusable assets that will be produced.
- Enterprise context: Factors relating to the enterprise applying PuLSE.
- For PuLSE-CDA these are: business objectives, enterprise skills, and available tool support.

PuLSE-CDA is customized through the detailed processes for gathering and modeling domain information and through the workproducts that make up a domain model for a project.

The customization of the process is concerned with who will do the activities and how, for example, through group discussions, interviews, literature searches, etc. This is split into two customization decisions: the process for the information gathering, and the process for modeling.

The customization of the products is split into two decisions: the workproduct types and the workproduct representations. The workproduct type captures which information and relations must be modeled. The representation decision defines the notations used to express the information and relations of the workproduct.

3.6   Tool Support: DIVERSITY/CDA

Domain modeling is a complex task for several reasons. During system analysis and modeling for single systems, a large set of complex and interrelated information from various sources has to be managed. In addition to this, domain analysts and modelers deal with multiple systems at once, which requires modeling both commonalities and variations among the systems. Tool support is essential to manage these complexities.

Several types of tool support exist that could be considered promising to automate domain analysis. General purpose analysis and design tools, and requirements engineering tools capture models at the same level of abstraction as a domain model. Another approach is to use specialized analysis tools that are available for different domains. As a third possibility, there are some domain analysis tools available, such as DARE [9], DOMAIN [11], or DOME [8].

Investigating these different types, we determined that there is not one tool that covers all of the required aspects: adaptation to different project situations, automated instantiation, support for intellectual control, and incorporation of existing information. Therefore, we created DIVERSITY/CDA (Domain and Variant Engineering Supporting Technology for the Customizable Domain Analysis) [5].

DIVERSITY/CDA provides support for — beside modeling in general — the four key concepts: customization to the target environment, instantiation of the models to generate specifications of particular applications, traceability among data in the domain model to support intellectual control, and integration of external information.

DIVERSITY/CDA supports *customization* (see Section 3.5) only through the work-products provided in a DIVERSITY/CDA version for a project. Customization of the process is actually not needed because process guidance is not integrated yet. For each project, the workproducts are determined through applying PuLSE-BC, and then created, adapted, or reused from the workproduct library for integration in the particular tool version. To facilitate customization, DIVERSITY/CDA has been developed as a product line itself. Its general capabilities — for example, database access, searching, and linking — have been separated from the workproducts. The interface between this general part and the workproducts is defined in such a way that different workproducts and combinations of workproducts can be plugged in to create efficiently customized versions of DIVERSITY/CDA for different projects.

To construct applications based on the domain model, DIVERSITY/CDA supports the construction of the domain decision model, as well as the *instantiation* of the domain model. The modeling views, which are part of DIVERSITY/CDA, integrate the workproduct-specific meta elements (see also section 3.2). The meta elements directly correspond to the set of simple decisions, the initial domain decision model (see also section 3.3). In the construction view for the domain decision model, a set of decisions is selected and a new decision is created. The new decision and its possible resolutions must be described. For each resolution, the constraints with respect to the resolutions of all selected decisions must be defined. Using DIVERSITY/CDA, the support for the instantiation of the domain model is separated from the construction support. The clear separation emphasizes the different product line phases, construction (especially PuLSE-CDA) and usage of the product line (i. e., PuLSE-I). The whole instantiation process is guided and interactive. It is guided by generating a useful sequence of decisions whose resolution completely instantiates the whole domain model. It is interactive by updating the representation of the instantiated domain model immediately after each resolution. The user can thus see the impacts of his/her resolution on the final instantiation.

The information captured in the different workproducts is interrelated. To explicitly capture these interrelations and exploit them, DIVERSITY/CDA has a linking mechanism. By providing a means to relate information in a domain model, links support *traceability* within the domain model. A link in DIVERSITY/CDA is a directed, typed reference from one workproduct element to another one. For each workproduct, it is defined which workproduct element (or part) can be linked. The reverse direction of a link can be navigated, too. For some links, the reverse direction expresses the same relation as the initial link, for others it is a reverse relation. Based on the workproducts present, DIVERSITY/CDA provides an initial, extensible set of link types, for example, 'Uses'/ 'Used by' (i. e., the use of a concept is described somewhere else) or 'Defines'/'Defined in' (i. e., a term is defined in a glossary entry). Through links, a network of relations is created connecting the information in a domain model. This network can be browsed using link inspectors.

To incorporate information that is not modeled with DIVERSITY/CDA in a domain model, we introduced *external workproducts*. There are basically three purposes of external workproducts: reuse of information from an already established application engineering process, linking information that is related but not part of the domain model

(e. g., PuLSE-Eco spreadsheets), and usage of external modeling tools for workproducts that are not supported by DIVERSITY/CDA (yet). An external workproduct is integrated by creating a representation of its internal structure within DIVERSITY/CDA using tags. These tags are linked to related parts of the domain model using the link mechanism described above and refer to positions in the external document. Hence, connections between domain model elements and positions in external documents can be established.

4 Analysis

The motivation for developing PuLSE-CDA was due to two problems we experienced with existing domain analysis methods: applicability and instantiation support.

The problem of applicability is supported through systematic customization of PuLSE-CDA to the context where it will be applied. Through PuLSE-BC, the framework for customization is supplied. The specifics for PuLSE-CDA are captured in the decision graph and strategies that support resolving the decisions. These specifics were developed based on our experience applying domain analysis and from literature. These will evolve over time with more experience.

The goal of PuLSE-CDA is not to necessarily create new concepts and models for domain analysis, but also to reuse existing models through defining what information models really capture and which models are needed depending on the context.

We have had success working with PuLSE-CDA on different projects. From these projects, we have developed workproducts for business process workflows, business rules, rationales, commonalities and variabilities, issues, glossaries, and to do lists. For a current project we are developing workproducts for variability extended UML diagrams.

All of these workproducts can potentially be reused in other projects if they are determined to be appropriate.

Instantiation support is handled with the domain decision model. Capturing the dependencies among variabilities and creating higher level decisions guides the instantiation and reduces the amount of decisions to be resolved. In addition, it ensures that single systems specifications are valid with respect to the constraints. Single system specifications are generated from a resolved domain decision model.

This generation can be expanded to support generation of an instantiated architecture as well. PuLSE-DSSA, the architecture development component of PuLSE, also provides a decision model for instantiating the architecture. This expanded instantiation can be achieved through mapping the domain decision model to the architecture decision model.

In addition to the customization and instantiation aspects of PuLSE-CDA, evolutionary aspects and tool support have been described above. These aspects are important for the practical application of PuLSE-CDA.

The requirements for the product line will evolve over time, therefore it is imperative to plan for this. Appropriate models and capturing relations explicitly increase understandability and traceability throughout the domain model. In addition, external links from sources of information and to other reusable assets support the evolution of the product line.

Tool support is essential for keeping intellectual control of the large amount and complexity of information involved. Therefore, Diversity/CDA has been developed. It makes applying PuLSE-CDA practical.

5 Related Work

In this section work related to PuLSE in general, PuLSE-CDA, customization (PuLSE-BC), and the PuLSE-CDA domain decision model is presented.

Domain engineering methods cover most of the same aspects as PuLSE. However, their focus is different, they lack customizability and they are complex to deploy. Domain engineering methods include Model-Based Software Engineering (MBSE) [14], Organizational Domain Modeling (ODM) [17], Synthesis [16], the Domain-Specific Software Architecture (DSSA) program [18], and the Evolutionary Domain Life-Cycle (EDLC) [10].

Domain analysis, requirements engineering, and knowledge engineering are areas that are related to the PuLSE-CDA component. There are many domain analysis methods, including those provided by each of the domain engineering methods mentioned above. Most stem from the work of Arango and Prieto-Diaz [1]. However, the models are either too specific to be applied in the different contexts of domain engineering projects, or they are meant to be tailorable, but lack support for this. CDA aims to improve upon these methods by providing a flexible domain analysis approach with adequate support. Requirements engineering has also provided input into the modeling workproducts, such as use-cases or state transition diagrams [13]. However, these models only support modeling of single systems; no variability modeling is provided.

The goal of PuLSE-CDA is not to develop new modeling technology per se, but to determine which models work best in which contexts and also to expand models developed for capturing single systems with variability capabilities for modeling families of systems.

The PuLSE-BC process for baselining and customization is grounded in work done on the CMM [12], the Reuse Adoption Guidebook [15], and Experience Factory packages [3]. This work is used in the BC component to support the baselining of an enterprise and customizing, or packaging, an appropriate process for the situation.

Decision models for supporting the instantiation of domain models do appear in Synthesis and in the Commonality Analysis [16,2]. The PuLSE-CDA domain decision model is based on this work, but extended with higher level decisions, relations among decisions, and variability from other workproducts (both Synthesis and the Commonality Analysis focus on creating models for a specific workproduct type known as Commonalities and Variabilities).

6 Conclusion

In this paper we presented PuLSE-CDA, a method to determine and capture the common and varying requirements for a product line of systems. PuLSE-CDA is an improvement over existing domain analysis methods because it is customizable to the context in which it will be applied and because it provides full instantiation support.

PuLSE-CDA can be used for both generative and component-based software engineering approaches, that is, the models created in PuLSE-CDA can support architecture and component development as well as language design.

Acknowledgements

The authors would like to thank all the other contributors to PuLSE: Oliver Flege, Cristina Gacek, Peter Knauber, Roland Laqua, and Klaus Schmid.

References

[1]   Arango, G. and Prieto-Diaz, R. (eds.) Domain Analysis Concepts and Research Directions. In *Domain Analysis and Software Systems Modeling*, pp. 9-31, IEEE Computer Society Press, 1991.

[2]   Ardis, M. and Weiss, D. Defining Families: The Commonality Analysis. *Proceedings of the Nineteenth International Conference on Software Engineering*, pp. 649-650, IEEE Computer Society Press, May 1997.

[3]   Basili, V., Caldiera, G., and Rombach, D. Experience Factory. *Encyclopedia of Software Engineering Volume 1:*469-476, Marciniak, J. ed. John Wiley & Sons, 1994.

[4]   Bayer, J., Flege, O., Knauber, P., Laqua, R., Muthig, D., Schmid, K., Widen, T., DeBaud, J.M. PuLSE: A methodology to develop software product lines.   In *Symposium on Software Reusability*, May 1999.

[5]   Bayer, J., Muthig, D., and Widen, T. Support for Domain and Variant Engineering: Diversity/CDA. *Submitted for publication*, May 1999.

[6]   DeBaud, J.M., Flege, O., and Knauber, P. PuLSE-DSSA: A Method for the Development of Software Reference Architectures. *In Proceedings of the 3rd International Software Architecture Workshop*, November 1998.

[7]   DeBaud, J.M. and Schmid, K. A Systematic Approach to Derive the scope of Software Product Lines. I*n Proceedings of the 20th International Conference on Software Engineering*, pp. 34-43, IEEE Computer Society Press, 1999

[8]   Domain modeling environment. The official web site. http://www.htc.honeywell.com/dome/. April 1999.

[9]   Frakes, B., Prieto-Diaz, R., and Fox, C. DARE: Domain Analysis and Reuse Environment. In *7th Annual Workshop on Software Reuse*, 1995.

[10]   Gomaa, H., Kerschberg, L., Sugumaran, V., Bosch, C., Tavakoli, I. and O'Hara. L. A knowledge-based software engineering environment for reusable software requirements and architectures. *Automated Software Engineering, 3(3,4)*, pp. 285–307, August 1996.

[11]   Higgins, J., Tracz, W., and Newton, E. Domain (DOmain Model All Integrated) User Guide. Technical Report ADAGE-LOR-94-06A, Loral Federal Systems, September 1994.

[12]   Paulk, M., Curtis, B., Chrissis, M., and Weber, C. Capability Maturity Model for Software (Version 1.1). *Technical Report CMU/SEI-93-TR-024*, February 1993.

[13]   Potts, C., Takahashi, K., and Anton, A. Inquiry-Based Requirements Analysis.

IEEE Software, pp. 21-32, March 1994

[14] Software Engineering Institute, Model-Based Software Engineering. http://www.sei.cmu.edu/technology/mbse/is.html, April 25, 1998.

[15] Software Productivity Consortium Services Corporation. Reuse Adoption Guidebook, Version 02.00.05, November 1993.

[16] Software Productivity Consortium. Reuse-Driven Software Processes Guidebook, Version 02.00.03. *Technical Report SPC-92019-CMC*, Software Productivity Consortium, November 1993.

[17] Software Technology for Adaptable Reliable Systems. Organization Domain Modeling (ODM) Guidebook, Version 2.0. *Unisys STARS Technical Report STARS-VC-A025/001/00*, Reston VA, June 1996.

[18] Tracz, W. and Coglianese, L. Domain-Specific Software Architecture Engineering Process Guidelines, *Technical Report ADAGE-IBM-92-02*, Loral Federal Systems, 1992.

A Grey-Box Approach to Component Composition

Hans de Bruin

Vrije Universiteit, Amsterdam, The Netherlands
hansdb@cs.vu.nl

Abstract. Despite the obvious advantages of reuse implied by component technology, component based development has not taken off yet. Problems that inhibit general reuse include incomplete component contracts and (undocumented) dependencies of a component on the environment, which makes it hard to assess whether a component will behave in a particular setting as expected. In principle, a black-box approach to component deployment should be favored. In practice, however, we require information that cannot be described solely in terms of externally visible properties of components. For instance, non-functional properties (e.g., space and time requirements), environmental dependencies, and variation points (e.g., places where a component may be adapted or extended) do require insight in the internal construction of a component. In this paper, a grey-box approach to component deployment is discussed. It is based on a scenario-based technique called Use-Case-Maps (UCM), which uses scenarios to describe how several components operate at a high abstraction level. UCM is an informal notation. Its strong point is to show how things work generally. In order to reason about component compositions, we have augmented UCMs with formal specifications of component interfaces. These interface specifications have been borrowed from the concurrent, object-oriented language BCOOPL (Basic Concurrent Object-Oriented Programming Language). A BCOOPL interface is more than just a set of operations, it also describes temporal orderings of operations and the parties that are allowed to invoke a particular operation. The combination of UCMs and BCOOPL interfaces gives us the opportunity to document intra and inter component behavior at a high, but formal abstraction level.

1 Introduction

Today, the notion of components is central in the development of software systems. The key idea is that a component encapsulates functionality, which can only be accessed through its interface published as part of the component's contract. In principle, we should favor a black-box approach to component deployment. That is, it should be possible to successfully deploy a component by just looking at its contract. Not only the functionality of a component, but also its non-functional properties, such as space and time requirements, must be specified unambiguously. Unfortunately, a black-box approach seems difficult to

K. Czarnecki and U.W. Eisenecker (Eds.): GCSE'99, LNCS 1799, pp. 195–209, 2000.
© Springer-Verlag Berlin Heidelberg 2000

realize in practice. For instance, space and time requirements may depend on specific component usages, which may be hard to describe in a contract. Another problem is that a component may work perfectly in one setting, but may fail to operate correctly in a different one due to (possibly undocumented) assumptions made on the environment [9]. This suggests a white-box approach with which we can investigate whether a component will perform correctly as part of a component system or not. However, it is not desirable to fully expose the internals of a component, since it can take a long time to master the details and we can become dependent on specific implementation details that might not survive the next releases of the component.

For the aforementioned reasons, we favor a grey-box approach that gives a high level view of the internals and clearly shows environmental constraints. We are not alone in our support for grey-box components. In [4], a justification for grey-box components is given following similar lines of reasoning. One can argue that a grey-box approach only partly describes the implementation and therefore is even worse than a white-box approach, which at least gives the full implementation. We do not agree with this point of view. By judiciously specifying the places where a component may be varied (e.g., extension or adaptation points), it is possible to avoid instable implementation dependencies. That is, a supplier of a component should guarantee that variation points remain invariant in subsequent releases. Moreover, a grey-box component can be specified without committing to a specific implementation yet. Such a specification can be seen as a type definition from which implementations can be derived all conforming to that type.

In this paper, we describe a grey-box approach to component-oriented system construction. The goal was to develop practical techniques for constructing systems out of components. With practical techniques we mean techniques that are easy to learn and to apply by software developers that do not necessarily have a formal computer science background. A second goal was to have a notation that can be used to validate the correctness of a system comprised of a composition of components. We use Use Case Maps (UCM) [5] for these purposes. UCM is scenario-based technique that bridges the gap between global requirement analysis models (e.g., use cases and class diagrams) and very detailed design models (e.g., interaction diagrams such as collaboration and message sequence diagrams). An important feature of a UCM is that it can show multiple scenarios in one diagram and the interactions amongst them.

However, a UCM is not a formal notation. Its strong point is that it can show in a glance how non-trivial systems work. Thus, UCMs alone are not sufficient to reason about system behavior in a formal sense. To suit our purposes, we annotate UCM with component interface descriptions. The notation for interfaces has been borrowed from the concurrent object-oriented programming language BCOOPL (Basic Concurrent Object-Oriented Programming Language) [6], a language specifically designed for component-oriented programming. An interface specification in BCOOPL is not just a collection of methods. It also describes the allowed sequences of method invocation and the parties that are allowed to do so. As such, a BCOOPL interface is comparable with a message sequence diagram.

By combining UCMs with BCOOPL interfaces we obtain an intuitive notation that, on the one hand, is easy to understand and, on the other hand, can be used to reason about properties of component-oriented systems in a more formal way.

This paper is organized as follows. After a discussion on component-oriented programming in general, we explain our grey-box approach. First, a short introduction to UCMs and BCOOPL is given, followed by showing how these two techniques can be combined. We end this paper with discussing related work and we give some concluding remarks.

2   Aspects of Component-Oriented Programming

In this section, we discuss aspects of component-oriented programming. In particular, we take a closer look at the contents of the component contract. Before we can define required properties of components, we must give a definition of a component. Here we adopt the definition given by Szyperski [11]:

A software component is a unit of composition with contractually specified interfaces and explicit context dependencies only. A software component can be deployed independently and is subject to composition by third parties.

According to this definition, a software component should be regarded as a blueprint that can be instantiated. This notion is similar to an object being an instance of a class. Indeed, components are frequently comprised of classes, but this is not a prerequisite, it can also be a library of functions or even a set of macros. Also, the client of a component should not be able to tell the difference, unless certain parts of the component are made public through its *provides* interface.

A software component should be sufficiently self-contained in order to be subject to composition in third party products. In particular, a component should exhibit as little context dependencies as possible. If there are dependencies, these should be made explicit by means of a *requires* interface.

A contract states what the clients should do to deploy a component, it also states what services are provided by the implementer of the component. Obviously, an interface description comprised of operations and their signatures should be part of the contract. Many popular component standards do not go much further than this. However, only enumerating operations is not sufficient to successfully deploy a component. For one thing, a set of operations does not specify the behavior. This leaves us with the question of what else should be part of the contract. This is very much a research question. What follows is a tentative list of key elements of a contract.

Context dependencies Components are seldom useful in their own right. They typically require a context in which they can function. Frequently, a component framework provides the context. The component's dependence on the environment can be formalized in a requires interface.

Semantics The name and signature of an operation defined in the provides interface does not give the semantics of the operation, although the name of an operation may strongly suggest the provided functionality. Also, the set of operations does not prescribe the required sequences of operation invocations. Typically, both omissions are remedied by stating the pre- and post-conditions for each operation. Unfortunately, pre- and post-conditions do not give the complete semantics of a component since they only say something about the state of an instantiated component and they do not reflect the semantics of interactions with other components. To fully capture the semantics of a component and its behavior in a particular environment, part of the internals that specify inter-component interactions should be exposed in the contract.

Non-functional properties Besides defining the functionality of a component, it is also important to define non-functional properties such as space and time requirements. The non-functional properties must be included in the contract since it states whether a component can function in a system with a given upper bound of resources.

Configuration Typically, a component can be configured prior to instantiation. Such a configuration could be comprised of associations in the form of key-value pairs to initialize attributes. Also, generically defined components that can be instantiated with concrete types can be considered as a form of configuration. Configuration information should be part of the contract since it defines usages of a component.

As noted before, this list is not complete. More requirements will be added as we gain a better understanding in component specification and deployment. The current state of the art in component technology, which includes CORBA, (D)COM(+), Active-X, and JavaBeans, do not even address all the aforementioned contract issues. For this reason, they are often referred to as wiring standards.

3   A Grey-Box Approach to Component Composition

As remarked before, the provides and requires interfaces of a component are not sufficient to fully capture the semantics of a component. Of course, a component can be understood by looking at its implementation, but this may be overwhelming, especially if a component has a complex behavior and interacts with many other components. Clearly, this level of detail is undesirable. What we need is a grey-box approach, which only exposes those details of a component that are required to assess different usages of a component. To this end, we combine Use Case Maps (UCM) [5] and BCOOPL [6] interface specifications. The result of this combination is component specification technique that captures the behavior of a component at a high level of abstraction, but at the same time is precise enough to reason about compositions of components.

3.1   Use Case Maps

A UCM is a visual notation for humans to use to understand the behavior of a system at a high level of abstraction. It is a scenario-based approach showing cause-effects by traveling over paths through a system. UCMs do not have clearly defined semantics, their strong point is to show how things work globally.

The basic UCM notation is very simple. It is comprised of three basic elements: responsibilities, paths and components. A simple UCM exemplifying the basic elements is shown in Figure 1. A path is executed as a result of the receipt of an external stimulus. Imagine that an execution pointer is now placed on the start position. Next, the pointer is moved along the path thereby entering and leaving components, and touching responsibility points. A responsibility point represents a place where the state of a system is affected or interrogated. The effect of touching a responsibility point is not defined since the concept of state is not part of UCM. Typically, the effects are described in natural language. Finally, the end position is reached and the pointer is removed from the diagram. A UCM is concurrency neutral, that is, a UCM does not prescribe the number of threads associated with a path. By the same token, nothing is said about the transfer of control or data when a pointer leaves one component and (re-)enters another one. The only thing that is guaranteed is the causal ordering of executing responsibility points along a path. However, this is not necessarily a temporal ordering, the execution of a responsibility point may overlap with the execution of subsequent responsibility points.

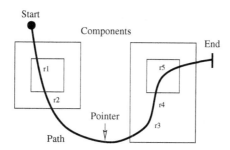

Fig. 1. UCM basic elements.

A more realistic example is shown in Figure 2 depicting a distributed client-server system. Because the client communicates with the server over a network that can fail occasionally, a proxy server is included to provide transparent access to the real server. The proxy server is modeled as a stub for which two implementations are given: a transparent proxy server which passes the requests to and the replies from the server unaltered thereby denying the possibility of network failures, and a proxy server with a timeout facility with which failures are detected. The notation used in the figure is supposed to be self-explanatory.

It is interesting to see that many things are unspecified in UCMs, but the intended meaning is suggested strongly. For instance, distribution aspects (e.g., connection mechanism and the amount of concurrency in a component) are not dealt with. However, the client, the server and the proxy server are distinct components that are connected by a network, which is also modeled as a component. By using these names, it is natural to assume that the components are distributed over a number of computer systems. But again, it is not specified, it is all in the eye of the beholder.

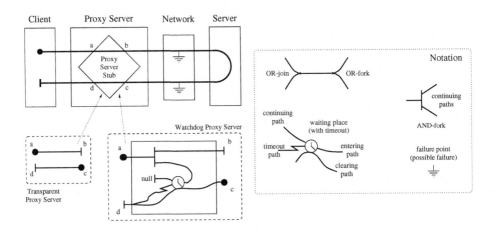

Fig. 2. Distributed Client-Server UCM.

3.2   BCOOPL

BCOOPL is a small, concurrent object-oriented programming language specifically designed to support component-oriented programming. BCOOPL has a long research history. It roots can be traced back to the concurrent object-oriented programming languages Procol [12] and Talktalk [3]. One of the strong points of BCOOPL is the built-in support of design patterns catering for component-oriented programming. In particular, BCOOPL supports the observer, the mediator and the bridge design patterns directly. Other design patterns frequently used in components, such as the facade and the proxy, can be implemented relatively easily in comparison with more traditional object-oriented programming languages like Java and C++.

Language Features BCOOPL is centered around two concepts: patterns and interfaces.

Patterns The concept of classes and methods specification have been unified in patterns and sub-patterns[1]. The term pattern has been borrowed from the object-oriented programming language Beta. The idea is that objects are instantiated from patterns and behave according to the pattern definition. A pattern describes the allowed sequences of primitives to be executed by an object after a message has been received in a so called *inlet*, which is implicitly defined in a pattern definition. A pattern may contain sub-patterns which also define inlets, and so on. When during the execution of a pattern one or more inlets are encountered, the execution is suspended until an appropriate message is received, which results in executing the corresponding sub-pattern. A pattern can therefore also be regarded as a synchronization mechanism coordinating the interactions with the object. It specifies when and which clients may communicate with an object. In this respect, a pattern resembles a protocol found in the concurrent object-oriented language Procol, which manages the access to an object.

A notification pattern is part of a pattern definition. It specifies the output behavior of a pattern in terms of notifications. Notifications are the OO abstraction of the call-back mechanism. In terms of design patterns, the call-back mechanism is known as the observer, the listener, the publish-subscribe and the dependency design pattern [8], while in the software architecture literature it is known as implicit invocation in event-driven systems [1]. An object interested in a particular notification of a publishing object can subscribe to that object. The subscription information is comprised of, amongst others, the name of the notification, the identity of the subscriber and the method to be invoked in the subscriber. A state change in a publisher will result in multicasting one or more notifications to the subscribers. Notifications are issued through an *outlet* by means of a *bang-bang* (!!) primitive. As a matter of fact, notifications are not only used for implementing the implicit invocation mechanism, but they are also used for getting a reply value as a result of sending a request to some object. The basic idea is to send a message to an object and then wait for a notification to be received in an inlet following the send primitive. The concept of notification patterns has been explored in Talktalk.

Interfaces The type or types of a pattern are provided by interfaces. A pattern that implements an interface has the type of that interface. Because a pattern may implement multiple interfaces, a pattern can have multiple types. A pattern implementing an interface must implement all the sub-patterns defined in the interface. The distinction between interface definition and interface implementation is not enforced by most popular languages. However, by adopting a disciplined programming style by using references to abstract classes only, the separation of interface and implementation can be realized in any object-oriented

---

[1] A pattern in BCOOPL should not be confused with a design pattern. The latter provides a solution for a design problem within a given context.

programming language. Java does support interfaces, although the use of inter-faces is not enforced in Java.

In short, BCOOPL embraces the principle of programming to an interface. As in Java, multiple interface inheritance is supported in BCOOPL. That is, an interface may extend one or more sub-interfaces. Note that interface inheritance does not break encapsulation as is the case in implementation (e.g., class) inher-itance. In contrast to Java, interfaces in BCOOPL contain sequence information specifying when a pattern may be invoked and by whom.

Interface Specification An interface is identified by a name and may extend one or more base interfaces. It is defined by means of an *interface interaction term*.

> **interface** *Interface Name*
>   **extends** [*interfaces*]$_{opt}$
> **defines** [
>   *interface interaction term*
>]$_{opt}$

An interface interaction term is specified using the following syntax:

> *client specifications* $\mapsto$ *Pattern Name (input args)* $\Rightarrow$ *(notification pattern)* [
>   *regular expression over interface interaction terms*
>]$_{opt}$

An interface interaction term corresponds with a (sub-)pattern definition that implements the interface. It defines the pattern name, the formal input ar-guments, a notification pattern that specifies sequences of notification messages, and client specifications. An interface interaction term is recursively defined as a regular expression over interface interaction terms leading to an hierarchical interface specification. The regular expression operators used for constructing an interface and their meaning are summarized in Table 1.

Expression	Operator	Meaning
$\ll E \gg$	synchronize	E is executed uninterupted
E ‖ F	interleave	E and F may occur interleaved
E + F	selection	E or F can be selected
E ; F	sequence	E is followed by F
E *	repetition	Zero or more times E
E [m, n]	bounded rep.	i times E with $m \leq i \leq n$

Table 1. Semantics of regular expression operators.

Client specifications denote the parties that are allowed to invoke the cor-responding pattern. They are defined by any combination of the following: by interface name, by interface name set (specified with the @ modifier), or by object reference set (specified with the $ modifier). The sets are used to dynamically specify the clients that are allowed to interact. A pattern implementing such an interface is responsible for the contents of a particular set.

Notifications issued by a pattern are guaranteed to be emitted according to the defined sequences specified in its notification pattern. Note that a pattern may issue multiple and distinct notifications. A notification pattern is defined as a regular expression over notification terms that are specified as follows:

Notification Name (output args)

The co- and contra-variance rules apply for specifying interfaces. An interface interaction term may be redefined in a derived interface. The types of the input arguments must be the same as or generalized from the argument types of the base interface (i.e., contra-variance rule). In contrast, a notification pattern may be extended in a derived interface, both in terms of notification output arguments having derived interfaces (i.e., co-variance rule) and additional notifications.

The interface *Any* acts as a base type for every other interface. That is, every interface extends *Any* implicitly. *Any* is defined as:

interface Any

As an example of interface specification, consider a User Interface (UI) component like a button. The button is derived from from the base interface *UIComponent*.

interface UIComponent

interface Button **extends** [UIComponent] **defines** [
    Any ↦ (properties : PropertyTable) ⇒
            (arm() ; (disarm() ; arm()) * ; activate() [0,1] ; disarm())*) [
        Any ↦ setProperties (properties : PropertyTable) ⇒ () *
    ]
]

After a button has been created, it can be initialized by sending it an anonymous message with a property table as argument. A property table is a dictionary comprised of name-value pairs. For instance, to set the label of the button, it can be initialized with a property table that contains the name-value pair having *Label* as name and the desired string as value. A button supplies suitable default values for properties, so only properties that must be overruled should be included in a property table. If required, the values of properties can be changed during the life-time of a button by invoking *setProperties*.

The button's notification pattern captures the idea that if a mouse is moved inside a button area and the end-user presses a mouse button, an *arm* notification is sent. Moving the mouse outside the area causes a *disarm* notification, and moving the mouse back inside results in an *arm* notification again. When the mouse button is released while the mouse is positioned inside the button area, an *activate* notification is sent followed by a *disarm* notification. Nothing happens if the end-user releases the mouse button outside the button area.

Note that this behavior cannot be deduced from the given notification pattern. For one thing, the relation between the notifications and the mouse events is not included in the interface specification. As will be shown later on, this relation can be clarified with a UCM.

3.3   Augmenting UCMs with BCOOPL Interface Specifications

In this section, we show how UCMs can be combined with BCOOPL interface specifications. The UCM notation has been augmented with extensions and notational shorthands in order to have a better match with BCOOPL's language features. The augmentations are depicted in Figure 3. The prime extension is the more rigorously defined semantics of a scenario in progress along a path within a component. As in BCOOPL, the *one-at-a-time* regime applies, which means that only one thread of control is active at any one time, although multiple threads may be in execution on an interleaved basis. However, a scenario in execution can claim exclusive control over a component by means of enclosing a path segment in ≪ and ≫ markers. Notational shorthands have been provided for the (creation) inlet, in which a message is received, and the outlet, which serves as a hook for connections to inlets.

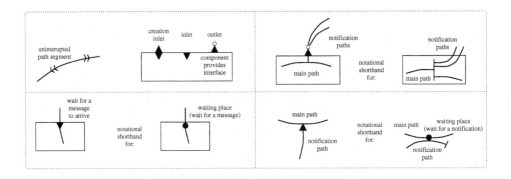

Fig. 3. UCM augmentations.

As an example, consider the previously introduced button again. The behavior of the button is captured in a UCM which is part of a so called specification sheet comprised of (see Figure 4):

- a description briefly describing the purpose of a component;
- a UCM showing the internal behavior of a component in terms of paths;
- a property table specification, consisting of the name of a property, its type and its default value;

- responsibility points describing in natural language how the state of a component is affected;
- the provides and requires interfaces specified as BCOOPL interfaces.

Specification Sheet: button

Description: A button is a UI component that allows the user to issue a UI command by "pushing" the button.

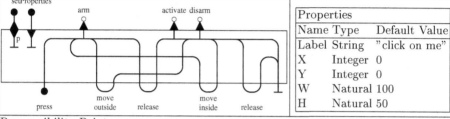

Properties		
Name	Type	Default Value
Label	String	"click on me"
X	Integer	0
Y	Integer	0
W	Natural	100
H	Natural	50

Responsibility Points:

p: the button is displayed with a label obtained with the property named Label, and is positioned at the coordinate obtained with the properties X and Y with a size given in the W(idth) and H(eight) property.

press: the mouse button is pressed with the mouse pointer positioned inside the button area move outside: mouse pointer is moved outside the button area while keeping the mouse button pressed
move inside: mouse pointer is moved inside the button area while keeping the mouse button pressed
release: the mouse button is released

Provides Interface:

```
interface Button extends [ UIComponent ] defines [
    Any ↦ (properties : PropertyTable) ⇒ ((arm() ; (disarm() ; arm())) * ; activate()[0,1] ; disarm())*) [
        Any ↦ setProperties (properties : PropertyTable) ⇒ () *
    ]
]
```

Requires Interface(s): *none*

Fig. 4. Button specification sheet.

Two kind of paths can be recognized, which can be defined in terms of external stimuli and notifications as follows:

press ; arm ;
(move outside ; disarm ; move inside ; arm) * ;
release ; activate ; disarm

press ; arm ;
(move outside ; disarm ; move inside ; arm) * ;
move outside ; disarm ; release

It is interesting to note that for each path infinitely many scenarios can be identified, since the mouse pointer can be moved inside and outside the button area infinitely many times.

The connection between a UCM and BCOOPL interfaces is established at two points:

- via the provides interface.
  Inlets (including the creation inlet) and outlets shown in a UCM must correspond with interface interaction terms in the provides interface.
- component interconnections via the requires interfaces.
  A component interconnection occurs when a path leaves one component and enters another one. If needed, an interconnection can be associated with a sub-expression of an interface. In most cases, however, an interconnection consists of linking an outlet of a used component to a path in the component being specified.

As an example of component composition, consider a dialog-box with which an end-user can be requested to enter a file name. The dialog-box is composed of several UI components, including buttons and a text field for entering a file name. The dialog-box acts as an intermediary synchronizing the notifications sent by its UI components thereby raising the abstraction level by providing a simple interface to its clients. Interacting with the dialog box results in issuing either a *fileName* notification or a *cancel* notification. The specification sheet is shown in Figure 5. This example clearly shows how the principle of abstraction is applied. The internal behavior of the UI components that are used in the dialog-box (i.e., the buttons and the text field) is abstracted away. A black-box approach has been taken by only showing the notifications issued by the UI components that are actually handled by the dialog-box. The UI components have a part-whole relation with the dialog-box. In particular, they exhibit the same life-time as the dialog-box and they are not shared with other components.

Although not shown in the examples, responsibility points can be used to state non-functional properties such as space and time requirements. This allows for the assessment of resource usage on a scenario basis. Responsibility points can also be used to further formalize a specification. At present, no such formalizations have been defined.

4   Discussion

In section 2, we have identified essential ingredients of a contract to successfully deploy a component. These include the specification of context dependencies, semantics, non-functional properties, and configurations. The combination of UCM and BCOOPL interfaces captures the essentials of a contract. Context dependencies are unambiguously specified with the requires interfaces specified as BCOOPL interfaces. They can be analyzed on a scenario-basis in the sense that typical usages of components or an agglomerate of components can be evaluated. The semantics of a component are defined by the combination of UCMs

---

Specification Sheet: fileNameDialogBox

Description: A fileNameDialogBox is a UI component with which a user can be requested to enter a file name.

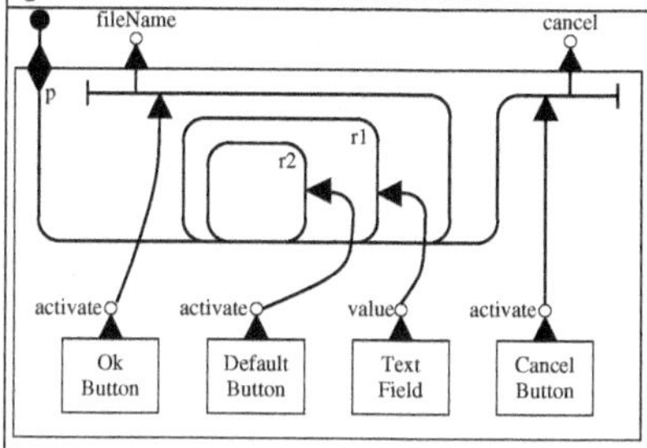

Properties		
Name	Type	Default Value
DefaultFileName	String	"component.doc"
X	Integer	0
Y	Integer	0
W	Natural	200
H	Natural	100

Responsibility Points:

> p: the dialog box is displayed with the text field containing the file name obtained with the property named DefaultFileName, and is positioned at the coordinate obtained with the properties X and Y with a size given in the W(idth) and H(eight) property.

> r1: the current file name becomes the string entered in the text field.
> r2: the current file name becomes the default file name.

Provides Interface:

```
interface FileNameDialogBox extends [ UIComponent ] defines [
    Any ↦ (properties : PropertyTable) ⇒ (fileName(name : String) + cancel()) [
        Any ↦ setProperties (properties : PropertyTable) ⇒ () *
    ]
]
```

Requires Interface(s):

```
interface Button extends [ UIComponent ] defines [
    Any ↦ (properties : PropertyTable) ⇒ ((arm() ; (disarm() ; arm()) * ; activate()[0,1] ; disarm())*) [
        Any ↦ setProperties (properties : PropertyTable) ⇒ () *
    ]
]

interface TextField extends [ UIComponent ] defines [
    Any ↦ (properties : PropertyTable) ⇒ (value(text : String) *) [
        Any ↦ setProperties (properties : PropertyTable) ⇒ () *
    ]
]
```

Fig. 5. FileNameDialogBox specification sheet.

and a BCOOPL interface. The effects of a scenario in progress are described by responsibility points and by interactions with other components. These interactions interactions are formally captured in the requires interfaces. Responsibility points are not only used to describe internal state changes, albeit in a informal way, they can also be used for specifying non-functional aspects (e.g., resource usage), which can also be analyzed on a scenario-basis. Finally, a component is configured by means of a property table, which provides the means to vary and extend its behavior.

What is missing is a formal notation to describe the internal state of a component in terms of attributes. The semantics of a component can then be further formalized by associating each operation with pre- and post-conditions to describe when an operation may be invoked and its effects. This approach has been taken in Catalysis [7], a component-based development approach compliant with the UML notation. In our approach, the pre- and post-conditions are partly described in BCOOPL's interface specifications which specify when, how and by whom certain operations may be invoked. Attributes and attribute manipulations can be incorporated easily in a UCM by formalizing the use of responsibility points, but as noted before, this is part of future work when we gain more insight in the aspects of components that we want to model. This goes further than the functional behavior and includes non-functional properties.

An important concept provided by BCOOPL interfaces is the built-in support of the implicit invocation mechanism, which provides a flexible way to compose new components from existing ones. Components provide their services through notifications. It is up to a client to link to the required services. This approach to composition is similar to the approach taken in the Real-Time Object-Oriented Modeling (ROOM) technique [10]. The basic building block in ROOM is the actor, which has both a structural and a behavioral definition. The structural part is defined in terms of input and output ports of an actor. Each port is associated with a protocol, a kind of abstract data type defining data and routines. Actors exchange information by sending messages conform a particular protocol. The behavioral part of an actor is expressed in ROOMcharts, which can be characterized as an hierarchical and concurrent state machine.

It interesting to note that UCMs and ROOM have been combined in the UCM-ROOM design method [2]. This method defines a forward engineering path starting at a high abstraction level with UCMs and ending with detailed specifications in the form of ROOM models. Message Sequence Charts (MSC) are used to bridge the rather large conceptual gap between UCMs and ROOM models. UCMs serve a different role in our approach. Here UCMs are used to provide a high level, grey-box view of the internal behavior augmented with BCOOPL interfaces to formalize the specification. The intent is to reflect how an already existing component works, rather than providing the first step in a forward engineering process. For this reason, MSCs do not have an added value in our approach. Moreover, they are already contained implicitly in BCOOPL interfaces.

5   Concluding Remarks

We have argued that a grey-box approach to component specification is required to promote reuse. UCMs seem to offer a lightweight notation that reveals critical aspects of a component in a glance. A scenario view is given that shows typical usage of collaborating components. UCMs in combination with BCOOPL interfaces strikes the balance between, on the one hand, high level of abstraction, and on the other hand, preciseness. We have indicated that not only behavior can be specified with UCMs, but they can also be used to express non-functional properties.

References

1. Len Bass, Paul Clements, and Rick Kazman. *Software Architecture in Practice.* SEI Series in Software Engineering. Addison-Wesley, Reading, Massachusetts, 1998.
2. F. Bordeleau and R.J.A. Buhr. The UCM-ROOM design method: from Use Case Maps to communicating state machines. Technical report, Department of System and Computer Engineering, Carleton University, Ottawa, Canada, September 1996. http://www.sce.carleton.ca/ftp/pub/UseCaseMaps/.
3. Peter Bouwman and Hans de Bruin. Talktalk. In Peter Wisskirchen, editor, *Object-Oriented and Mixed Programming Paradigms*, Eurographics Focus on Computer Graphics Series, chapter 9, pages 125–141. Springer-Verlag, Berlin, Germany, 1996.
4. Martin Büchi and Wolfgang Weck. A plea for grey-box components. Technical Report 122, Turku Centre for Computer Science (TUCS), Turku, Finland, August 1997. WWW: http://www.tucs.fi/publications/techreports/TR122.ps.gz.
5. R.J.A. Buhr. Use Case Maps as architecture entities for complex systems. *IEEE Transactions on Software Engineering*, 24(12):1131–1155, December 1998.
6. Hans de Bruin. BCOOPL: Basic Concurrent Object-Oriented Programming Language. WWW: http://www.cs.vu.nl/~hansdb/bcoopl/, 1999.
7. Desmond Francis D'Souza and Alan Cameron Wills. *Objects, Components, and Frameworks with UML: The Catalysis Approach.* Object Technology Series. Addison-Wesley, Reading, Massachusetts, 1998.
8. Erich Gamma, Richard Helm, Ralph Johnson, and John Vlissides. *Design Patterns: Elements of Reusable Object-Oriented Software.* Professional Computing Series. Addison-Wesley, Reading, Massachusetts, 1995.
9. David Garlan, Robert Allen, and John Ockerbloom. Architectural mismatch: Why reuse is so hard. *IEEE Software*, 12(6):17–26, November 1995. Carnegie Mellon University.
10. Bran Selic, Garth Gullekson, and Paul T. Ward. *Real-Time Object-Oriented Modelling.* John Wiley and Sons, New York, 1994.
11. Clemens Szyperski. *Component Software: Beyond Object-Oriented Programming.* ACM Press, Addison-Wesley, New York, 1997.
12. Jan van den Bos and Chris Laffra. Procol: a concurrent object language with protocols, delegation and persistence. *Acta Informatica*, 28:511–538, September 1991.

An XML Based Component Model for Generating Scientific Applications and Performing Large Scale Simulations in a Meta-computing Environment

Omer F. Rana, Maozhen Li, David W. Walker, and Matthew Shields

Department of Computer Science, Cardiff University, POBox 916, Cardiff CF24 3XF,
UK

Abstract. The architecture of a component based environment for constructing scientific applications – generally referred to as a Problem Solving Environment (PSE), is described. Each component is a self-contained program, and may be a sequential code developed in C, Fortran or Java, or may contain internal parallelism using MPI or PVM libraries. A user visually constructs an application by combining components from a local or remote repository as a data flow graph. Components are self-documenting, with their interfaces defined in XML, which enables a user to search for components suitable to a particular application, enables a component to be configured when instantiated, enables each component to register with an event listener and facilitates the sharing of components between repositories. The data flow graph is also encoded in XML, and sent to a resource manager for executing the application on a workstation cluster, or a heterogeneous environment made of workstations and high performance parallel machines.

Components in the PSE can also wrap legacy codes. We also describe the architecture and implementation of a molecular dynamics application based on the Lennard-Jones code [18], containing MPI calls, executed on a cluster of workstations, and based on our generic component model. A user can submit simulation data to the application remotely using a Java based user interface. Users need not download any softwares for the simulation and do not need to know the exact implementation.

Keywords: Component-Based Development, Component Interface/Re-use, Metaprogramming Systems, Parallel Computing, Application Generators

K. Czarnecki and U.W. Eisenecker (Eds.): GCSE'99, LNCS 1799, pp. 210–224, 2000.
© Springer-Verlag Berlin Heidelberg 2000

1   Introduction

A Problem Solving Environment (PSE) [1] is a complete, integrated computing environment for composing, compiling, and running applications in a specific area. PSEs have been available for several years for certain domains, but most have supported different phases of application development, and cannot be used cooperatively to improve a programmer's productivity, primarily due to the lack of a framework for tool integration and ease-of-use considerations. Extensions to current scientific programs such as Matlab, Maple, and Mathematica are particular pertinent examples of this scenario. Developing extensions to such environments enables the reuse of existing code, but may also severely restrict the ability to integrate routines that are developed in other ways or using other applications. Multi-Matlab [2] is an example of one such extension for parallel computing platforms. Similarly, data flow approaches for constructing scientific applications range from tools such as Khoros, AVS, WebFlow to Iris Explorer.

The modern concept of a PSE for computational science [3] is based on the availability of high performance computing resources, coupled with advances in software tools and infrastructure which makes the creation of such PSEs for computational science a practical goal. PSEs have the potential to greatly improve the productivity of scientists and engineers, particularly with the advent of web-based technologies, such as CORBA and Java, for accessing remote computers and databases. At a 1995 NSF workshop on PSEs [4], the need to develop and evaluate PSE infrastructure and tools was stressed. Subsequently a number of prototype PSEs have been developed. Most focus on linear algebra computations [5] and the solution of partial differential equations, and as yet only a few prototype PSEs have been developed especially for science and engineering applications [7]. However, this is likely to change over the next few years. Tools for building specific types of PSEs include PDELab[11], a system for building PSEs for solving PDEs, and PSEWare[12], a toolkit for building PSEs focused on symbolic computations. More generic infrastructure for building PSEs is also under development, ranging from fairly simple RPC-based tools for controlling remote execution to more ambitious and sophisticated systems such as Legion[13] and Globus[14] for integrating geographically distributed computational and information resources. However, most of these PSEs lack the ability to build up scientific applications by connecting and plugging software components together.

Component-based software engineering (CBSE)[15] is receiving increasing amounts of interest. One goal of CBSE is to reduce development cost and improve software reuse. To apply these technologies to the construction of an effective framework of PSEs is becoming vital and challenging. Similarly, free computational resources are increasingly becoming available on the Internet. A user who wants to utilise these resources must look for the appropriate library or set of libraries needed for his specific computational problems.

We describe a domain-independent PSE for scientific computations and large-scale simulations. In this environment, a user can visually construct domain-specific applications by plugging together software components written in various languages. We describe the interface of components within such as environment in detail, using an XML-based representation. We believe the universality of this approach will enhance component reuse, and enable sharing between numerical and tool repositories. We have created a molecular dynamics PSE (MDS-PSE) by wrapping a legacy code – a pre-existing MPI-based molecular dynamic simulation program written in C, into Java/CORBA objects. A user can submit input simulation data to the MDS-PSE and then receive the simulation results without downloading the MDS-PSE. The principal advantage is that behind the interface, the client need not know the exact implementation details. Wrapping can be accomplished at multiple levels: around data, individual modules, subsystems, or the entire system. This paper is organised as follows. Section 2 describes the architecture of our PSE, and section 3 describes the component model in detail. Section 4 shows the implementation of the molecular dynamics application, and we conclude the paper in section 5 with extensions and ideas for the future.

2   The Software Architecture of the PSE

The architecture of our generative environment consists of a Visual Program Composition Environment (VPCE), the Intelligent Resource Management System (IRMS), and CORBA Wrappers for legacy codes, as illustrated in Figure 1.

2.1   VPCE

The VPCE enables a user to develop an application by combining a diverse range of components that may come from different vendors. The components may be sequential codes written in C, Fortran, or Java, or they may be parallel implementations that make use of MPI or PVM libraries. Legacy codes, in Fortran for instance, can be wrapped as CORBA objects. The VPCE is itself a CORBA object, and can communicate with other applications using the ORB interface, as illustrated.

The main component of the VPCE is the Program Composition Tool (PCT), which is a visual tool that enables a user to build and edit applications by

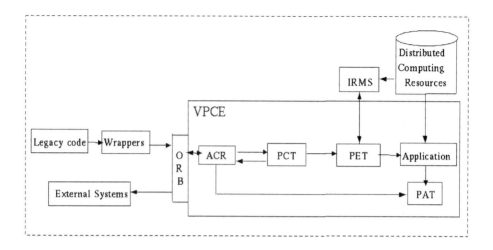

Fig. 1. *The CB-PSE Architecture*

plugging together components, by inserting application components into pre-defined templates, or by replacing application components in existing programs. The PCT allows a user to connect two components only if their interfaces are compatible. The PCT also enables a user to create new application components and place them in the Application Component Repository (ACR). The Program Execution Tool (PET) develops the task graph generated for each application, encodes this into XML (described in section 3), and passes the graph to the IRMS. The VPCE also includes a Program Analysis Tool (PAT) for displaying the hierarchical structure of an application component, describing the purpose and interface of each of its components, as well as of itself. Each component has a well defined interface defined in XML, and associated constraints on its I/O behaviour. When creating a new application component or placing it in the ACR, the user is prompted to optionally supply this information.

2.2   Wrapper

The Wrapper enables a program written in another programming language, to be converted into a CORBA object. The services provided by Wrapper are the same as those implemented in the legacy code. Either the complete legacy application may be wrapped as one object, or the application may be divided into smaller objects, provided the structure of the application is known. The granularity of a wrapped application is therefore dependent on how much is known about an application, whether the application can be successfully sub-divided, and whether constraints on the interfaces of components of a sub-divided application can be derived. The use of hierarchy in the VPCE facilitates the sub-division and the use of wrappers.

2.3 IRMS

The IRMS parses every task graph obtained from the PET. Based on the resources available and a performance model of components, it assigns tasks to resources. Through the IRMS, an application built in the VPCE may be scheduled onto single or multiple processor machines. The IRMS provides local scheduling and allocation for tasks obtained from PET, and negotiates with local scheduling systems such as LSF and Codine, where available, to build a possible schedule.

3 The Component Model

Each component is either a Java or CORBA object, with its interface specified in XML, according to a standard data model applied to all components within the environment. Components are stored in the Component Repository using this format, and any binary data associated with a component must also be identified by tags. XML tags may be used to automatically derive help on particular components already present in the repository, or may be used to query the availability of particular types of components. User-supplied components must also have their interfaces defined in XML.

The XML-based component model ensures uniformity across components, and helps to abstract component structure and implementation from component interface. Our XML definition enables the division of a component interface into a set of sections, where each section is enclosed within predefined tags. A parser capable of understanding the structure of such a document can identify and match components which meet this interface. The Document Type Definition (DTD) identifying valid tags does not need to be placed with each interface, as it can be obtained from a URL reference placed in the document header, and identified by the `href` tag. The XML definition can be used to perform information integrity (such as the total number of inports and outports), check the suitability of a component for its intended use, the types of platforms that may support the component and internal component structure when available. The tags are divided into: `context` and `header`, `ports`, `execution` specific detail, such as whether the component contains MPI code, a user specified `help` file for the component, a `configuration` file for initialising a component, a `performance model` identifying costs of executing the component for use by the resource manager, and an **event** handler, which enables registering or recording of particular types of events. A component may also contain specialised constraint tags in addition to the mandatory requirements identified above. Constraints can include security or license constraints, where a component is required to run on a particular machine or cluster. For instance, a data analysis component within the repository may be described as:

```
<?xml version="1.0" href=URL?>

<preface>
  <name alt=DA id=DA01>Data Analyser</name>
  <pse-type>Generic</pse-type>
  <hierarchy id=parent>Tools.Data.Data Analyser</hierarchy>
  <hierarchy id=child></hierarchy>
</preface>

<ports>
 <inportnum>2</inportnum>
 <outportnum>1</outputnum>
  <inportype id=1>float</inportype>
  <inport id=1 type=real>
    <parameter=regression value=NIL/>
  </inport>
  <inport id=2 type=float>
    <parameter=bayesian value=NIL/>
  </inport>
 <outportype> real </outportype>
</ports>

<execution id=software>
 <type>parallel</type>
 <type>MPI</type>
 <type>SPMD</type>
 <type>binary</type>
</execution>


<execution id=platform>
 <type> </type>
</execution>
```

```
<help context=instantiate>
<href name=file:/home/pse/help/data-analyser.txt value=NIL>
</help>
```

The XML-based DTD contains the following types of tags:

- Context and header tags: used to identify a component and the types of PSEs that a component may be usefully employed in. The component name must be unique, with an alternative alphanumeric identifier, however any number of PSEs may be specified. These details are grouped under the preface tag, hence:

```
<!ELEMENT preface    (name pse-type+)>
<!ELEMENT name       (name-list+)>
<!ATTLIST name       alt %PCDATA
                     id  %PCDATA>
<!ELEMENT pse-type   %PCDATA> ...
```

The hierarchy tag is used to identify parent and child components, and works in a similar way to the Java package definition. A component can have one parent, and multiple children. In the example, 'DA01' has no children, indicating that it is at the bottom of the hierarchy.

- Ports: used to identify the number of input and output ports, and their types. An input port can accept multiple data types and this can be specified in a number of ways by the user. Input/output to/from a component can also come from/go to other types of sources, such as files or network streams. In this case, the inport and outport ports need to define an href tag, rather than a specific data type. We standardise our href definition to account for various scenarios where it may be employed, such as:

```
<ports>
<inport id=1 parameter=regression type=stream value=NIL>
 <parameter=regression value=NIL/>
 <href name=http://www.cs.cf.ac.uk/PSE/ value=test.txt>
</inport>
</ports>
```

or when reading data from a file, the href tag is changed to:

```
<ports>
<inport id=1 parameter=regression type=stream value=NIL>
 <parameter=regression value=NIL/>
```

```
<href name=file:/home/pse/test.txt value=NIL>
</inport>
</ports>
```

This gives a user much more flexibility in defining data sources, and using components in a distributed environment. The user may also define more complex input types, such as a `matrix`, `stream` or an `array` in a similar way.

- Execution: a component may have execution specific details associated with it, such as whether it contains MPI code, if it contains internal parallelism etc. If only a binary version of a component is available, then this must be specified by the user also. Such component-specific details may be enclosed in any number of `type` tags. The execution tag is divided into a `software` part and a `platform` part. The former is used to identify the internal properties of the component, while the latter is used to identify a suitable execution platform or a performance model.

- Help: a user can specify an external file containing help on a particular component. The `help` tags contains `context` options which enables the association of a particular file with a particular option, to enable display of a pre-specified help file at particular points in application construction. The contexts are predefined, and all component interfaces must use these. Alternatively, the user may leave the `context` field empty, suggesting that the same file is used every time help is requested on a particular component. If no help file is specified, the XML definition of the component is used to display component properties to a user. Help files can be kept locally, or they may be cross references using a URL. One or more help files may be invoked within a particular `context`, some of which may be local.

- Configuration: similar to the `help` tag, a user can specify a `configuration` tag, which enables a component to load predefined values from a file, from a network address or by using a customiser or wizard program. This enables a component to be pre-configured within a given context, to perform a given action when a component is created or destroyed, for instance. The `configuration` tag is particularly useful when the same component needs to be used in different applications, enabling a user to share parts of a hierarchy, while defining local variations within a given context.

- Performance model: each component has an associated performance model, and this can be specified in a file, using a similar approach to component configuration defined above. A performance model is enclosed in the `performance` tag, and may range from being a numerical cost of running

the component on a given architecture, to being a parameterised model that
can account for the range and types of data it deals with to more complex
models that are specified analytically.

– Event model: each component supports an event listener. Hence, if a source
  component can generate an event of type XEvent, than any listener (target)
  must implement an Xlistener interface. Listeners can either be separate components that perform a well defined action – such as handling exceptions, or
  can be more general and support methods that are invoked when the given
  event occurs. We use an **event** tag to bind an event to a method identifier
  on a particular component.

```
<event target="ComponA" type="ouput" name="overflow" filter="filter">
 <component id=XX> ... </component>
</event>
```

The **target** identifies the component to initiate when an event of a given
type occurs on component with identity **id**, as defined in the **preface** tag
of a component. The **name** tag is used to differentiate different events of the
same type, and the **filter** tag is a place-holder for JDK1.2 property change
and vetoable property change events support. Also, the filter attribute is
used to indicate a specific method in the listener interface using which the
event must be received for a particular method to be invoked.

Event handling may either be performed internally within a component,
where an event listener needs to be implemented for each component that
is placed in the PSE. This is a useful addition to a component model for
handling exceptions, and makes each component self-contained. Alternatively, for legacy codes wrapped as components, separate event listeners may
be implemented as components, and may be shared between components
within the same PSE. Components that contain internal structure, and support hierarchy, must be able to register their events at the highest level in
the hierarchy, if separate event listeners are to be implemented. An simple
example of an event listener is as follows:

```
<preface>
  <name alt=DA id=DA02>Data Extractor</name>
  <pse-type>Generic</pse-type>
  <hierarchy id=parent>Tools.Data.Data_Extractor</hierarchy>
  <hierarchy id=child></hierarchy>
</preface>

<event type="initialise" name="start" filter="">
```

```
<script>
  <call-method target="DA01" name="bayesian">
</script>
</event>
```

The `script` tags are used to specify the method to invoke in another component, when the given event occurs.

– Additional tags not part of the component model may be specified by the user in an

```
<add> ... </add>
```

section towards the end of each section. We will not support variable tags in the first version.

All applications that employ our PSE must adhere to this component model. A user may specify the component model using tags, or may have it encoded using a Component Model editor, which also acts as a wizard and enables customisation. The editor works in a similar manner to an HTML editor, where a user is presented with a menu based choice of available tags, and can either choose one of these predefined tags, or (different from an HTML editor) may define their own. The Component Model in XML forms the interface between the VPCE and other parts of the PSE, and is used to store components in the repository. The XML representation is therefore pervasive throughout the PSE, and links the VPCE to the IRMS. Various representations can be obtained from the XML description in *Scheme, Python, Perl, CORBA-IDL* etc, for connection to other systems that may be attached to the PSE.

The use of tags enables component definitions to be exchanged as web documents, with the structure available at either a single or at particular certified sites. Hence, changes to the DTD can be made without requiring changes to component definitions held by application developers, and will be propagated the next time a user utilises a component interface.

Component interconnectivity is also specified in XML, in the form of a directed graph. Component dependencies are enclosed in `dependency` tags and include constructs such as `parent-of`, `child-of` and `sibling-of`, enabling distant relationships to be constructed from recursive applications of these three basic types. Such dependencies can also be embedded within a JAR file, for instance, where multiple components may be stored in a single file for transfer over a network. Based on OSD [9], 'push'-based applications can automatically trigger the download of particular software components as new versions are developed. Hence, a component within a data flow may be automatically downloaded and installed, when a new or enhanced version of the component is created. This approach is linked to event handlers, with specific events to identify when a new version of a particular component is available.

The use of the component model also requires that each component has a unique identifier across the PSE workspace, and is registered with a component repository. This is particularly significant when handling events, as event types will need to be based on component identities and their particular position in the data flow. The component models mentioned here have been influenced by IBM's BeanML [8] and Microsoft's OSD [9] XML-based frameworks.

4   The MD Application

The code used in the MDS-PSE is a three-dimensionsal molecular dynamics code for simulating a Lennard-Jones fluid. The code has been parallelised, and makes use of the MPI message passing library. The code models short-range atomic interactions by using a link-cell (geometric hashing) algorithm where all particles are hashed into three-dimensional $N_b \times N_b \times N_b$ cells. The cell size is at least the cut-off distance (r_c) used in the short-range force evaluation so that each particle interacts only with particles in the same cell or in the neighbouring cells. The symmetry of Newton's Third Law is exploited so that atoms in only 13 (instead of 26) neighbouring cells need to be examined. The code assumes an $N_c \times N_c \times N_c$ Face Centered Cubic (FCC) periodic lattice with a total of $N = 4N_c^3$ atoms. A "shifted-force" [17] Lennard-Jones 6-12 potential ensures that the potential and its first derivative are continuous at the cut-off distance. Particle positions are updated at each time step using a simple Verlet [18] leap-frog scheme. Details of the molecular dynamics algorithms used are described in the book *Computer Simulation of Liquids* [19].

A spatial decomposition [20] is used which distributes the cells in blocks over a three-dimensional mesh of processes, so that each process is responsible for the particles in a rectangular sub-domain. Point-to-point message passing is necessary to perform two tasks in the algorithm. First, particle information in cells lying at the boundaries of a process must be communicated to one or more neighbouring processes. This is necessary because these particles must interact with particles in neighbouring processes. The standard approach of creating "ghost" cells around the boundary of each process is used, and the communication can then be performed in a series of six shift operations (one for each face of the rectangular sub-domain). The second type of point-to-point communication arises when particles migrate from the sub-domain of one process to that of another.

Again this communication can be performed in a series of shift operations. In the message passing code the communication of boundary data and particle migration are combined to reduce the frequency (and hence the overhead) of message-passing.

4.1   The Architecture of MDS-PSE

Figure 2 illustrates the architecture of the MDS-PSE.

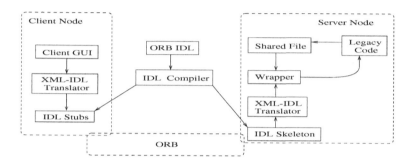

Fig. 2. *The MDS-PSE Architecture*

We use an XML to Java IDL translator and a CORBA-compliant ORB shipped with JDK1.2, as the fundamental infrastructure for defining component interfaces in MDS-PSE. The Wrapper packages the legacy code in the server node as a CORBA object. It is responsible for communication with the legacy code through a shared file and provides services to the Client. Since the operations are pre-defined in the MDS-PSE, a Client invokes the Wrapper with the IDL stub on the client side and uses the corresponding IDL skeleton on the server side.

Client The Client provides a graphical user interface (GUI) to the user for input, as illustrated in Fig. 3. Using the GUI, a user can input simulation parameters such as the number of processors in each co-ordinate direction. After submitting the input simulation data, the user can view the simulation results, as in Fig. 3, such as the `temperature`, `pressure` and `energy` during the simulation.

Wrapper The Wrapper performs two functions. First it initialises the ORB, and then registers itself as `WrapperRef` with the ORB Naming Service, and waits for the Client request to invoke the MDS legacy code. The Wrapper uses the Java

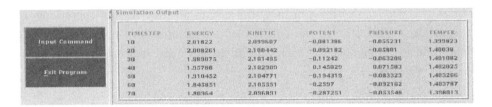

Fig. 3. *The simulation output in MDS-PSE*

Native Interface (JNI) to communicate with a C function (`NativeC()`) to invoke the MDS-PSE. All Client and Wrapper objects must be registered with the ORB Naming Service to be used in the MDS-PSE.

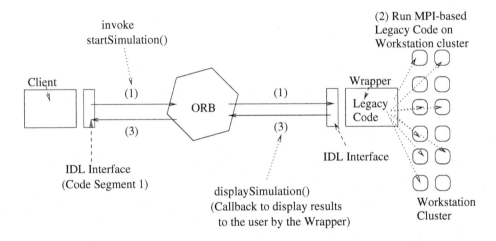

Fig. 4. *The invocation sequences of the MDS-PSE*

Figure 4 illustrates the MDS-PSE, and the sequence of steps involved in running an application program. The legacy code is run on multiple machines and has internal parallelism using MPI calls.

We have also divided the MD code into computational sub-tasks, and wrapped these as separate CORBA objects. Each object maintains its local data distribution, and objects need to be run in a pre-defined sequence, with data sharing taking place through intermediate files.

5 Conclusion and Future Work

We describe an environment for generating scientific computing applications by combining components. The environment is based on the Java programming language, with components being Java or CORBA objects defined with XML interfaces, and with support for parallelism provided, for example, via MPI libraries. The framework is currently under development as part of a larger multidisciplinary Problem Solving Environment (M-PSE) project.

The current MDS-PSE may be used to explore possible methods for wrapping legacy codes for use in a CORBA environment. The MDS-PSE may be extended to: 1) provide different level wrappers for the legacy code, and divide the MPI-based legacy code into distributed objects, with embedded message passing calls; 2) explore approaches to wrapping different computational resources and providing different wrappers as components for constructing applications. At present we do not handle any errors or exceptions that may occur during this client-server interaction, delegating this task to the underlying ORB. We will be considering specialised error messages in the future.

References

1. E. Gallopoulos, E. N. Houstis and J. R. Rice, "Computer as Thinker/Doer :Problem-Solving Environments for Computational Science", IEEE Computational Science and Engineering, Vol. 1, No. 2, pp. 11-23, 1994
2. Vijay Menon and Anne E. Trefethen, "MultiMATLAB: Integrating MATLAB with High-Performance Parallel Computing", SuperComputing97, 1997.
3. E. Gallopoulos, E. N. Houstis and J. R. Rice, "Workshop on Problem-Solving Environment:Findings and Recommendations", ACM Computing Surveys, Vol. 27, No. 2, pp 277-279, June 1995
4. J. R. Rice and R. F. Boisvert, "From Scientific Software Libraries to Problem-Solving Environments", IEEE Computational Science and Engineering, Vol. 3, No. 3, pp. 44-53, 1996.
5. H. Casanova and J. J. Dongarra, "NetSolve: A Network-Enabled Server for Solving Computational Science Problems", Int. J. Supercomputing Appl. Vol. 11, No. 3, pp. 212-223, 1997.
6. Alan W. Brown, Kurt C. Wallnau, " The Current State of CBSE", IEEE Software, September 1998.
7. K. M. Decker and B. J. N. Wylie, "Software Tools for Scalable Multilevel Application Engineering", Int. J. Supercomputing Appl. Vol. 11, No. 3, pp. 236-250, 1997.
8. Sanjiva Weerawarana, Joseph Kesselman and Matthew J. Duftler "Bean Markup Language (BeanML)", IBM TJ Watson Research Center, Hawthorne, NY 10532, 1999

9. The Open Software Description Format, See Web page at http://www.w3.org/TR/NOTE-OSD.

10. G. Spezzano, D. Talia, S. Di Gregorio, "A Parallel Cellular Tool for Interactive Modeling and Simulation", IEEE Computational Science and Engineering, Vol. 3, No. 3, pp. 33-43, 1996.

11. S. Weerawarana. Proceedings of the Second Annual Object-Oriented Numberics Conference, Sunriver, Oregon, April 1994.

12. R. Bramley and D. Gannon. See Web page on PSEWare at http://www.extreme.indiana.edu/pseware.

13. A. S. Grimshaw, "Campus-Wide Computing: Early Results Using Legion at the University of Virginia", Int. J. Supercomputing Appl. Vol. 11, No. 2, pp. 129-143, 1997.

14. I. Foster and C. Kesselman, "GLOBUS: A Metacomputing Infrastructure Toolkit", Int. J. Supercomputing Appl. Vol. 11, No. 2, pp. 115-128, 1997.

15. Alan W. Brown, Kurt C. Wallnau, " The Current State of CBSE", IEEE Software Sep. 1998.

16. S. Browne, The Netlib Mathematical Software Repository. D-lib Magazine, Sep. 1995.

17. J. G. Powles, W. A. B. Evans, and N. Quirke, "Non-destructive Molecular Dynamics Simulation of the Chemical Potential of a Fluid", Mol. Phys, Vol. 46, pp. 13476–1370, 1982.

18. L. Verlet, "Computer Experiments on Classical Fluids I. Thermodynamical Properties of Lennard-Jones Molecules", Phys. Rev., Vol. 159, pp. 98–103, 1967.

19. M. P. Allen and D. Tildesley, "Computer Simulation of Liquids", Claredon Press, Oxford, 1987.

20. S. Plimpton", "Fast Parallel Algorithms for Short-Range Molecular Dynamics", J. Comput. Phys., Vol. 117, pp. 1–19, March 1995.

Author Index

Lecture Notes in Computer Science

For information about Vols. 1–1865
please contact your bookseller or Springer-Verlag